RETHINK
DESIGN GUIDE

Architecture for a post-pandemic world

RIBA Publishing

Published by RIBA Publishing, 66 Portland Place, London, W1B 1AD

ISBN 978-1-85946-980-4

British Library Cataloguing-in-Publication Data
A catalogue record for this book is available from the British Library.

Commissioning Editor: Elizabeth Webster

Project Manager: Caroline Ellerby

Production: Richard Blackburn

Designed and typeset by Mercer Design, London

Printed and bound by Pureprint Group, East Sussex

Cover image Bill Bragg

www.ribapublishing.com

MIX
Paper from responsible sources
FSC® C022913

CONTENTS

ST JOHN BOSCO

INTRODUCTION

'No-one will be even thinking about social distancing in a year's time,' said one optimistic architect to me fairly early on in lockdown. While it looks like he's wrong about the lasting impact of the pandemic, it's fair to say that even though the short-term consequences are becoming clear, few can predict with any certainty the long-term changes that COVID-19 will bring to building design.

So much depends on developing a reliable vaccine, and when that can be delivered sufficiently widely. Until then, it's a question of adapting to the 'new normal' of finding safe ways to go about our lives while maintaining social distancing. And even with a vaccine, there's the spectre of other pandemics that may be heading our way in the years to come. At least COVID-19 will have taught us how to develop a pandemic mode of operation that can be overlaid when required.

COVID-19 has also taught us that dramatic change is possible, first in lockdown, and subsequently as we rethink everything about our daily lives in the name of COVID-safety. How can this impetus be harnessed to drive broader change, and meet other significant societal challenges, like Black Lives Matter or the climate crisis?

In this design guide, architects and designers with expertise in different building typologies consider both the short- and longer-term impacts of COVID-19 on the design of these buildings, for better as well as for worse. Chapters range from schools and housing through to healthcare and infrastructure, offering a broad range of insights into the new context for architecture.

Figure 1 St John Bosco Arts College, Liverpool, designed by BDP and completed in 2014. The shed-like form is designed for maximum flexibility in the case of conversion to a new use in the future.

While it's clear that each sector produces its own specific conditions and challenges, it is possible to discern some common threads, in particular the need to design for flexibility and adaptability. This is a way of future-proofing a building, not only against any further pandemics, but against societal and market changes that could make its original use obsolete (see Figure 1).

As post-COVID safety chimes with the challenges of the climate crisis, there is also likely to be an increased emphasis on buildings that are designed sustainably and to promote wellbeing and interaction with nature and the outdoors. In this way, formerly niche design interests such as biophilia and wellbeing look likely to be heading for the mainstream. It is clear that there is great opportunity for positive change.

This is particularly the case in the housing sector, with the long months of lockdown revealing – and deepening – existing significant problems. Chapter 3 author Julia Park sees COVID-19 as the catalyst for long-overdue change, highlighting the importance of the simple basics that everyone should be able to take for granted, yet can't, such as access to green space, good daylight and views out, ventilation, a controllable indoor ambient temperature and clean air. She sets out a need for fundamental change in how housing is commissioned and delivered – only then will there be a realistic understanding of how much good, long-lasting, net-zero-carbon buildings cost, and how long they take to achieve. In all this, architects have an important part to play by understanding how to achieve net-zero-carbon homes and by encouraging their clients to be early adopters, as understanding of what constitutes 'good' evolves.

It's not just about cities. In her chapter on masterplanning and infrastructure, Sarah Featherstone and fellow members of VeloCity – a multidisciplinary team of industry experts – urge the embracing of 'gentle radicalism' to both tackle the housing crisis and achieve more sustainable rural development. 'Now more than ever there is an appetite for change,' they say, advocating the need to slow down and evolve a long-term strategy for rural development rather than a post-COVID rush to build. VeloCity embraces people over cars, compact development rather than sprawl, and connection rather than isolation. The aim is to build sustainable places with resilience, health and wellbeing – wishes that resonate all the stronger in the midst of the pandemic. Rather than being parochial backwaters, the VeloCity team envisage that rural areas 'can drive innovation and be a true place for gentle radicalism'.

Workplace is a particularly interesting sector following the working-from-home revolution. After the first lockdown, there was only a very slow, partial return to office working, which in turn had a significant knock-on effect on city-centre businesses such as the cafés and restaurants that rely on office trade. Many of us, it seems, are happy to remain as home-workers, whether entirely or partially. And now that home working has been proven to be effective, that perceived barrier has gone forever, although in truth this trend was already growing. As a result, it seems highly unlikely that the workplace will ever go back to what it was, vaccine or no vaccine.

The immediate impact of COVID-safety arrangements runs contrary to trends in workplace design over the last five or 10 years, where the direction has been towards agile, flexible workspaces with an emphasis on collaborative working and serendipitous meetings around the office. On the other hand, the recent trend towards workplaces that prioritise wellness may well receive a boost (see Figure 2).

So what will change beyond the new safety protocols of handwashing, social distancing, clear screens, assigned seating and new circulation routes? Nicola Gillen of Cushman & Wakefield discusses how COVID-19 has questioned the fundamentals of how and where work should be delivered, and the impact on how offices are designed and occupied. She expects to see increased homeworking combined with a shift away from centralised offices towards smaller core office hubs including local workplace hubs. These will be supplemented by on-demand space provision for events and collaborative working as required. As Gillen states in her chapter, 'The pace of change could be rapid, as the average remaining lease length across the world has decreased to three years … giving time for organisations to redeploy their portfolios.'

What will be the challenges for the architects of workplaces? Gillen's colleague Sophie Schuller considers the future of the employee experience as the use of a centralised workplace decreases, and looks at the role of both architects and facilities management in delivering this. She likens the future role of architects as more akin to a film director 'designing an immersive 9D cinematic experience of the workplace', spanning place, sound, light and customisable spaces for teams and individuals across a network of locations, both in the real and virtual worlds. Already a growth area before COVID-19, co-working spaces could also be the beneficiaries of post-pandemic changes in workplace culture, with their appealing mix of flexible sized and timed tenancies.

While COVID-safe offices run contrary to recent trends in workplace design, in the retail sector the pandemic is accelerating trends that were already established – such as the inexorable shift towards online shopping, which has surely been turbo-charged by COVID-19. Trends towards

Figure 2 Deloitte HQ, 1 New Street Square, London, designed by Sheppard Robson and completed in 2018. This was the first workplace of its kind to achieve WELL Gold and BREEAM Outstanding certification.

incorporating mixed uses rather than just retail into shopping centres will surely also gain traction. In his invigorating retail and hospitality chapter, Adam Scott of experience masterplanning agency FreeState describes retail as facing a giant crisis that is also a giant opportunity – but only if retailers, developers and the planning system play their cards right by ripping up the rules of the game and planning a new way forward. To succeed in these Amazon-dominated, pandemic-disrupted times, physical shopping areas have to offer what online can't. This 'co-created campus' could be a latter-day agora, offering a rich mix of human-centred uses and above all focusing on 'the experience of being out'. Scott calls for more flexibility in planning use classes, in particular to encourage 'meanwhile' uses and greater use of Compulsory Purchase Orders, as well as the introduction of Compulsory Selling Orders and Investment Orders. Developers, meanwhile, need to understand that being socially useful can go hand in hand with commercial acumen. And designers need to 'design for delight' by encouraging curiosity, sociability and creativity.

The closure of education buildings to the vast majority of students was one of the most significant features of the first lockdown. In her chapter on schools, Helen Taylor draws on UK and international examples to consider how the design of education buildings can respond to the pandemic and its aftermath. During the long period of school closure, a number of architects and designers have looked not only at how schools could be adapted to meet the safety protocols required for reopening, but also how these buildings could be more fundamentally redesigned to meet new criteria for wellbeing and sustainability. In doing so, she says, they can be future-proofed not only for COVID-19 and other pandemics, but also for climate change. Examples range from concepts for outdoor learning to England's first Passivhaus school in Sutton, south London. This future-proofing goes way beyond the school environment itself. As Taylor points out, as schools are reinvented, they have the potential to be far more than monofunctional institutions and to additionally integrate more closely with the local community.

When it comes to higher education, it is architects who are best placed in the design team to rise to the challenge of the new post-COVID priorities, according to Chapter 7 author Ian Taylor. While acknowledging the impact of social distancing on student interaction and learning, he suggests that the pandemic has presented an opportunity to address some historical wrongs in the university and college sector and accelerate the delivery of 'the university of the 21st century' for the benefit not only of those who study and work there but also for the planet. In so doing, universities and colleges are safeguarding their own futures by appealing to the Extinction Rebellion generation. Taylor identifies a set of new client values that will become the drivers for innovation in higher- and further-education buildings – economy, adaptability, carbon neutrality, health, equality, wellbeing and biophilic/regenerative design. Flexibility is particularly important, and with retrofit (see Figure 3) rather than new-build the first port of call, buildings

designed to be bespoke to just one function may be increasingly rare in the future. Architects have a crucial role to play but they can't do it alone. Taylor urges the higher-education establishment to take the lead in prioritising healthy, adaptable spaces.

Adaptability and flexibility certainly shine through as key attributes in the chapter on civic and cultural buildings led by Pippa Nissen. She considers whether the COVID-19 legacy will be a combination of base builds that allow changeable configurations combined with short-life, sustainably produced surface 'skins'. Use of technology may also change. Elsewhere in the chapter, Finn Ross talks about the end of the touch era, with touch interactives and screens being replaced by cleanable personal devices. On a broader level, the chapter also considers whether lockdown will drive the desire for new creative experiences away from the computer screen, and whether there will be increased scope to enhance public spaces 'simply and joyfully, celebrating what it means to be human'.

Figure 3 Bath School of Art and Design, completed by Grimshaw in 2019. The project repurposes the former Herman Miller furniture factory, designed by Farrell/Grimshaw in 1976, for its new educational use.

Figure 4 ICÔNE, a new office complex in Belval, Luxembourg, due for completion in 2021. Designed by Foster + Partners, the 18,000sqm building aims to promote collaboration and wellbeing and promises to be filled with light and greenery.

Concerns for post-COVID safety may also intersect with the Black Lives Matter (BLM) agenda, by further encouraging cultural institutions to embrace diversity, inclusion and equality. Those who run our museums and galleries have had plenty of time to reflect on the nature of their own institutions during the long months of closure, especially as they watch footage of BLM demonstrations including the stunning chucking of the statue of slave-owner Edward Colston into the Bristol Harbour. There are signs that these activities may be leading some cultural organisations to reassess both their collections and how these are presented, or certainly spur on initiatives already underway towards more inclusive and ethical practices relating to race, gender and disability. The Pitt Rivers Museum in Oxford, for example, had already been conducting a lengthy ethical review of its collections and has recently removed a number of shrunken heads from its display. It is also talking to descendant communities about the future of many items of human remains within its collections. While the COVID-19 overlay of social distancing and carefully choreographed circulation may – we hope – be temporary, these more fundamental changes in approach will hopefully be here for the long haul.

The pandemic has provided huge lessons for healthcare, as explored by Sumita Singha in her wide-ranging chapter on the sector. She urges a holistic approach to healthcare linked not just to the provision of hospitals, medicine and equipment, but to broader infrastructure and the design of places. In taking this approach, she contends, all architects work in healthcare, whether directly or indirectly: with city design and decent housing an important part of pandemic prevention for the future. She looks ahead to 2025 and considers what post-COVID changes may have taken root by then, from remote consultation to greater use of human-centred, empowering technology. She also looks at the hospitals of the future, and how these could further embrace sustainable design principles in both new-builds and retrofits. More generally, she believes, architects and planners can apply lessons from the pandemic to not only dealing with future pandemic emergencies but promoting health for all.

One of the few silver linings of COVID-19 is that its legacy may assist the increasing efforts to design in a more sustainable way and consider retrofit over redevelopment. In particular, this pandemic has shone a brighter light on the need to design environments that promote health and wellbeing, with a greater emphasis on engagement with nature and the outdoors (see Figure 4).

Speaking this September on Radio 4's *Today* programme, RIBA president elect Simon Allford summed up the long-term impact of COVID-19 as encouraging design that is long-life, loose-fit and low-energy. With a growing recognition of the climate emergency, this was already the direction of travel in the profession. COVID-19 might just provide it with a much-needed further boost.

PAMELA BUXTON

CHAPTER 1

WORKPLACE

NICOLA GILLEN

Dimitris Vlachopoulos

Thomas Vazakas

Sophie Schuller

Joe White

Naomi Cleaver

Richard Howard

NICOLA GILLEN

Nicola is a Partner and Head of Total Workplace EMEA at Cushman & Wakefield. She specialises in the relationship between design, behaviour and the built environment. An architect and author, she is widely recognised as an industry leader on workplace strategies and change management. Based in London, Nicola draws from 25 years' experience delivering workplace strategy and innovation across EMEA, US and APAC. She is lead author of the RIBA Publishing book *Future Office*, published in 2019.

Introduction

Past pandemics have accelerated social and economic change, forcing societies to adapt their present and reimagine their future. COVID-19 raises fundamental questions of how and where 'work' should be delivered. The pandemic-driven changes in economy, workforce and organisations will shape long-term impacts on real estate. The immediate impact of COVID-19 led to most offices, retail units, leisure and sporting facilities standing empty.

More than ever, the current crisis is forcing various workplaces to shift from physical to virtual work styles. In the first half of 2020, many organisations realised that they can operate within these new modes. Sundar Pichai, CEO of Google, has said that the pandemic has been an 'opportunity to reimagine' how the company works.[1]

1 J. Elias, 'Google CEO Tells Employees Return to Office Won't Happen Until At Least June', CNBC website, 28 April 2020, https://www.cnbc.com/2020/04/28/google-ceo-says-return-to-office-wont-happen-until-at-least-june-1.html.

The opportunity to reimagine the workplace is reinforced in the Experience per Square Foot™ (XSF) research conducted during the pandemic by Cushman & Wakefield. XSF is a proprietary tool that statistically uncovers real-estate and workplace metrics relating to employee engagement and experience.

At the outset of the pandemic, Cushman & Wakefield expanded its XSF survey with an XSF@Home tool to gauge how new working conditions were affecting employees. The survey's indices look at five main areas driving employee productivity: the ability to focus; collaboration in a team; bonding with colleagues; renewal of energy throughout the day; and continuous learning (see Figure 1.1).

The findings compare 2.5 million data points driving workplace experience from the pre-COVID-19 era with 2.5 million data points from more than 55,000 respondents worldwide in their work-from-home environment. The findings point to the future role of offices, with observations including:

- Collaboration increased by 10% through homeworking.
- Colleagues working from home struggle to maintain personal connections, which impacts their learning and connection to company culture.
- Younger generations, especially, are struggling with maintaining a sense of connectedness while working remotely.
- 73% want flexible working to continue.
- The new normal will be a 'total workplace ecosystem' – leveraging home, office and third places.

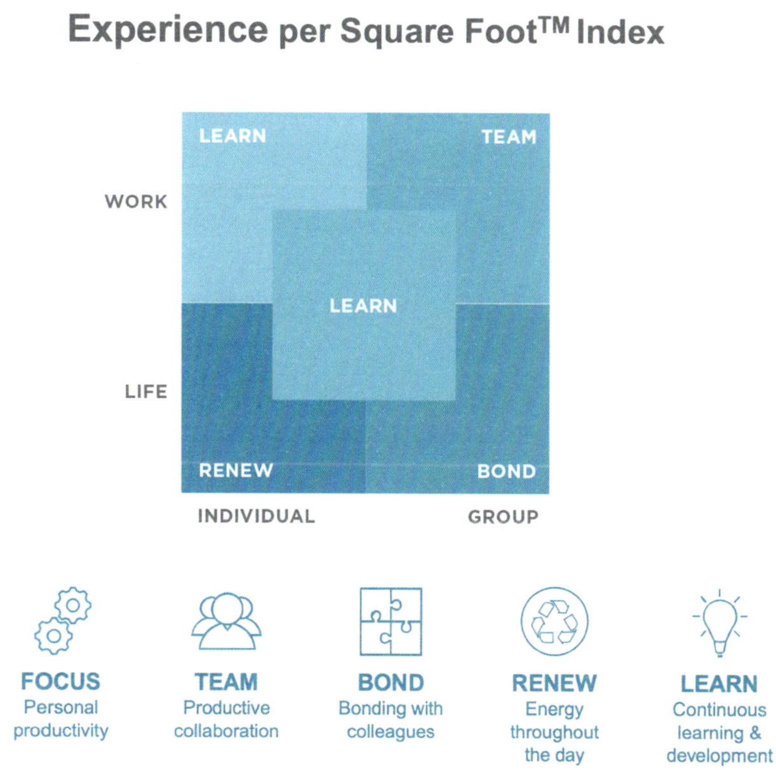

Figure 1.1 Experience per Square Foot™ Index, Cushman & Wakefield.

Office occupiers and investors alike are looking at the long-term implications of COVID-19. When and where will tenants want to occupy space? What typologies will be needed and how much of each will be required? How can people feel connected, safe and productive while working across a variety of locations? It's not just about the office, it's about a wider ecosystem in which as much as half of the future workforce will likely be working across the office, home and elsewhere.

The current crisis has shown that the ability to operate virtually is not only business critical, but it also opens new channels for more equal collaboration and potentially gives access to untapped sources of talent as more employees can access work from wherever they are.

COVID-19 could also impact how we design public realm. Previous pandemics impacted public spaces – like the boulevards and sewers of Paris, and Central Park in New York[2] – to create healthier spaces and air quality, promoting public health. This is important for health and wellbeing, with cities like London beginning to take lessons from places like Amsterdam in promoting cycling and walking. We are reclaiming the spaces between buildings and opening up ground floors to drive better experience, wellbeing and social equity.

Coming out of the crisis, occupiers will rethink the role of offices: from purpose to location and how many offices there should be. Recognising that remote working works for

2 C. Klein, 'How Pandemics Spurred Cities to Make More Green Space for People', HISTORY website, 27 April 2020 (updated 28 April 2020), https://www.history.com/news/cholera-pandemic-new-york-city-london-paris-green-space.

many, there could be less need to have cohorts of employees commuting daily to underutilised offices in expensive capitals, with the associated carbon footprint.

The shift of core offices towards physical meeting and collaboration spaces could accelerate, and this would most likely continue to take place in vibrant urban centres and regional knowledge clusters. Virtual collaboration and individual work will happen from an increasing variety of locations closer to talent pools. Many organisations could therefore potentially shift from centralised models to distributed, on-demand space provision.

The idea of the distributed workplace is not new. Its intellectual history can be traced back to Frank Duffy and DEGW.[3] As gleaned from the DEGW Archive, they have been key in linking the changing nature of work to the way we conceptualise, design and use office spaces.[4] Duffy argues: 'The unit of analysis is no longer the shorthand of office buildings and departmental boundaries – how anachronistic the term "headquarters" already seems – but the sum total of all the many and varied spaces and places within which and between which highly mobile, electronically networked, knowledge workers are already operating successfully.'[5]

3 F. Duffy *et al.*, *Design for Change: The Architecture of DEGW*, Haslemere / Basel: Watermark / Birkhäuser, 1998.

4 https://collections.reading.ac.uk/special-collections/collections/degw-archive/; H. Patel and S.D. Green, 'Beyond the Performance Gap: Reclaiming Building Appraisal Through Archival Research', *Building Research and Information*, 48(5), 2020, pp 469–84.

5 F. Duffy, 'About This Book', in B. Hardy *et al.*, *Working Beyond Walls*, Office of Government Commerce, 2008, p 6, https://assets.publishing.service.gov.uk/government/uploads/system/uploads/attachment_data/file/394153/Working-beyond-Walls.pdf.

Since COVID-19, rather than concentrating on standalone offices, organisations will likely operate across a workplace ecosystem including the following components:

- **Core hubs – smaller and higher quality:** the core office function would focus on collaboration, learning and development, and client meetings, creating a sense of belonging and brand. Post social distancing, employees may still be expected to spend regular time in these key hubs to ensure informal collaboration and connection to corporate culture. Requirement for individual desking could decrease, but more companies will target central and accessible urban locations for event spaces.
- **On-demand event spaces and third spaces:** for companies' increasing remote work or even completely shifting to virtual, there could be a new requirement for on-demand event/collaboration spaces for recurring company and team meetings. Demand for these would be in accessible and memorable locations such as city centres, main transportation hubs including airports, and out-of-town destination hotels. There will be continued demand for third spaces, i.e. people working in cafés, hotel lobbies and in transit.
- **Flexible 'touch down' space:** in larger metropolitan areas with extended employment catchment areas it would make sense to provide additional space on demand, leased on flexible terms. These hubs would be smaller and in less central areas, still surrounded by

amenities and public transport. They could welcome employees that want to benefit from corporate workplace infrastructure within reasonable commute distance.

- **Local community hubs:** to avoid longer commute times and tap into wider employment catchment areas, people could access local community workplace hubs close to where they live. These could be in regional cities, out of town or on local high streets. High-street retail units could be rejuvenated to provide innovative workspaces within walking or cycling distance. These hubs would also satisfy employee appetite for greater engagement within their own communities and increased movement.

The overall requirement for office provision is likely to decrease, allowing for smaller core hubs in attractive urban areas as well as a variety of other locations. Occupiers adopting distributed portfolios, with workspace provision closer to employees, will ensure better resilience in times of crisis.

Large cities will most probably continue to attract employment, but the likely acceleration of remote and flexible working will decrease the time spent in core office hubs. It is possible that demand for traditional office space will slow down or even decrease in large cities, and rebalance into regional hubs and attractive regional cities. The pace of change could be rapid, as the average remaining lease length across the world has decreased to three years according to Cushman & Wakefield's data, giving time for organisations to redeploy their portfolios.

Overall, rather than new workplace strategies emerging we see the potential for the acceleration of current trends with hybrid

Figure 1.2 The Total Workplace Ecosystem, Cushman & Wakefield, 2020.

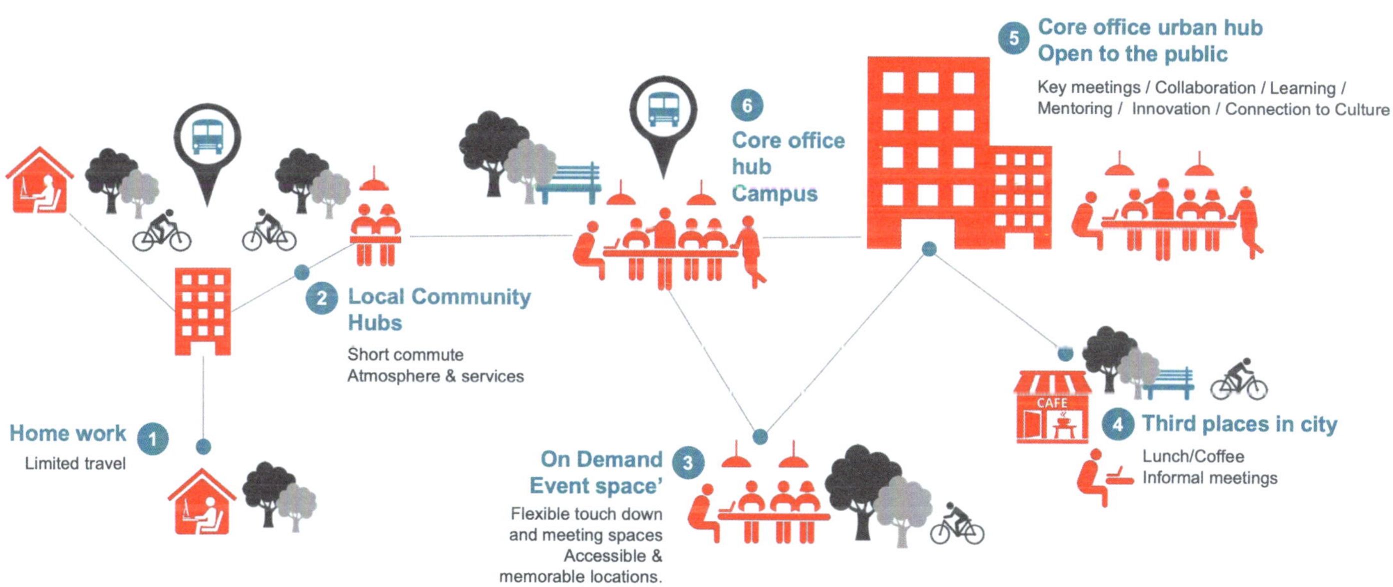

workplace scenarios. The old way of doing things is fundamentally in question: both occupiers and investors need to make this pivot to drive long-term value, improve the employee experience, minimise negative environmental impact and create thriving workplace ecosystems.

With work becoming more distributed and virtual, the role of physical place, and the office, to meet, socialise and learn is more important than ever. This presents a great opportunity for designers of the built environment to create places, both physically and virtually, for communities to connect and create a sense of belonging.

Figure 1.3 King's Cross, London mixed-use connective public realm.

DIMITRIS VLACHOPOULOS

Partner – Head of Location Strategy EMEA, Cushman & Wakefield

The Future of Location Strategy and the 'Disappearing City'

The city of everywhere and nowhere

A virus, that keeps us contained in our homes for months, that changes the way we work, create, socialise, consume, learn and live. COVID-19 sweeps away many of the artificial barriers to move more of our lives online, to fully leverage the capabilities of cloud computing and digitisation. This is a glimpse of the future. Ironically, the future appears to take us back almost 90 years, when Frank Lloyd Wright in his 1932 book *The Disappearing City* introduced us to the radical concept of the Broadacre City.[6]

This was a model that would completely disperse the city as we know it, giving each family at least an acre of land on which to live but also to raise its own food. *The city should be everywhere and nowhere.* Professionals would work near home; people would spend more time with their families and not so much time travelling unnecessarily. Electrical power and communication would collapse distances.[7]

Almost 90 years later, and we are not any closer to Frank Lloyd Wright's vision. In fact, the suburbanisation that began in the 1950s is a light version of the Broadacre City model that didn't fully live up to expectations, and since the late 1990s talent and companies have started moving back to cities.

From physical to digital: the new norm?

Since Frank Lloyd Wright we have embraced digital life, constantly connected to online. We increasingly shop, work and socialise online. But so far, this digital activity has been complementary to our default analogue mode; the city hasn't been disappearing yet. However, perhaps it has already started … Have you been in the City of London on a Friday daytime or commuted during a Friday morning 'peak' time before the COVID-19 lockdown? Over the last few years, with more and more people working from home on Fridays, the City of London has indeed been 'disappearing'. According to the recent ONS Labour Force Survey, before the pandemic more than 1.54 million people in the UK already worked from home for their main job – a 74% increase within 10 years.[8] The trend in America has been similar with 8.25 million people, or 5.3% of the population, now reporting home as their primary work location.[9] A recent survey showed that nearly two-thirds of people worked remotely

6 Frank Lloyd Wright Foundation, 'Revisiting Frank Lloyd Wright's Vision for "Broadacre City"', 8 September 2017, https://franklloydwright.org/revisiting-frank-lloyd-wrights-vision-broadacre-city/.

7 T. O'Donnell, 'Decentralization Integration: Frank Lloyd Wright's Broadacre City', Urban Utopias website, 1 January 2020, https://urbanutopias.net/2020/01/01/broadacre-city/.

8 Office for National Statistics, 'Homeworkers by UK region, 2008 compared to 2018', 2019, https://www.ons.gov.uk/file?uri=/employmentandlabourmarket/peopleinwork/employmentandemployeetypes/adhocs/009913homeworkersbyukregion2008comparedto2018/regionalhomeworkers0818.xls.

9 United States Census Bureau, 2018, https://data.census.gov/cedsci/.

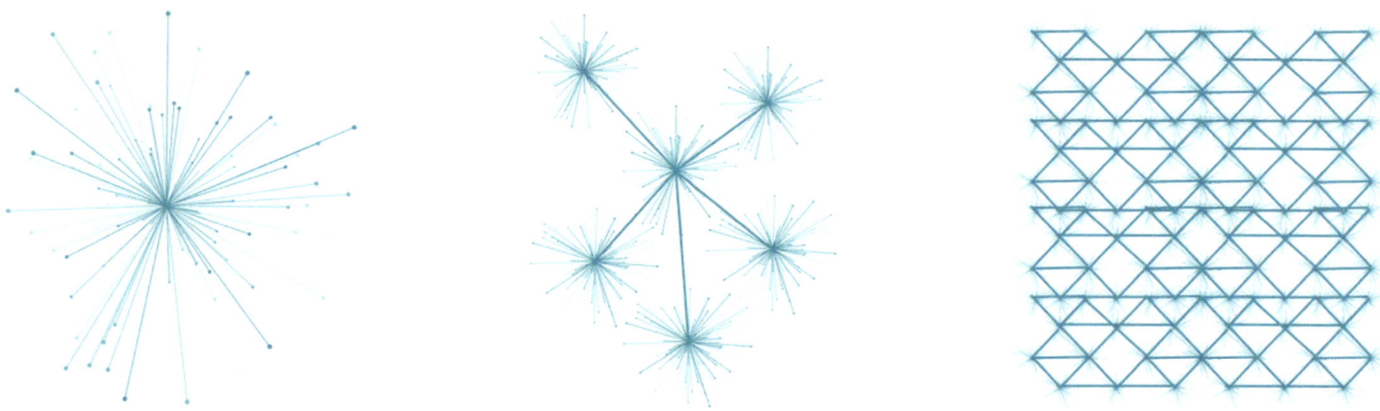

Figure 1.4 Diagrams of three key operating models: centralised, decentralised and distributed.

before the pandemic, at least occasionally.[10] The advantage of having fewer distractions and the flexibility to weave personal obligations into the day are cited as benefits.

Let's imagine how the city would look if this practice extended beyond Fridays. This is what we have experienced with the COVID-19 outbreak. By necessity, the analogue mode is temporarily unavailable. COVID-19 has forced us to switch fully to the digital mode and social distancing. Now that the genie is out, it will be almost impossible to put it back in the bottle when this unprecedented period of global quarantine ends.[11] According to Cushman & Wakefield's XSF@ Home survey, 73% of respondents would like their companies to embrace long-term or permanent flexible working policies post COVID-19.[12]

10 Owl Labs, 'State of Remote Work 2019', https://www.owllabs.com/state-of-remote-work/2019.

11 L.-H. Liang, 'How Covid-19 Led to a Nationwide Work-From-Home Experiment', BBC website, 9 March 2020, https://www.bbc.com/worklife/article/20200309-coronavirus-covid-19-advice-chinas-work-at-home-experiment.

12 'Cushman & Wakefield Predicts New Normal for Workplace', Cushman & Wakefield website, 27 May 2020, https://www.cushmanwakefield.com/en/news/2020/05/research-predicts-new-normal-for-workplace.

The future of location strategy

If we can do most of these activities from anywhere in the world, how relevant will a company's office location be? Do companies need to be where the talent is, or can they employ global talent connected virtually via the company's Cloud platform? Which factors are expected to become more critical for location selection? And is demand for core urban areas going to continue at the same level as today?

We expect the following trends to play a critical role in influencing corporations' future location strategy.

1. Global talent sourcing – virtual presence everywhere

Companies will be able to source untapped talent pools. Over the past 20 years we have been experiencing a shift from a centralised operating model to a decentralised one, with companies setting up shared service centres and centres of excellence in lower-cost regional locations. We now expect a shift to a distributed model where companies have presence everywhere, as the employee address becomes the virtual office address.

2. Regional cities winning ground
Virtual equality and agile working policies could ensure fewer employees feel the pressure to relocate to capital cities to access better career opportunities. Talent will be able to choose where they live and proximity to work will become less important. Smaller cities with good universities could rise in popularity for talent as well as all areas offering a combination of quality of life and affordability.

We have already started partially experiencing this with the 'north shoring' trend in the UK. In the last 10 years the percentage of people leaving London who have bought or rented homes in the north has increased more than tenfold.[13] In Leeds, for example, HMRC is opening a new hub with 6,000 employees; whilst Sky, which already employs 1,300 people in the city, has announced plans for a new Studios Innovation Hub, creating an additional 1,000 jobs by 2022.[14]

3. A radical shift on city selection criteria
New types of locations are expected to emerge as strong contenders for establishing core HQ or satellite hubs, as an internationally distributed workforce is expected to impact the criteria for selecting cities. Factors that could become more important include:

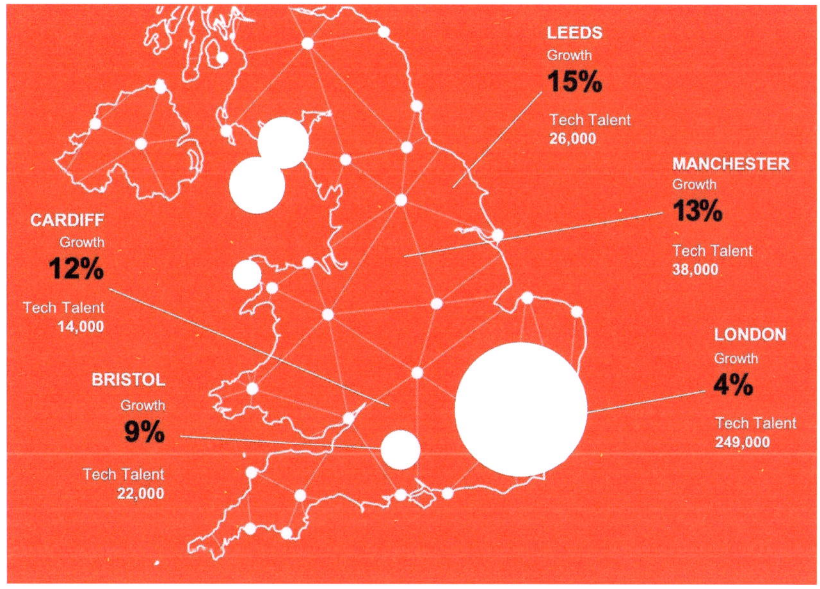

Figure 1.5 UK map showing the growth of tech talent job posts in regional cities versus London.

- **broadband speed and reliability** for virtual collaboration
- **air/ground connectivity** to the geographically dispersed workforce – considering that teams will occasionally need to meet face to face
- **alignment on labour and tax regulation** to enable seamless cross-border business operations – which means locations in countries that are members of international trade and economic unions could be better positioned (e.g. European Union, Eurozone)
- **quality of life and affordability**, to attract talent who will be able to first choose where to live. Locations that have already proven attractive to digital nomads reveal pointers as to some of the elements that can position a city to attract remote workers: these are places with strong performance in cost of living, climate conditions, cultural vibrancy, lifestyle etc.

13 R. Booth and L. Campbell, '"Escaping the Madness": Steep Rise in Londoners Moving to Northern England', *The Guardian*, 14 February 2020, https://www.theguardian.com/uk-news/2020/feb/14/rising-tide-of-londoners-moving-to-northern-england?CMP=fb_gu&utm_medium=Social&utm_source=Facebook#Echobox=1581691561.

14 K. Worsley, 'New Sky Studios Innovation Hub to Open in Leeds', *TheBusinessDesk*, 18 September 2019, https://www.thebusinessdesk.com/yorkshire/news/2043974-new-sky-studios-innovation-hub-to-open-in-leeds

4. A combination of urban and suburban

Most people are likely to choose where to live based on community, amenities, access to transport hubs, education, quality of housing and natural resources. As lifestyle preferences around home and workplace evolve with age and life-stage changes, workplace location preferences will continue to vary:

- **Urban locations** typically provide a high density of transportation infrastructure, cultural, commercial and educational amenities, human capital and demographic diversity.
- **Suburban locations** typically provide an environment that supports wellbeing, with more space for housing and outdoor activities, and a small-town feel.

Winning globally

Organisations will become more global, fluid and virtual, with location becoming a broader and more complex concept that sits between the physical and the virtual. As a result, competition for talent and business is expected to intensify. Changes are also required on the workplace supply side to address the perennial issues of fragmentation as well as lack of feedback from end users.[15]

Cities need to take significant steps to ensure they can seize this opportunity through actions such as:

- continuing to invest in telecommunications infrastructure (broadband, 5G)
- upgrading urban public transport infrastructure with a forward-thinking agenda that addresses future environmental and operational considerations – for example, expansion of cycle lanes and pedestrian networks
- improving air and ground accessibility to regional cities – upgrading and modernising regional airports, rail infrastructure etc.
- incentivising the upgrading of office stock and the development of new types of working space (serviced offices, co-working space) to enable international corporations to set up small-scale regional hubs
- integrating further with international economic or political entities (e.g. the European Union) in terms of employment and tax regulation, to facilitate seamless cross-border employment
- providing tax or other incentives to retain and attract internationally experienced talent
- continuing to invest in education and research to build and strengthen an ecosystem of innovation.

As Facebook founder Mark Zuckerberg has said, 'Enabling more remote work is going to be very positive towards creating more broad-based economic prosperity.'[16]

This is a once-in-a-lifetime opportunity for new locations to emerge and is a potential challenge for those long established.

15 F. Duffy, 'The Office and The City: Twelve Propositions', in *Stream 02 – After Office*, Paris: PCA Editions, 2012, https://www.pca-stream.com/en/articles/the-office-and-the-city-twelve-propositions-39.

16 Facebook live-streamed town hall, 21 May 2020, https://www.youtube.com/watch?v=yVJbVkBa4uM.

THOMAS VAZAKAS

Associate Director, Energy, Infrastructure & Sustainability EMEA, Cushman & Wakefield

A Sustainable Workplace

The COVID-19 pandemic represents the biggest shock to the global energy system in more than seven decades. According to the Global Energy Review report, released by the International Energy Agency in April 2020, the projection for 2020 is for a record annual decline in carbon emissions of almost 8% and a 6% reduction in energy demand.[17] However, this projected reduction is just in line with the 7.6% reduction in carbon dioxide emissions required every year for the next decade, in order to meet the 1.5°C Paris Target, according to the United Nations Report from November 2019.[18] As after previous crises, however, the rebound in emissions may be larger than the decline, so it is very important that we restart the economy in a more energy-efficient way, in order to maintain these projected carbon reductions over the years.

As the COVID-19 crisis spread around the world, vast numbers of people started working from home, with immediate and varied impacts on energy use. Large commercial buildings remained empty and consumed no energy. Energy consumption from transport was also significantly reduced. As a result of less road traffic there was a widespread decline in air pollution. One of the steepest was in New Delhi, where average levels of nitrogen dioxide were around two-thirds lower, during lockdown, compared with the weeks leading up to it.[19]

In 10, 50 or even 100 years into the future, humanity will look back at 2020 as a year that significantly changed our lives. Pandemics tend to have this effect.

The bubonic plague in the 14th century killed at least a third of the European population. However, it also helped to inspire the opening of larger and less crowded public spaces and the appointment of building professionals, like architects, who led the urban improvements of the Renaissance in the next two centuries. Similarly, the 19th-century cholera and smallpox outbreaks, happening at the same time as the Industrial Revolution, helped drive the creation of larger streets in our cities, the implementation of indoor plumbing and city-wide sewer systems and the development of suburban areas. During the 20th century, typhoid, polio and Spanish flu breakouts prompted urban planning, slum clearance and waste management.[20]

17 International Energy Agency, 'Global Energy Review 2020', April 2020, https://www.iea.org/reports/global-energy-review-2020.

18 UN Environment Programme, 'Emissions Gap Report 2019', 26 November 2019, https://www.unenvironment.org/interactive/emissions-gap-report/2019/.

19 D. Crow and A. Millot, 'Working From Home Can Save Energy and Reduce Emissions. But How Much?', International Energy Agency website, 12 June 2020, https://www.iea.org/commentaries/working-from-home-can-save-energy-and-reduce-emissions-but-how-much.

20 S. Lubell, 'Past Pandemics Changed the Design of Cities: Six Ways COVID-19 Could Do the Same', *LA Times*, 22 April 2020, https://www-latimes-com.cdn.ampproject.org/c/s/www.latimes.com/entertainment-arts/story/2020-04-22/coronavirus-pandemics-architecture-urban-design?_amp=true.

Remote working can save energy and emissions

Before the COVID-19 pandemic, an estimated 7.9% of the global workforce was working exclusively or mainly from home, according to the International Labour Organization.[21] This is expected to significantly increase post-COVID-19.

As homeworking increased, oil demand shrank but residential electricity use surged.

Figure 1.6 is based on Google mobility data and shows the change in people movement in the UK based on a baseline day, which is defined as the median value from the five-week period from 3 January to 6 February 2020. The graph illustrates the effect of remote working, showing a significant reduction in the time people spent in transit with a small increase in time spent at home.

Even though there is a slow shift back to baseline figures for both workplace and transit presence, it is still evident that this new trend is here to stay. As trends start to stabilise, and more people work from home, fewer people will commute to the office every day.

Figure 1.6 People's change in mobility since the beginning of the pandemic in the UK.

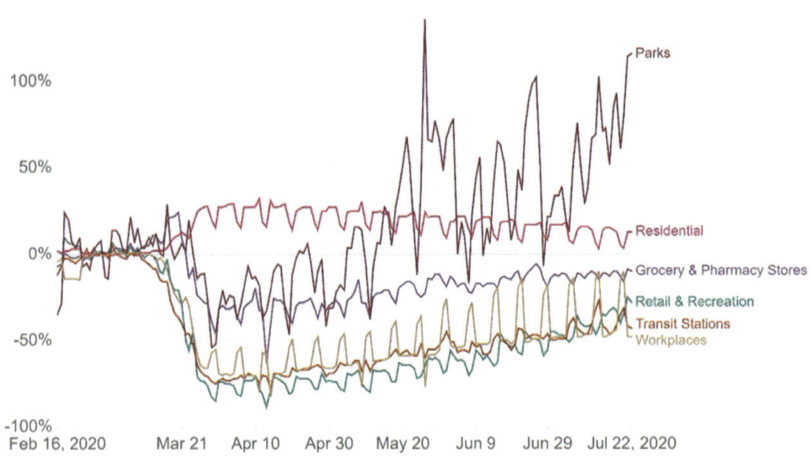

Source: Our World in Data

According to the Google mobility data, the effect of the pandemic on people's mobility is different in big cities that rely heavily on public transport compared to cities where the use of a private car is more common. For example, in London, for June 2020 a 58% reduction on use of public transport is reported against the baseline, compared to just 44% in Leeds and 41% in Los Angeles County.

COVID-19's impact on energy consumption and emissions

The COVID-19 crisis has had staggering consequences for the transport sector. Government lockdowns triggered a fall of 50% to 75% in road traffic around the world. With the majority of employees in affected countries working from home, the effect on rush-hour road traffic was even more striking.[22] Major cities saw a reduction in rush-hour congestion of 65% to 95%.[23]

Energy utilities reported increased residential demand as a result of people spending more time at home (online searches for blenders in the UK have almost doubled since 2019!). In the UK, residential electricity consumption leapt up by 15% in the days after the first lockdown began, with peak demand during lunch hours.[24]

21 International Labour Organization, 'Policy Brief', April 2020, https://www.ilo.org/wcmsp5/groups/public/---ed_protect/---protrav/---travail/documents/briefingnote/wcms_743447.pdf, p 2.

22 Eurofound, 'Living, Working and COVID-19: First Findings – April 2020', 6 May 2020, https://www.eurofound.europa.eu/publications/report/2020/living-working-and-covid-19-first-findings-april-2020.

23 Crow and Millot, 'Working From Home'.

24 Crow and Millot, 'Working From Home'.

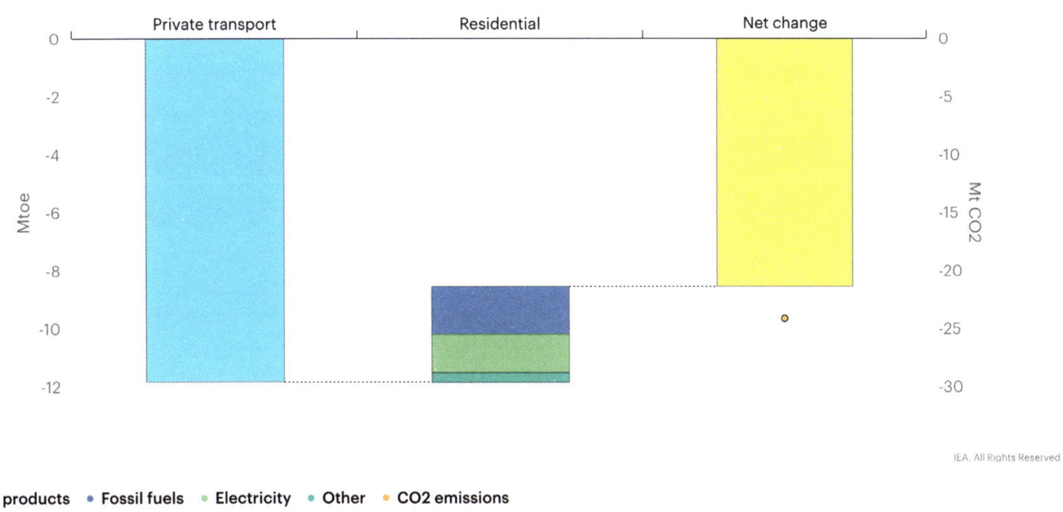

Figure 1.7 Net savings from teleworking.

Source: IEA (2020), https://www.iea.org/commentaries/working-from-home-can-save-energy-and-reduce-emissions-but-how-much. All rights reserved.

The impact of remote working on transport varies widely depending on the region and the time of year. In the United States, the average one-way commute by car is around 18km, and over three-quarters of car commuters travel alone, according to the US Census Bureau. In Europe, the average one-way car commute is 15km, and in China it is 8km. Differences in fuel efficiency, local geography and the use of air-conditioning also matter.[25]

For commuting by car, a day working from home would in general reduce energy consumption and CO_2 emissions. However, for short commutes by car (less than 6km in the United States, 3km in the European Union and 2km in China), as well as for those made by public transport, working from home could lead to a small increase in emissions as a result of extra residential energy use. The net effect would depend on the residential fuel mix; however, according to the International Energy Agency, the overall energy saved as a result of less commuting is still around four times larger than the increase in residential energy consumption, as presented in Figure 1.7.[26]

On a global level, oil savings are around 11.9 million tonnes of oil equivalent (Mtoe) per year – or about 250,000 barrels a day, corresponding to about 1% of road passenger transport consumption. After including the extra residential demand, overall energy use falls by around 8.5Mtoe, resulting in a drop of 24Mt in annual CO_2 emissions.[27]

For companies to see the biggest benefits from homeworking, it needs to be widespread enough that they can ensure offices make the best use of space and maximise energy savings. However, people who usually work from home often live

25 Crow and Millot, 'Working From Home'.

26 Crow and Millot, 'Working From Home'.

27 Crow and Millot, 'Working From Home'.

further away from their office, meaning that they have much longer journeys on the days they do commute, which may offset much of the savings. For example, one study of UK workers found that those who work from home have, on average, a 17.2km-longer commute than those who are solely office-based.[28]

A sustainable future workplace

It is evident that the future workplace environment will be significantly different. How we design our buildings to support the swift changes in work patterns, ensuring the best use of technology, maximising the wellbeing of the building users, without ignoring the big white elephant in the room – climate change and sustainability – is the key question for all building professionals.

When designing the office, sustainability will be paramount. The following seven principles will be key.

Low energy consumption

Buildings will have to reduce their energy consumption to match the needs of their occupants. We see buildings currently designed to full occupancy but in reality, the average utilisation in a typical office in EMEA is 61%.[29] As a result, large parts of the building are conditioned for no reason. Smart buildings with building management system (BMS) optimisation can save energy whilst ensuring the wellbeing of their occupants.

28 C. Edmond, 'Working From Home Might Not Cut Energy Use As Much As We'd Hoped', World Economic Forum website, 10 June 2020, https://www.weforum.org/agenda/2020/06/remote-working-energy-use-coronavirus/.

29 Cushman & Wakefield, occupancy database 2020.

Modular buildings

As the pandemic has grown, the most pressing need has been speed: the quick creation of emergency facilities like hospitals, quarantine centres, testing sites and temporary lodgings. That demand has prompted an overwhelming response, much of it employing techniques outside the mainstream, with modular construction – prefabricating standardised components in a factory, then assembling them quickly on site. This technique has huge advantages in speed, but also in reducing waste and energy consumption. Moreover, flexible components like moveable walls can help buildings adapt to future needs.

Design for reuse

More than 80% of buildings that will be standing in 2050 are already built, so upgrading these is key. This is even more important if changes in use may be required for older, less desirable commercial buildings, due to increased remote working. It's clear that we'll need more efficient, effective and flexible reuse plans for future uses.

Healthy buildings

COVID-19 has made people realise the importance of wellbeing, and the impact buildings and work itself have on health. Expect more people to embrace a healthy building movement, an approach to improving health through strategies like greater natural light, improved ventilation, fewer toxic substances and the incorporation of plants and other natural materials. Think skylights, large windows, rooftop terraces, balconies and courtyards. Spaces for exercise and meditation could become standard, along with home offices. Health and wellbeing are key pillars for sustainability.

Convergence of residential, office and hospitality

With increased remote working, residential projects need to cater for homeworking. Mixed-use developments with workplace, residential and leisure accommodation will increase in popularity. Workplaces need to become more like hotels, offering a range of meeting and leisure spaces. This more sustainable approach will reduce the direct and indirect environmental impact of our buildings and improve their social impact in our cities and regions.

Building certifications

Third-party building certifications like BREEAM, LEED, WELL or Fitwel are already common and demand is likely to increase. Certifications will be used by investors to attract tenants and by occupiers to attract employees. Regulators (i.e. planning policies such as the London Plan) will ask for these to demonstrate compliance with their sustainability and energy targets.

Circular economy

With continued organisational change, reuse of existing buildings, and a focus on reducing energy use and increasing wellbeing, a shift towards a circular economy and embodied carbon is inevitable. According to the Ellen MacArthur Foundation, the circular economy is based on the principles of designing out waste and pollution, keeping products and materials in use, and regenerating natural systems.[30] Already the London Plan has produced the *Design for a Circular Economy Primer* to help support organisations in the built environment sector understand how they can embed circular economy principles into their projects and design processes.[31]

SOPHIE SCHULLER

Partner – Integrated Facilities Management EMEA, Cushman & Wakefield

Employee Experience

The relationship between architecture and facilities management

Architecture and facilities management (FM) can be considered traditionally at opposite ends of the workplace life cycle, with the practice of architecture dealing with the design and conception of the physical space, and FM bringing the use of the space to life through activity-based services and managing the asset over the long term.[32] However, as an Edinburgh University review of the interactions between FM and architecture points out, 'FM [included]

30 Ellen MacArthur Foundation, 'The Circular Economy in Detail', undated, https://www.ellenmacarthurfoundation.org/explore/the-circular-economy-in-detail.

31 Mayor of London, *Design for a Circular Economy: Primer*, undated, https://www.london.gov.uk/sites/default/files/design_for_a_circular_economy_web.pdf.

32 M. Fenker and F. Lautier, 'Architecture and Facilities Management: Design implications of the Growth of Service Activities', RAMAU International Workshop Architecture and Facilities Management, Paris, 17–18 April 2008, pp 1–3, https://www.ramau.archi.fr/IMG/pdf/problematiquefm-eng-2.pdf.

at the design stage will add value to the facility by ensuring less "rework", emphasizing value for money, efficient control of the supply chain and teamwork.'[33] Essentially, it is hard to successfully design a space without input from the people responsible for managing the experiences within it.

What is employee experience and how can it be curated?

In order for architects and FM professionals to effectively navigate the impact of COVID-19, we must first understand the 'employee experience'.

Facilities management, long seen as the less attractive end of the real-estate life cycle, has in recent years been undergoing a quiet revolution. It seems that clean lavatories, gym services and free soft drinks actually make employees happier and can increase productivity. According to a 2015 study of over 1,000 respondents by US grocery-delivery service Peapod, 'while the majority, 56%, of full-time employees are "extremely" or "very" happy with their current job, that number jumps to 67% among those who have access to free food'.[34] You don't need to search further than the bountifully stocked kitchenettes in Bloomberg's, Google's and Facebook's offices to see this in action.

Facilities management has been slowly migrating from the delivery of functional workplace services (reception, security, light bulbs) to curating a series of experiences for employees and office dwellers through which to enrich their day, increase their enjoyment of the workplace and essentially keep them working longer and more efficiently.

But in a post-pandemic environment where employees' experience is typically limited to their choice of virtual conferencing rooms, what does the future of employee experience look like and how could this shift the landscape of workplace design?

Initially we should acknowledge that experience in its very nature is subjective and personal. In the XSF@Home survey, conducted during the recent global lockdown, Cushman & Wakefield found that 70% of Generation Z respondents reported challenges working from home.[35] Not all experiences of recent working practices have been positive.

This highlights that curating an employee experience is not a 'one-size-fits-all' effort. Does the current architectural curriculum offer enough training for architects on the anthropological aspects of placemaking? Is that curriculum equipping students to undertake user research that could enable not just building,

33 A. Enoma, 'The Role of Facilities Management at the Design Stage', in F. Khosrowshahi (ed.), *21st Annual ARCOM Conference*, 7–9 September 2005, SOAS, University of London, Association of Researchers in Construction Management, vol. 1, pp 421–30.

34 H. Malcolm, 'Study: The Key to Happiness at Work is Free Snacks', *USA Today*, undated, https://eu.usatoday.com/story/money/2015/09/16/study-says-snacks-affect-happiness-at-work/72259746/.

35 D. Katsikakis, B. Berthold, S. Zatta and D. Brown, *The Future of Workplace; How Will COVID-19 and Data Shape the New Workplace Ecosystem?*, London: Cushman & Wakefield, 2020, p 9, https://www.cushmanwakefield.com/vi-vn/insights/covid-19/the-future-of-workplace.

but the critical evaluation and constant revival of a knowledge base for the profession?[36]

In addition, there is the consideration of experience for whom? The employee as an individual? Their learning, working preference, family situation, geographical location, experience with each other? Or is it an experience of the corporate culture? Cushman & Wakefield's *The Future of Workplace* research paper found that of 55,000 people polled globally, 73% feel disconnected from corporate culture.[37] With homeworking undoubtedly playing a larger role in the future of work, it begs the question. How will corporate culture develop when people don't sit together every day?

With consideration of the above, it could be argued that the future role of architects is more akin to that of a film director: designing an immersive 9D cinematic experience of the workplace. A 9D workplace experience could provide its inhabitants with a pair of VR glasses, allowing them to step into a 3D, 360-degree visual version of the workplace. Body sensors on handheld devices or wearable monitors allow you to 'walk' around. The built-in sound and light functions expand the realism of the experience and could be customisable to the inhabitant's individual or group preferences. With this lifelike technology-based experience, people could connect and gather in a fully immersive, more realistic way as opposed to the decidedly 2D experience of our current Zoom and Microsoft Teams channels.

New working practices enable more people to 'experience' work

Do recent events create an opportunity for employees who could not previous experience work, to join in?

In days gone by, work was something you did in the building you went to '9 to 5'. The recent global experiment during lockdown has taught us that homeworking does not reduce company productivity. A May 2020 *Forbes* article reports how a California-based company had tracked a 47% increase in worker productivity across 30,000 respondents using non-invasive spyware.[38] We spend longer on email, phone and instant messaging; we are more connected than ever.

People previously living in the Outer Hebrides or on remote islands off the coast of Iceland have been limited to certain jobs and work. People with physical or psychological barriers have been limited to certain jobs and work. In a recent review the UK House of Commons reported that 46% of people living with a disability within the UK are unemployed and that people with disabilities have an employment rate that is 28.6 percentage points lower than that of people without disabilities, commonly referred to as the

36 F. Duffy, 'Facilities Managers and New Developments: The Experience of Broadgate and Stockley Park', in W.F.E. Preiser (ed.), *Professional Practice in Facility Programming*, New York: Van Nostrand Reinhold, 1993, pp 85–102.

37 Katsikakis *et al.*, *The Future of Workplace*, p 8.

38 C. Westfall, 'New Survey Shows 47% Increase In Productivity: 3 Things You Must Do When Working From Home', *Forbes*, 20 May 2020, https://www.forbes.com/sites/chriswestfall/2020/05/20/new-survey-shows-47-increase-in-productivity-3-things-you-must-do-when-working-from-home/#1ab31aa780dc.

'disability employment gap'.[39] Does an online world offer an opportunity to close this gap?

If so, what should the experience for these people be? How can architects create opportunities for such employees to experience corporate culture in a virtual or lower-touchpoint way?

A future career for architects may involve the creation of online spaces. Perhaps these could be curated Microsoft Teams backgrounds and online virtual spaces for people to connect and 'live' in a commercial version of Animal Crossing™ or a modern-day The Sims™. Virtual reality (VR) design tools provide architects with just this opportunity. Could this be extended to not only use VR as a design tool, but as the product itself?

The future of employee experience

Within the traditional envelope of 'the office', cultivating employee experience through FM is well defined. However, in a post-pandemic world, the definition and shape of the office has radically changed.

The workplace profession has long considered the need for offices to facilitate social engagement and connectivity, but within the new world, does the scope of this go further? If the home is to function as an office and the office is to function as a home, what does socialisation look like in an office environment? Walking meetings and outdoor gatherings appear to provide some with assuredness and the ability to socialise once again. Will we see the first 'outdoor' offices; gardens and farms staged into weatherproof office experiences?

Soho House and other high-end private members' clubs have long known it, but could the private members' clubs make a mainstream return for the masses? They could offer a 24/7 experience for employees with the provision of hotels, spas and gym facilities to take care of employee's health and wellbeing, and state-of-the-art meeting rooms to ensure that absent colleagues can share in the experience of today's work agenda. As Lipton Rogers, the developers behind 22 Bishopsgate, London say, these could be 'vertical villages' providing 'wellbeing every day of the week, not just the weekends'.[40]

A radical shift for in-office facilities management

Traditional FM services such as cleaning and catering are also undergoing a key change. Cleaning often delivered in the dead of night by an invisible workforce is suddenly performed frequently and in full visibility – a psychological reminder that in a post-pandemic world the office is a safe space; cleanliness has become synonymous with safety.

In addition, catering services typically provided as a full-scale daily buffet of hot and cold options is in the new world no longer hygienically possible. Demand-based catering options selected alongside booking a desk

39 A. Powell, 'Research Briefing: Disabled People in Employment', London: House of Commons Library, 13 August 2020, pp 3–6, https://commonslibrary.parliament.uk/research-briefings/cbp-7540/.

40 22 Bishopsgate website, https://22bishopsgate.com.

on the office app are increasing in popularity and visibility amongst those within the FM industry. With a growing and mainstream focus on sustainability, reduction of waste and consumption of plastic by organisations such as Unilever, IKEA and sports brand Patagonia, brands not focusing on these topics will be in the minority.

Employee experience and homeworking

On the other side, we have homeworking. In a recent interview with the *Wall Street Journal*, Mark Zuckerberg confirmed that Facebook would start '"aggressively opening up remote hiring", expecting that about half its workforce would work remotely over the next five to 10 years'.[41]

Whilst there have always been 'homeworkers', this category of employees has historically been small in population and had limited attention from an FM perspective. According to the Office for National Statistics, the proportion of the UK workforce who worked 'mainly' at home went from 4% to 5% in the UK between 2015 and 2019. Post-COVID-19, this number is reported as being approximately 49%.[42]

In response to the COVID-19 situation, we saw corporations curating packages of office furniture and computer screens for employees to work safely in an invisible environment. What is the role of architecture in homeworking environments?

The long-term effect on the intersection between mental health, wellbeing and productivity of employees and, as a result, the requirement for space to facilitate and support homeworking, is still in its infancy.

Finally, does this new way of working offer us a second chance at globalisation where the boundaries of work, previously designed to cater for the commute and office experience, are enhanced by IT and events? This could pose an interesting dynamic where your workspace is not dictated by your physical presence and your ability to connect is not limited to 'who is in the office'. IT becomes part of FM. The role of the architect is to design both physical and virtual environments, in the home and workspace. Where 'going to work' no longer becomes a destination, but rather an ecosystem from which the employee can choose their work location. And where people can commune or retreat in a world that has during 2020 dramatically shifted to include a life to be lived online.

41 S. Usborne, 'End of the Office: The Quiet, Grinding Loneliness of Working From Home', *The Guardian*, 14 July 2020, https://www.theguardian.com/money/2020/jul/14/end-of-the-office-the-quiet-grinding-loneliness-of-working-from-home.

42 Office for National Statistics, 'Coronavirus and the Latest Indicators for the UK Economy and Society: 18 June 2020', https://www.ons.gov.uk/peoplepopulationandcommunity/healthandsocialcare/conditionsanddiseases/bulletins/coronavirustheukeconomyandsocietyfasterindicators/18june2020#main-points.

JOE WHITE

Associate Director and Head of Technology Client Care EMEA, Cushman & Wakefield

The Digital Workplace

There are two main drivers differentiating smart or digital buildings:

- operational efficiency
- occupier experience.

Both are equally important. The one common factor in all smart building initiatives is data.

The value of data

The research company Gartner predicted in 2017 that there would be 20 billion internet-connected things (excluding PCs and smartphones) by the end of 2020.[43] We are connected in more ways than we could ever have imagined even a decade ago. Tens of billions of devices are all online, all contributing data, and all, if used effectively, with the capacity to make fundamental and long-lasting recommendations for change. Whilst there is a lot of discussion around smart buildings, they only become smart when the data is harnessed and utilised in an appropriate way. Capturing the data is important, interrogating the data is key, but making data-led decisions that improve the built environment for occupiers is the purpose.

43 M. Hung (ed.), 'Leading the IoT: Gartner Insights on How to Lead in a Connected World', Gartner Inc., 2017, https://www.gartner.com/imagesrv/books/iot/iotEbook_digital.pdf.

Digital twins in practice

A prominent example of using data to drive value is the concept of digital twins. A digital twin is a digital version of a physical asset. This technology can make a huge impact in commercial properties. An example of digital twins in practice is fault detection and diagnosis (FDD) in HVAC equipment. The European Centre for Disease Prevention and Control (ECDC) has stated that poor ventilation in confined environments is associated with increased transmission of respiratory infections,[44] and therefore the importance of cleaning and maintenance of HVAC systems is key. Utilising FDD when designing a building will provide proactive insights into performance and potential issues. The use of FDD and sensors to enable proactive maintenance will be a requirement of buildings in the future. Sensors could become literally 'part of the furniture', ensuring that everything that can be measured, is measured.

Beyond occupancy sensors

A study of the major players providing sensors suggested the global occupancy sensor market was valued at $2.45 billion in 2019 and is expecting to rise to $6.7 billion by 2025.[45] With this clear increase in occupancy sensors, it is likely that growth will also occur in other types of sensors such as those gauging light, indoor

44 European Centre for Disease Prevention and Control, 'Heating, Ventilation and Air-Conditioning Systems in the Context of COVID-19', 22 June 2020, https://www.ecdc.europa.eu/sites/default/files/documents/Ventilation-in-the-context-of-COVID-19.pdf.

45 Mordor Intelligence, 'Occupancy Sensor Market – Growth, Trends, and Forecast (2020–2025)', 2019, https://www.mordorintelligence.com/industry-reports/occupancy-sensor-market.

air quality, assets and equipment, especially in view of COVID-19. Designing sensors into the building to gather data on how the building is working or incorporating the concept of 'Digital Ceilings'[46] will help drive the green building ethos and attract investors and occupiers to use data to make better decisions.

The lag between building design and technology maturity

Digital twins are one example of technology that risks trying to run before it can walk.[47] The digital twin industry was valued at $3.8 billion in 2019 and is expected to grow to $35.8 by 2025.[48] We can expect that some early adopters will learn lessons and experience failures. After many years the industry is still only starting to embrace BIM.[49]

Whilst much of this technology exists today, much of it is immature or has inflated expectations. Technology needs to be tested at scale. The implementation process is likely to test to the limits and potentially end in more failures than successes. Many of the buildings that will be built in 2025 are already being designed now. Many of the office buildings we will occupy in 2025 are already built and occupied today. There is an inherent lag between building design and construction and technology maturity. By 2025 the tools that are either at a consumer level or are being piloted now will have significantly improved and will be more commonplace in the corporate real-estate environment.

Tenant/building user experience

In terms of tenant/building user experience, occupiers are becoming much more reliant on and even expectant of certain levels of technology. Building designers need to respond and embed technology in the design process. Experience apps can give users access to data from sensors, enable them to book a space, control light intensity and even adjust temperature, to their preference. Giving occupiers this kind of control will not only improve their experience but is also likely to reduce the cost of unnecessary callouts.

The impact of COVID-19 on smart buildings

With more than 75 million daily active users of Microsoft Teams during the pandemic (an 894% increase since early February 2020),[50] employees are clearly adapting to the use of virtual meetings and collaboration. In a post-pandemic environment, occupiers will seek fewer touchpoints when entering a building. Apps that integrate building access control, calling lifts and visitor management will mean that users can interact with common multi-

46 Cisco, 'Cisco Digital Ceiling: White Paper', 2016, https://www.cisco.com/c/dam/global/zh_cn/assets/pdf/white-paper-c11-736542.pdf.

47 J. Adams, 'Is Construction Ready for Digital Twins?', *BIM+*, 11 May 2019, https://www.bimplus.co.uk/opinion/construction-ready-digital-twins-john-adams/.

48 J. Harris, 'As Important as the Internet: Are Digital Twins the Next Big Thing for Construction?', *Building*, 13 November 2019, https://www.building.co.uk/digital-transformation/as-important-as-the-internet-are-digital-twins-the-next-big-thing-for-construction/5102682.article.

49 A. Lapsley, 'Technology Shifts from Design Process to Design Product', DesignIntelligence website, 23 May 2017, https://www.di.net/articles/technology-shifts-design-process-design-product/.

50 T. Warren, 'Microsoft Teams Jumps 70 Percent to 75 Million Daily Active Users', *The Verge*, 29 April 2020, https://www.theverge.com/2020/4/29/21241972/microsoft-teams-75-million-daily-active-users-stats.

user touchpoints without physically touching anything.[51] Incorporating digital signage with these touchpoints enables both wayfinding and access to key building information. Specific and customised messages can target people as they walk past, such as 'your next meeting is on the 3rd floor', or 'avoid the Victoria line due to delays'. These apps (such as MODO™ (modolabs.com), DISTRICT™ (https://district-tech.com/), HqO™ (https://www.hqo.co/) and RISE™ (https://www.risebuildings.com)) will become an important part of corporate community communication and engagement. They will be key in enabling people to connect with each other, order lunch, arrange meetings and share information. This is likely to become increasingly important as more people work virtually.

Biometric design in buildings

Taking this one step further, biometric design is becoming more prevalent, i.e. using your face or your thumbprint as a password. Biometric access will allow people to walk up to access gates and navigate to the space they will use for the day. This space could already be customised to their preferred environmental conditions.

Sales of voice assistants for consumer use are increasing. The Gartner IT Symposium in 2019 published a summary of the top strategic trends for 2020,[52] one of which suggested a reduction in physical buttons being pressed or screens being swiped in favour of multi-experience through conversational, immersive and sensory experiences. This retail disruptor is likely to translate into the corporate real estate. Voice activation should be built into building infrastructure, allowing occupiers to interact with their environment through voice or digital assistants.

The building of 2025 will rely heavily on capturing, digesting and most importantly generating value from building data. A post-pandemic world is likely to shape both the types of buildings that are designed, as well as the use of these buildings. The building of 2025 will not purely be a place where an employee or visitor goes to work; it will be an asset they interact with using experience apps. Buildings will be designed with many of the technologies readily available today and focused on improving both operating efficiencies and occupier experience.

51 J. Mudditt, 'How Offices Will Change After Coronavirus', BBC website, 15 May 2020, https://www.bbc.com/worklife/article/20200514-how-the-post-pandemic-office-will-change.

52 K. Panetta, 'Gartner Top 10 Strategic Technology Trends for 2020', Gartner Inc. website, 21 October 2019, https://www.gartner.com/smarterwithgartner/gartner-top-10-strategic-technology-trends-for-2020/.

NAOMI CLEAVER

Interior designer

Co-work (Live)

The co-work sector, and its co-conspirator, co-live, were already pretty dynamic sectors pre-COVID-19. Iterations abounded and boundaries blurred: The Department Store in London's Brixton is home to design firm Squire & Partners, but also offers a neighbourhood co-work space with the added feature of model-making workshops and a large basement for lectures and parties. Big and Tiny in Silver Lake, California is an illuminating example of another co-work space with added benefits, namely a crèche for working parents.

In the wake of the COVID-19 pandemic and associated 'social distancing', designing shared co-work space for a wide community of usually sole traders and SMEs is a stimulating creative challenge that accelerates ideation in this field.

Versatility, connectivity and, to a greater or lesser degree, a 'bottom-up' management strategy, are strengths core to the success of the most viable co-work spaces to date. They are also the survival skills of any endeavour in the face of economic, social and cultural vicissitudes.

Homeworking

Already in the first quarter of 2020, 18% of all UK employees were self-employed, with over 30% of those working from home.[53] One month later, by April 2020 and in the teeth of lockdown, nearly half (47%) of people in employment did at least some of their work from home,[54] revealing to many individuals and companies new possibilities in 'how to do work' and enhance that often elusive work/life balance, as well as balance sheets.

The inherent flexibility in co-work space puts it in pole position to provide workspace that fits new ways of working. Many employees have come to realise during lockdown that they would actually prefer to work either at home, or much closer to home, some or perhaps all of the time.

And this could even make employees more productive, but crucially only if this is their choice; productivity can improve by 13%, according to a 2015 study by Nicholas Bloom, a senior fellow at the Stanford Institute for Economic Policy Research (SIEPR), and colleagues.[55] (Conversely, Bloom has also observed through lockdown that those forced to work from home, with the challenge of poor

53 Office for National Statistics, 'Dataset EMP14: Employees and Self-Employed by Industry', 11 August 2020, https://www.ons.gov.uk/employmentandlabourmarket/peopleinwork/employmentandemployeetypes/datasets/employeesandselfemployedbyindustryemp14.

54 Office for National Statistics, 'Which Jobs Can Be Done From Home?', 21 July 2020, https://www.ons.gov.uk/employmentandlabourmarket/peopleinwork/employmentandemployeetypes/articles/whichjobscanbedonefromhome/2020-07-21.

55 N.A. Bloom, J. Liang, J. Roberts and Z.J. Ying, 'Does Working From Home Work? Evidence from a Chinese Experiment', *The Quarterly Journal of Economics*, 130(1), February 2015, pp 165–218, https://nbloom.people.stanford.edu/sites/g/files/sbiybj4746/f/wfh.pdf.

broadband connectivity and the distractions of family, or a lovely sunny day, could create a productivity disaster for firms.[56])

Similarly, companies have learnt that they could relinquish costly real estate and rents where co-work space can offer cost-effective 'desks' on flexible contracts, accommodating employees who don't want or need to commute but want to get out of the house.

The value in the spontaneous cross-pollination between individuals from different companies working under one roof is not to be underestimated either, where co-work space is fertile ground for creativity.

Modular is the message here.

Taking the office to the workers

What this means for the design of co-work space is first the opportunity to liberate co-work operations from typical city locations into towns and even rural areas, taking the office to workers instead of workers commuting to the office, though success will be contingent on access to secure high-speed broadband.

It means a continuing commitment to mutable space and a smorgasbord of tenancy contracts that can adapt according to immediate tenant need – perhaps only servicing monthly team meetings – realised in spaces with ambitious design aspirations informed by communal values of environmental sustainability and emotional and physical wellbeing, instead of a singular company mission statement, where materials are durable and high-quality to withstand promiscuous use, and lighting and power networks are multi-layered and so eminently flexible.

Co-work also posits a point of difference in a competitive jobs market, where the concomitant features of co-work space, achievable through economies of scale, could secure the best candidates. Popular programmes of events for self-improvement, mental and physical, are well established in this sector.

A crèche is one example of taking services that add value a step further. Dog daycare is ubiquitous in 'multi-family' residential schemes in the US and would be compelling in a co-work offer in a country where dog ownership runs at 23% of all households.[57] As well as a gym, why not a spa? Or organic grocery? Laundry and dry cleaner's? Barber's and hair salon? Co-work space that offers these other features – effectively 'life support' and close to home – would make the office a place people really want to be.

Local co-work

Here co-work space has the opportunity to be the fulcrum of new communities, redistributing wealth through always-more-effective-than-government-intervention market forces and regenerating regional and local businesses.

56 R. Molla, 'Working From Home Can Make People More Productive. Just Not During A Pandemic', *Vox*, 20 March 2020, https://www.vox.com/2020/3/20/21187469/work-from-home-coronavirus-productivity-mental-health-nicholas-bloom.

57 'Leading Pets, Ranked by Household Ownership in the United Kingdom (UK) in 2019/20', July 2020, Statista website, https://www.statista.com/statistics/308218/leading-ten-pets-ranked-by-household-ownership-in-the-united-kingdom-uk/.

High Street House, designed by architects Teatum+Teatum and built by the practice's development company Noiascape in West London, is a pioneering case study of how the traditional intersection between commerce and the community – the high street – could be revivified by creating co-work space, converting neglected shopfronts through inventive architectural interventions, with co-live accommodation attached. Imminent (at the time of writing – August 2020) changes to permitted development rights will no doubt unleash activity in this vein.

Health and wellbeing

The scale of a co-operative can also equate to being better equipped to manage hygiene and physical health, where electronic contactless devices, such as doors and taps, could be more affordable. More simply, the natural environment has its role to play. Viruses like COVID-19 are much less likely to be transmitted outside and the biophilic benefits of nature are well documented. Co-work space with outdoor space – for work and recreation, such as outdoor meeting areas and relaxing games zones – will attract a premium.

Community

But it is in the zone where co-work and co-live coalesce that things become particularly dynamic – where a nomadic workforce, on the wings of the internet, are discovering that they can work in any number of exotic locations and operations are emerging to respond to that desire. This will continue, notwithstanding pandemic-related travel restrictions, where co-live operations will also offer well-equipped co-work space, and vice versa.

The Collective is a co-living brand that opened its second site in 2019 in London's Canary Wharf. A different kind of exotic, it is the largest co-living scheme in the world. Complete with swimming pool, spa and restaurant, it also offers co-work space. But more than that, it has realised a much-needed resource for large City corporations whose graduate employees have, to date, been faced with less-than-appealing housing at a price they can't even really afford.

Banks and accountancy firms are block booking apartments so they can offer jobs with the added benefit of somewhere well-located, good-looking, fully serviced – they even clean your room and launder your bed-linen and towels for you – affordable and all-round life-enhancing to live. Corporations are also taking apartments to accommodate staff from overseas on project work.

Of course the risk with this kind of buy-in, in such a large building, is an erosion of the concept of community on which The Collective is founded. But here a combination of scale and careful management is the solution that underpins all the benefits of collaboration.

And in any case, the management of the community is purposefully 'bottom-up'. Community Hosts on staff, together with tenant Community Ambassadors, support residents in creating their own events, where inspiration, innovation and the creativity that comes with being with a group are motivational values.

Figure 1.8 The Collective, Old Oak, London: example of social space in this innovative co-living scheme.

Figure 1.9 The Collective, Old Oak, London: example of quiet space.

A blackboard in the reception area chalks up ideas and records interest, running at an average of five events a day with a pre-lockdown uptake of 60% and a during-lockdown uptake of virtual events, focused on mental and physical health, of 75%.

Additionally during lockdown staff re-organised to procure groceries and have them delivered to the door, as well as providing a support phone line, connecting residents with experts on mental and physical health issues but also specialists in human resources, accountancy and banking.

In the teeth of the COVID-19 pandemic, The Collective – with two other sites in Old Oak, London (see Figures 1.8 and 1.9) and the Paper Factory, Long Island, New York – became a showcase of how people can live and work together in the 21st century, creating new kinds of communities, resilient through co-operation and human-centred purpose, where loneliness, the curse of modern life, is transplanted by fellowship to create capital of all kinds.

RICHARD HOWARD

Head of London Leasing and International Partner, Cushman & Wakefield

From Buildings to City Quarters

London's DNA

A principal attraction of London is its ability to provide true 'villages' within a world-class metropolis. Soho, Mayfair and Clerkenwell, for example, all have very different characteristics and attractions, and yet are all inherently part of London's DNA. Dorothy Parker is often credited with the line about Los Angeles being '72 suburbs in search of a city'; London is the antithesis of this, and one of the key reasons for this has been its ability to stitch its component parts together to constitute a truly global city. Any successful new city quarter in London would need to become part of this narrative and make sense within it.

What clustering has come to mean

King's Cross reinvented a large part of central London to the extent that it is now a new city quarter which attracted some of the city's most dynamic companies, organisations and institutions. A key reason for this attraction is that occupiers have shown themselves to be increasingly willing to move relatively large distances across London if they feel they identify with the location. Today, there is very little of the specialist clustering that was prevalent (for example the newspaper industry in Fleet Street) in London until relatively recently. 'Clustering' is therefore different – in fact it is more likely to be a truly dynamic and versatile proposition that will attract occupiers, and the 'cluster' is of different organisations, companies and institutions who see a real value in sparking off a variety of neighbours.

The wider place

If a place is successful, people will want to spend time there, in any capacity: work, recreation or indeed living. Public realm and amenities are a key element of convincing an occupier to be footloose – addressing the dining culture that has been growing over the last decade, and the demand to be located within striking distance of a wider range of eating, drinking and even broader nightlife experiences, are all key factors in making a thriving place. Other highly important ingredients for public realm are open spaces, which can become focal points in themselves (such as the fountains in Granary Square in King's Cross (see Figure 1.10), where families, workers and visitors gather to pass time and enjoy themselves). These amenities need to be accessible and nearby. There is genuine demand for art and culture around the office environment. In short, occupiers are looking well beyond the office building itself in assessing where they want to be.

Buildings in context

The successful interaction between an office and its environment is not entirely one-way; the building itself should form part of the wider place and draw people in. An early example of buildings that engaged with their environment and drew people in is Kings Place in King's Cross (2008,

Figure 1.10 Granary Square fountains in King's Cross, London enjoyed by visitors.

designed by Dixon Jones; see Figure 1.11) with its canal-side setting and restaurants, conference facilities and even a concert hall. Most recently The White Chapel (2016) and Brunel Buildings (2015) in East London, both by Fletcher Priest, have been seen as being very attractive because they have integrated with, and added to, the place that they are located in. If this can be achieved, and then coupled with excellent public realm, true community engagement and an active arts and events programme, then businesses that are looking to make a positive impact in their local community, and that have a desire to feel connected with that community, will want to be there. R7 at King's Cross (2017, by Duggan Morris Architects), with its gym, cinema, bar, restaurant and nightclub, is a truly engaging building, but its attraction is significantly magnified by the wider proposition.

Building features

Workplace requirements, never static, will undoubtedly change again in a post-COVID-19 world. Greater flexibility than ever will be needed – buildings will have to be chameleon-like in their ability to flex between collaboration zones, meeting areas, lecture theatres, recreation places and training space as well as straightforward workspace. Occupiers will need, more than ever, increased connectivity, vertically as well as horizontally. Light, fresh air, amenities and certifications will be high on the agenda.

Figure 1.11 Green spaces in between buildings at King's Cross.

Buildings and the space within them will have to address sustainability and wellbeing in a tangible way, not just as marketing whitewash. Large roof terraces – arguably pioneered in London by The Angel Building (2010, by AHMM) – will be more and more in demand as occupiers focus on the buildings that add an extra dimension to the experience of working in them.

A continuing evolution

Worldwide events in 2020 have shown that decision-makers will want to feel that they are offering their employees something that makes

Figure 1.12 Permanent art in London's Lewis Cubitt Park, King's Cross, by Eva Rothschild: *My World and Your World*, April 2020.

them want to leave home to come to work, both in terms of the workspace itself and, increasingly importantly, what is going on around that workplace. Brent Cross Town (under development by Argent) will be a new part of London and will need to offer an environment that is all of the above in order to be successful. The intention is that it should lead the next stages of London's evolution – breaking new ground in terms of enhanced amenity, proximity to nature, wellbeing, and genuine engagement with sustainability and reduced carbon consumption. There will be many components to Brent Cross Town – perhaps one of the most striking is the intention to create one of the best participatory sports facilities in the world, where access to these facilities is open to all regardless of ability, age, race or gender, thereby giving an entirely new resonance to the wellbeing agenda. If successful, these facilities alone will put Brent Cross Town on the world stage.

Figure 1.13 World-class sports and amenity planned for Brent Cross Town, one of the UK's largest developments in North London.

CHAPTER 2

CIVIC AND CULTURAL

PIPPA NISSEN

Finn Ross

Zerlina Hughes

Lu Mansell

Marie-Lise Oulmont

Jim Richards

Dr Sushma Jansari

Jane Samuels

PIPPA NISSEN

Pippa is a trained architect and a theatre designer, and director and co-founder, with Jim Richards, of the multi-disciplinary Nissen Richards Studio which they set up to work on cultural projects including the design of museums, galleries, exhibitions and performance spaces. Pippa has taught architecture for over 20 years, and enjoys debating the subject and its future.

Introduction

The pandemic has been as devastating for our cultural organisations and enterprises as it has for the many communities they serve. For designers and architects, both the pandemic and the post-pandemic world pose new pressures and significant challenges.

At Nissen Richards Studio we see the pandemic as a transformative moment that will and should drive and accelerate change in terms of how we think about the design and architecture of cultural spaces. Sometimes, important creative thinking comes out of adversity and constraint. Some changes will respond to practical needs, such as the use of materials and the need to accommodate safe distancing, but we should also use this moment to embrace more aspirational changes, driven by the need to create a more equal and sustainable world.

We asked frequent collaborators and clients of our studio, together with other experts, to help shape this chapter, thinking ahead to the next five years and telling us how we can redesign the future to be more sustainable, more caring – and safer.

The key theme that comes through for us is designing flexible and adaptable public spaces. Where these spaces already exist, we need to find new ways through, whilst also rethinking our relationships to materials – creating less 'perfect' surfaces, for example, whilst understanding how we can accelerate the sustainability race. Overconsumption and seamless, bespoke surfaces now seem inappropriate. How can we incorporate craft and the 'hand of the maker' into our designs, using local suppliers? Marie-Lise Oulmont from our practice and Lu Mansell from contractors Factory Settings discuss this important topic, as well as how the relationship between contractors and architects can adapt to create partnerships for change.

Are there ways in which the whole architecture of buildings can become changeable and flexible, so that we create the base-build and then add skins produced by digital films and light, which are changeable and adaptable, so that we re-clad buildings using only surfaces that are less burdensome to the environment and less permanent? Finn Ross, creative digital artist from FRAY Studio, is responsible for some of the most

Figure 2.1 Materials have a quality about life, and humanity. Shown here, part of the National Trust site at Sutton Hoo, Suffolk.

interesting moving film in theatre and exhibition today. He discusses the future of where cultural experiences could move, post pandemic.

In the post-lockdown world, how will our appetite for the beautiful and extraordinary be increased and how will we want our imaginations to be sparked? We may seek anything that is different from the computer screen aesthetic of a homogeneous, flat world. Lighting designer Zerlina Hughes of Studio ZNA, who works across theatre and cultural buildings, looks at how light fits into this debate. What are the most sustainable solutions, and how can we sate our thirst for fantasy?

The Black Lives Matter movement has accelerated a re-examination of public collections. This chapter will also talk about how we can create spaces that reflect today's and our future society. The discussions we've been having with access specialists over the years are the same ones that we need to have during the COVID-19 pandemic – discussions about how we might feel more secure and safe in our spaces and comfortable as we visit public buildings. Jane Samuels from the Natural History Museum focuses on this and discusses the future of accessibility.

How do we display objects that make them feel relevant to us today? Sushma Jansari of the British Museum looks at this and how buildings' architecture can affect how relevant these feel to us.

Live music performance has all but stopped in lockdown. How can venues be shaped and adapt, if indeed they can? How might we create a new economic model for performance? Jim Richards, my partner in Nissen Richards Studio, explores these questions with the directors of Broadwick Live – creators of venues such as Printworks – discussing how they can change the public's experience whilst maintaining the excitement and essential connection between performer and audience.

Changing Times – Our Eyes are Opened

We are rapidly redesigning and learning from our change in sentiment following the COVID-19 lockdown. Our appetites have changed, whilst the practicalities of social distancing – or the aftermath mindset – may be with us for some time, meaning that spatial configurations can no longer be the same. Some types of venues have been affected more than others, including theatres and music venues, and we wait to see how government guidance changes over the months and years to come. As we write, plenty of venues can do practical things, but ultimately need to wait until social distancing laws change in order to reopen fully.

New ways to guide people through spaces

One key factor in these changes has been guiding people through spaces in a linear progression. During the pandemic, we've been adapting existing buildings, or looking at interventions and exhibitions, as one-way circuits. The key has been about giving people enough empowerment to judge the way ahead for themselves and gauge distances they feel comfortable with.

We put together a series of diagrams (see Figure 2.2) to illustrate this and to help clients choose how they configure a public building, whether as a route with passing places, or by understanding the whole of a space before going inside. If visitors have maps and can see where exits are, as well as spaces being less cluttered so there is more space to move around, then environments feel safer, clearer and less complex or daunting.

Going hand in hand with this remodelling of buildings is a layer of information that tells you at a quick glance where to go and what you're doing, allowing you to keep an eye on your process. This could be a new layer of floor vinyl and signage that changes as guidance changes, or subtle but elegant grids on the floor and walls to empower the visitor to keep their distance and follow a route. The language of safety is probably here to stay, bright and bold, and we must accept this, sitting alongside our elegant and carefully choreographed architecture.

Personally, I have hugely enjoyed the routes museums have developed during lockdown. Rather than being restrictive, they feel like a curated voice leading you through a chosen series of rooms or ideas. I have been introduced to unexpected new artists and collections as I have been led around – with little description but increasing the associations that I have been making between the more familiar and the new. This should become a more normal formula: the flexible weaving and changing of routes and collections.

Figure 2.2 Routes through buildings – passing places and views of exits.

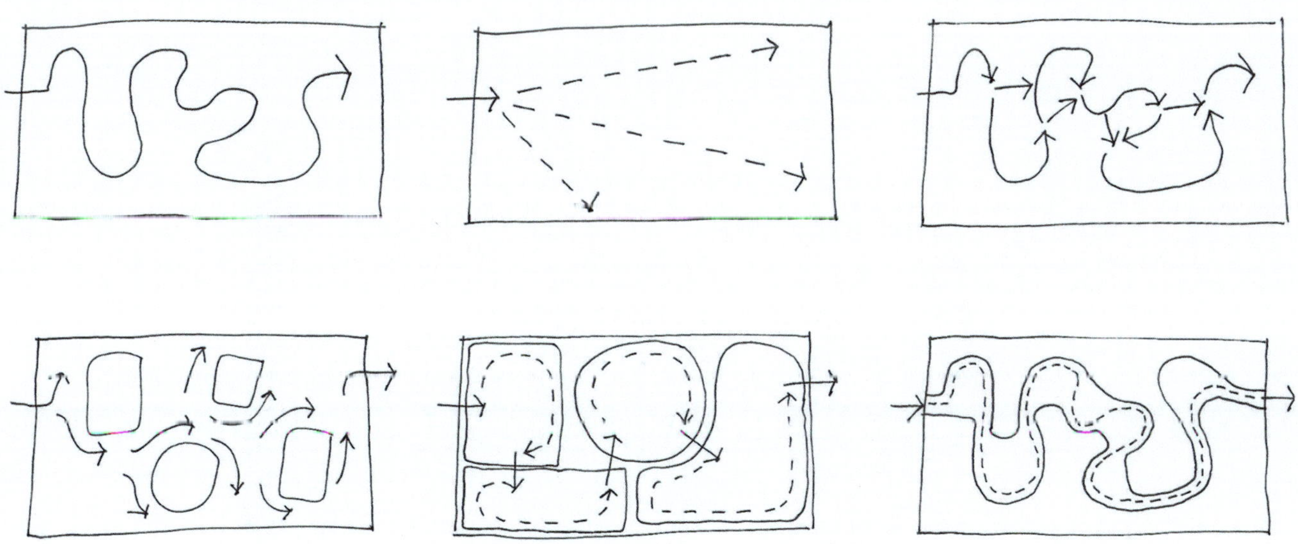

Figure 2.3 Paper cladding for an exhibition about the history of book-making at the National Library of Norway, held from September 2019 to January 2020.

The drive to be sustainable

As we react to the situation around us, we have become more attuned to the fact that we live in one world and that travel and long distances – although enabling faster connection – should not necessarily be feeding each other across the world by transporting materials vast distances. The fragility of our supply chains has also been exposed, increasing awareness of the need to de-globalise supply. We shall talk about materials later in this chapter, but wonder whether the drive to be sustainable and save money will particularly impact on cladding and surface treatments? Where we once were trying to put up buildings and temporary architecture as seamless statements, could it be that we now want to scale down what we build, using materials that are totally sustainable and accepting the flaws and imperfections that come with this?

Nissen Richards Studio recently built an exhibition out of paper in Norway and enjoyed the way this thin skin shifted and changed according to the humidity of the room it was in (see Figure 2.3). It had character, and a personality, even if it could only withstand being there for a few months. Perhaps we might accept a shorter life for our finishes, whilst the base build remains robust, allowing a more sustainable way for the messages and content of shows to flex around? This idea of a framework could either be totally flat-packed and stored, or else permanent – perhaps holding wires and infrastructure? The surfaces could then either be smooth, with additional digital layers being used to transform them, or else quick and easy to put up and sourced from suppliers that are local, or else specially crafted in some way.

A new design language

New surfaces could speak of our fragility and humanity; a painted surface or plaster where you can still see the brushstrokes – or wallpaper – digitally made to take us to a place far away. We love the energy of a Bauwerk paint surface – a new type of paint developed without any artificial or toxic materials, that replicates the quality of pigment in water.

'Less' is definitely part of this new design language too. Fewer people, fewer objects in museums – and certainly less money to import stone from across the world to put onto our buildings and structures. We need to find ways to sculpt and mould, and dream around our spaces (see Figure 2.4).

For exhibitions and gallery spaces, clients have been thinking more about reusing and adapting builds, with the same build fabric thought of for three or four shows together – finding clever ways to repurpose structure, such as by using pivoting walls, moving archways and pieces of design that can be reordered and reassembled in creative ways like a kit of parts. The lyrical quality of spaces is then rendered through temporary and changeable recyclable skins and by light and film.

Figure 2.4 Temporary materials used within a 2016 exhibition Nissen Richards Studio designed for King's College London, titled 'Paths to Utopia'.

Flexible and temporary adaptations

The flexibility to enable performance is something that may become one future option, so that, at key moments when buildings become redundant, spaces are used in different ways. If there is a future spike in COVID-19 or the emergence of a new strain of this or a different virus, spaces could be shuttered up, with objects, displays or performance spaces emerging instead, which can be safely viewed from the perimeter walls or remote viewpoints.

The rise of drive-in movies or comedy performances has been interesting, with companies such as Secret Cinema and Rooftop Film Club reinventing themselves, allowing people to inhabit their own space and control this via a 'live' broadcast in their car. This could be taken further to reappropriate larger spaces within cultural buildings for other types of performances; new stages where the atrium circulation spaces are used as 'boxes' for the audience, so that you get a glimpse of the action but hear the performance on your own device or hired headphones.

How about temporary stages in unusual locations or else linear performances, where you get part of a story that unfolds across a circuit? It reminds me of two devised projects Nissen Richards Studio developed for Aldeburgh Festival some time ago, in 2007. *Elephant and Castle* was a devised opera performance, consisting of a series of stages and surfaces forming backdrops and spaces that changed through film and lighting and where the audience travelled between. Performers were hidden in the landscape and popped out of trees, parked lorries or reed-beds, and you travelled around and found your own viewing space (see Figure 2.5).

Figure 2.5 Theatre and music performance *Elephant and Castle* was staged outside and in a series of smaller stage sets and moments for Aldeburgh Festival 2007.

The 2010 project *The Way to the Sea* was even looser as a venue. A series of events and acting doubles were planted along a route which the visitor, map in hand, could come across to piece the story together. It was rather like a live video game in structure, where only a couple of complete 'scenes' were initially set up. Companies such as Punchdrunk have been developing large-scale events such as these for years. Could other more traditional performances be reworked in this way?

Obviously, this idea does not work for all, but technology could certainly piece together larger casts and musicians to maintain live elements. In this way, larger casts and orchestras could be included but managed separately in order to keep audiences on the move, in control and safe, with the performers also in smaller groups.

Perhaps the future of public buildings will find form in a series of totally flexible spaces, where technology and infrastructure are set up and space can shift and change as needed (see Figure 2.6). For example, a café could become a display area for objects presented on packing cases with Perspex hoods, with a temporary stage brought in for performances. Gallery spaces could be conceived so they can be split

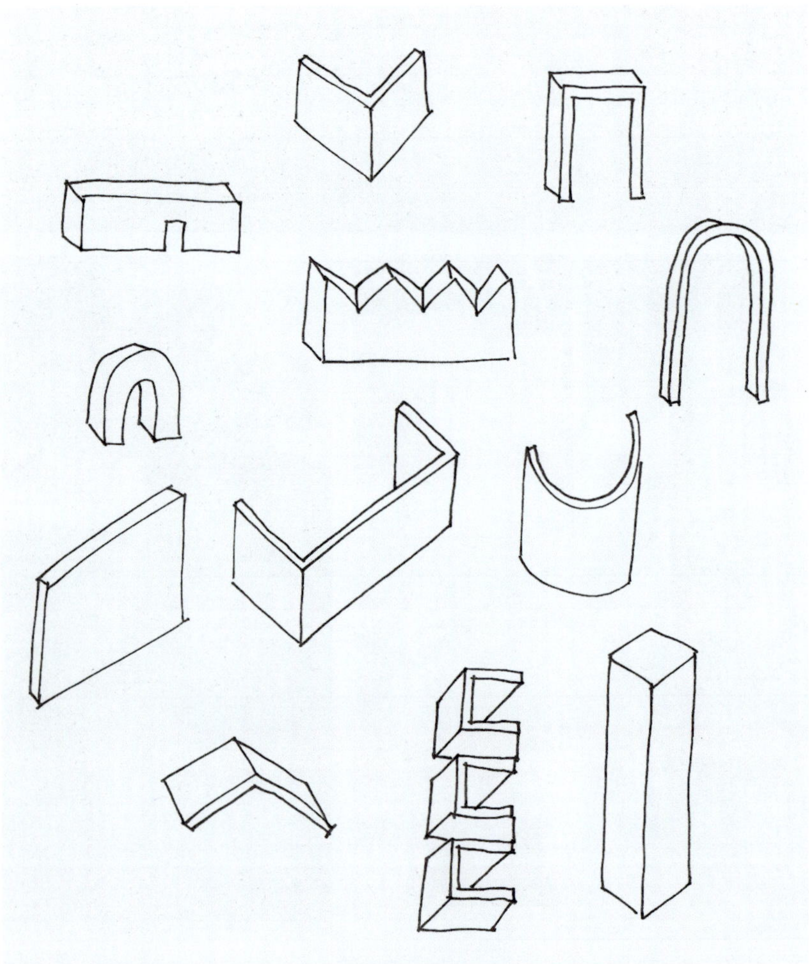

Figure 2.6 Kit of parts of shapes and walls to reconfigure as spaces repurpose.

into smaller spaces too. Theatres might consider performances that can be triggered remotely, inhabiting spaces within the corridors and bars of their buildings – part live and part relayed over headphones as you walk around.

Humility and community

All these issues come hand in hand with a sustainable approach to design and reusing and adapting rather than building anew, culminating in fewer expensive, over-the-top built statements.

It's time for the return of the humble, where design comes with use, returning to the bare bones of spaces and what they make you feel and how you can develop this further through clever adaptation.

It is also interesting to see how we may be able to tap into the new sense of community and empathy we have hopefully become more attuned to through lockdown, thereby halting some of the trends around for conspicuous consumption and grand gestures. As we move forward, we should look to use technology to empower and create slightly different kinds of shared experiences, where we visit places, but where our sense of being part of something just takes a bit more time. We could physically go somewhere – hearing a performance or seeing an exhibition slowly – with this functioning as a kind of taster menu, whilst we connect with other people later through shared photos and sound downloads, with communities forged and collated around maps and visualisations provided through data and the internet.

This would change our buildings forever. Cultural buildings would become maps or music boxes with hidden drawers and revolving stages. The entire buildings could become like the technical backstage of theatres and music venues, unpacking and shifting over time as our needs change.

A sense of joy and wonder

Over the last few years, clients have consistently asked for designs that include a sense of 'joy and wonder', underscored by the idea that we all want to be a part of an immersive experience. Perhaps this will in fact be easier to achieve after lockdown when space itself, different in configuration and effect from people's homes, will feel joyous to be within, just as I felt when I first went back to our much larger office space from home or first visited a large public museum after lockdown. We can then enhance these spaces simply and joyfully, celebrating what it means to be human, through the use of colour, shapes, scratches, splashes, streaked surfaces – like the giant post-war Jackson Pollock canvases, full of energy and life, or the bold and bright shapes of Ellsworth Kelly marching through a space!

Already, scriptwriters are being asked to avoid including crowd scenes in new films. As architects, we may be asked either to avoid designing large and open spaces or else to create spaces that can easily be repurposed for a different function. Perhaps cultural sharing will happen less in a shared physical space and more in digital spaces – meeting, greeting, chatting, watching shows together, sharing ideas. There have been many successful examples of this, such as the creative association MIMproject Space from Estonia, who ensured their theatre had a global audience over lockdown.

Could our cultural and civic buildings change in flavour from being design statements, to canvases for a poetry created in a completely different way through changing thin-skin layers of digital and light?

Figure 2.7 Joy: celebratory colour was part of Nissen Richards Studio's designs for the exhibition 'Forgotten Masters' at the Wallace Collection, held from December 2019 to September 2020, showing the work of Indian master painters in the late 18th and 19th centuries.

FINN ROSS

Director, FRAY Studio

Digital Spaces – Modular Flexibility

It's fascinating to have the chance to sit and look to the future during this moment of pause for our industry. One thing that has certainly been playing on our minds as a practice has been 'more with less'. Clients and producers are not going to want to make the huge spends they are used to. In theatre, directors are increasingly favouring digital approaches to scenery, as they can commit at a later point, whilst the museum world hasn't really harnessed the full potential of digital yet or its ability to respond to change quickly and remain current. Setting up a simple content management system (CMS) can influence what a museum or institution does on a daily basis, so that information can respond to world events and can change rapidly. If you're looking for an experience to last over a length of time, there are ways in which it could evolve or adapt. Time-based components are regularly used in our theatre shows, so that the experience is a little bit different every day, depending on variables such as the weather or the number of visitors.

We're going to see the end of the touch era, however and whenever the current crisis resolves. Touch interactives and screens will go, shifting more to cleanable personal devices. These can be pre-loaded with the right software, then taken and pointed at something to give you a layer of augmentation over it. You point at a dinosaur skeleton for example, so that the dinosaur appears around it. Without needing to build any surface, you can effectively reimagine existing museum collections, which is a really interesting starting point.

In the future, you could invest in the infrastructure and respond to a changing architecture through digital technology to transform surfaces in the physical and virtual world. The versions of buildings we at FRAY Studio make don't have any health and safety requirements, after all, and they don't have to stand up! There would be an initial set-up cost of mapping out a building and, once that's produced, then for many years you should be able to vary what architectural images sit within these. You could change the way an exhibition looks by allowing it to evolve according to multiple factors – time, space, current events or even the people in the building that day. The curatorial possibilities are really quite interesting. You could pull out layers to alternate experience at different times too.

Another interesting place to go with digital is the power of video to transform spaces. One thing video really likes is modularity. This makes me think of TAIT Towers in the US, who build a lot of rock'n'roll stages. They have modular sections, which are like a giant LEGO® system, put together in different configurations. One will go off to Beyoncé and come back to be reconfigured for the

Foo Fighters the next day. You design your thing and send it to them and they send it back built out of 'TAIT' building blocks. They're designing for large pictures without the finer detail of course, but this concept of modularity could really save money.

Big set-up costs are involved in preparing systems for visualising your content in, to present to various stakeholders as you progress through a project; whereas if you're essentially reassembling it out of blocks, it becomes more about putting together pre-programmed elements. As we know what resolution this is going to be and what size it is going to be, it would take so much guesswork out of the process, which would be fantastic.

Our processes are already changing. We're moving to more real-time ways of working. The rendering happens in real time. If you take the modularity of architecture and move this into the content side, you could have building blocks made up of layers of 'looks', which you could then combine and add the information into via a CMS. Obviously, the casualty of this would be that nothing is as bespoke any more.

There's a lot we can learn from gaming too, so that digital isn't just a film that plays in the space, but something that responds to a person or can be influenced by them. The way people learn about a museum exhibit, for example, could be that they play a game. Theatre, gaming and exhibition are all blurring together. We call this 'gameification'. Technology is at the point where this can happen. We're using traditional game engine tools to make video content or do quick, rendered visualisations for clients that will all start to come together because of an interactive layer that responds to people.

Everyone's journey through a game is different, so that the story being told is a broad-reaching thing with many avenues and people can choose their individual path. In a museum experience, people can really drill down into the thing they're interested in via the deeper layers of information, whereas someone else might look at it in a different way. You could create varying tracks through an experience, ranging from total beginner to deeply knowledgeable.

This way of working is also transferable to theatre. It's about changing the way in which people experience performance, but, as all these disciplines are ultimately about storytelling, shows could be performed in many ways – on the outside of a theatre building, for example. People standing outside or sitting at home could watch, but there is still the live element of theatre. Different things could happen on different sections of a building, where some aspects are live but where a layer of 'gameification' means viewers can decide what happens next.

I think of theatre as a huge snowball that rolls down the hill and gathers everything around it, repurposing for its own end. Within the future evolution of digital spaces there will be lots of cross-pollination between art forms. Differing technologies can now can all talk to each other

Figure 2.8 Physical surfaces were used for digital storytelling in 'You Say You Want a Revolution?', an exhibition designed for the Victoria and Albert Museum, London, and held from September 2016 to February 2017.

via application programming interfaces (APIs) and more things can be interfaced without the need for vast development teams.

We will have to change the way we write and create theatre or exhibitions. We need to think more flexibly and in a more micro way. If we're trying to do more with less, one thing we can do sustainably and with far fewer resources is work more closely with writers to really inform visitors. The value that they get is not just the built environment or the finish, but what they take away. At a moment in time when everything else seems to have been taken away, the one thing that is primal, simple and goes back to the beginning of time is the human need to tell stories.

ZERLINA HUGHES

Director, Studio ZNA

Lighting Cultural Buildings – Finding the Poetry

Our practice as lighting designers spans museum, gallery, heritage, theatre, opera and dance sectors. In some cases, our work goes unseen by the non-specialist eye, whilst being nonetheless intrinsic to the successful delivery of content, atmosphere and messaging. In other scenarios, however, it can be so much more. Lighting can elevate a space or an object or bring a particular focus and interpretation to a narrative, adding a dynamic, rhythm and depth. It's the context of these dual aspects – the dialogue between art and science, the poetic and the practical, the creative and the technical – where we want to frame our thoughts on the relevance of our work in this 'new' landscape.

On the arts side, we've seen a massive rise in recent years in the popularity of public lighting installations via international festivals such as Lumiere London and the work of light-specialist artists such as Olafur Eliasson and James Turrell. There's real interest in the sensory experience these works provide, with Eliasson's *The Weather Project* installation in Tate Modern's Turbine Hall almost a spiritual experience for many.

During lockdown, a recurrent theme has been people connecting with nature and becoming more aware of and having a hunger for the cycles of the natural world; something we all experience in such individual ways. These cycles and our responses are the preoccupation of many light art installations – works which provoke more primal responses and play with our circadian rhythms, but which can also be meditative. Every religion and culture has its version of 'Let there be light' and, with that, a way of grappling with the unknown and the bigger questions of humanity and spirituality. In response, our larger public spaces could become spaces for contemplation, where people can experience light installations that provoke a sense of wonder and connectivity, but which can be experienced either alone or at a distance.

On a practical level, the lighting industry is in a good place to offer products that can be incredibly flexible in terms of colour-mixing capabilities, via moving heads with programmable positions and beam angles. The fittings using LED technology are smaller, lighter and more energy-efficient, requiring less maintenance. Once the infrastructure is installed, small crews of technicians can set up very different bespoke visual experiences in short periods of time.

In exhibition design, the same is true. A space can appear transformed by its changed lit quality, minimising the need for large, unsustainable set works. There has been a financial requirement in public buildings in recent years to ensure spaces have multiple functions. A gallery can transform into a wedding venue, for example, or a conference or fine-dining space to secure venue hire fees. Where this would previously have been approached as a one-off temporary installation for each event,

Figures 2.9 and 2.10 Light creating the atmosphere for an exhibition at the British Library and for the production of 'The Feeling of Going' at the Malmö Opera House.

more recent installations have utilised flexible lighting technologies incorporated into the gallery infrastructure, securing better fees per event but also minimising potential damage to a building and collection by reducing the amount of additional equipment brought on site for temporary events.

In a sense, this newly flexible approach was already starting to be adopted, but could now be adopted more widely. Preparation for events could be done in advance and off site by using computer models and equipment profiles. Off-site programming would allow for reduced crews to work in tight turnaround times and could be visualised via real-time programming shown in the model for client sign-off. This is often done for large rock-and-roll or theatre and opera tours but could also be applied to museum, gallery and public space programmes.

The fact these newer technologies can offer a huge range of possibilities means it is as important as ever for a designer to harness and understand these possibilities to create beautiful designs with visual sophistication and creative integrity. A great example of a recent event made and enjoyed in lockdown was 'Nick Cave Alone at Alexandra Palace', which saw the artist alone with his piano in a vast empty space. Of course, the emotive music was a powerful element, and a gig normally enjoyed as a collective was streamed only once and therefore watched at the same time all over the globe. This showed how the live event could adapt to a different collective experience, whilst also acknowledging the current need for physical isolation. The event was a keen metaphor for our current circumstances but also, significantly, showed the beauty of architecture laid bare and rendered in strong beams of light which was minimal in design, but changed over time in hue and intensity with each piece of music. This in itself was emotional, a sensory display which appealed to both our need for the sublime and for contemplation.

LU MANSELL

Director, Factory Settings

A Contractor's Viewpoint – Better Relationships

Like it or not, we are all going to be poorer as a nation and an industry in the immediate future. Luxury, high-spec presentations will not only be tone-deaf, but for most institutions unaffordable, on current financial models at least. Designers and clients will need to find ways to do more with less. Whilst there was already a huge pressure towards this pre-COVID, it tended to manifest itself as an escalation of ambition for shows, without a corresponding increase in budget or time resources.

More innovative clients had been looking at ways to mitigate some of the costs added by the procurement process. Moving to a two-stage tender process has, in our experience, yielded far higher value-per-pound for clients. It allows us to bring our experience of design development and realisation to bear on projects and find ways to achieve design intent that designers and contractors rarely have time to develop under the single-stage model.

Moving forward under the hitherto-unimaginable pressures now prevalent in the industry will require much more willingness to innovate, if institutions are to survive in anything resembling pre-pandemic states. Where many in the industry have been trying for years to bring in more financially and environmentally sustainable methods of exhibition build, there have been numerous hurdles hindering progress. The desire among clients and designers to present something visually distinct from other shows and the lack of modular or reusable products actually delivering on their promised benefits, as well as the paucity of storage space in venues (in London at least) and the relatively high cost of labour versus materials have all been factors restricting progress.

The peculiar effects of working under procurement and contract processes co-opted from the construction industry (often with elements that are unsuitable or counterproductive) can deliver less value to clients and contractors alike, and can be limiting to collaborative approaches, especially where the procurement process has been set up to consider contractors as the adversary. As a design-led company which loves collaborating with designers and clients and innovating to give better outcomes, this makes me die inside a little every time.

If you add in the array of specific requirements for museum shows – security, fire safety for people and objects, conservation, accessibility, environmental controls, durability, working in historic buildings, working in buildings whilst they are open to the public – the concept of achieving innovation without compromising other requirements begins to resemble a Gordian knot.

What opportunities lie ahead of us?

1. Less restrictive contractual approaches. If clients can find ways to manage their risk and still be compliant with competition law, they can find better value. Design and build? Two-stage tenders? Framework agreements?
2. Longer timelines to facilitate design development input from contractors and suppliers, who often have greater experience.
3. Good faith and mutual support. This really makes a material difference to outcomes.
4. Multi-show designs, so that build elements can be reused or reinterpreted. These would need to be conceived and scoped at the beginning of the project cycle, if not before.
5. Modular approaches to show presentation.
6. Simpler design principles with less focus on high-end finishes.
7. Understanding of how to design for easiest construction (see point 2).
8. Earlier involvement/appointment of contractors, to facilitate their resource planning and reduce risk to projects.
9. Multi-show appointment of contractors to facilitate more stable business models and allow planning, which will enable volume efficiency and better pricing.
10. Higher proportion of spaces given to ticketed shows, to balance reduced footfall against stagnation of offer.

We might summarise by saying: better process, better design, better relationships.

Figure 2.11 Testing out ideas and working with the client: the Courtauld Gallery, London.

Large, publicly funded institutions are not renowned for their ability to pivot with agility, but smaller, non-publicly funded organisations may be much more responsive in their approach. In either case, speed of adaptation will be critical.

The recognition of the value of specialist supply chains, together with the breadth and depth of experience that resides in specialist contractors will also be important. Without client-side support and commitment, suppliers may end up leaving the market.

As an industry we need to innovate, and we need to do it now. The future of the industry will depend on whether this can be understood and responded to by institutions that are often ponderous in nature. Change was already coming before COVID-19. Nobody wanted the current catalyst but it's here and we can't ignore it. For the museum and cultural sector, it's time to adapt or die.

Figure 2.12 Lightweight changeable surfaces with big images fixed in a flexible way: detail of an exhibit for the 'Great Exhibition of the North'.

MARIE-LISE OULMONT

Associate at Nissen Richards Studio and currently working on cultural projects including Courtauld Connects

Material Change – Surfaces with Meaning

Following the pandemic, we are having to interrogate our relationship with the built environment.

The importance of material qualities and surfaces with which we come into contact has shifted, especially in public and cultural buildings. Our senses have been heightened and we are now more aware and mindful that these should be robust, easily cleanable and convey a sense of reassurance and resilience. Through our design practice, we have started to draw up various parameters for this to take place – datum points, where this idea of robust and easily cleaned materials manifests itself within a clarity of space.

The challenge, however, is to select natural materials which can achieve this whilst also ensuring we are not creating sterile spaces but rather environments that are engaging and welcoming – and of quality – in order to maintain a high standard of cultural experience.

Nissen Richards Studio is currently working on a wonderful transformative project for the Courtauld Institute of Art, where we have been able to alter our specifications to reflect the radical change in priorities. Corian, with its non-porous material quality, has been the material of choice for all surfaces within this public datum (where the public comes into contact with surfaces). The choice of a matt, sanded surface creates a beautiful honed finish, whilst the speckled, sandy colour brings a warmth and textured quality to the surfaces. Furthermore, timber elements have been retained but with a more durable matt lacquer finish applied to ensure the new stringent regimes can still be achieved. Patinated metal elements are then used as accents within the space, with a beautiful mottled surface finish achieved through a hand-applied artisan process.

Above this public datum, the opportunities are endless. Our practice in the exhibition sector has its roots in researching experimental and meaningful materials, which assist in the interpretation of the exhibition's themes. Recently, this has really come to the forefront of our practice, where we have focused on new sustainable materials and sustainable processes of work: interrogating materials, sourcing locally, using recycled materials, such as plastics, paper and textiles, and creating a lighter, less wasteful approach.

Being honest about the material application and the surfaces we use, as well as accepting their imperfections and textures and celebrating their provenance, has always been a key principle of the practice but has now been reflected in the priorities for many institutions. The sustainable agenda is now clear for all – everyone from designers and architects, contractors and clients to the public needs to make this a priority.

Within our exhibition design, structures and materials are essential but should be easily reconfigured and reused. The principle of de-cladding and re-cladding structures with non-disposable or lightweight surface materials is a solution we are beginning to implement. A move away from a dispensable, one-use system is essential.

A more collaborative relationship with clients and contractors is needed, in which we are not looking at one project at a time but at multiple projects and the consequent efficiencies. As discussed earlier in this chapter by Lu Mansell from Factory Settings, collaboration and exchange with contractors are often not taken to their full potential because of stringent contractual rules. The process of a two-stage tender can bring so many efficiencies where we as designers are able to benefit from their particular expertise, and where we can work together to solve issues. Efficiencies can be made in drawing and specification and through workshops and dialogue.

In cultural buildings, the public is a witness to design – as well as being witness to the material choices made by designers, clients and contractors, as we all work hard to find ways through the new challenges we are facing and break away from previous patterns of a highly disposable system. This is a new opportunity to bring together craftsmen, makers, designers and clients to forge a new approach to design while maintaining a high-quality cultural experience.

Figure 2.13 Material showing a sense of craft and articulation at 'Opplyst', a permanent exhibition for the National Library of Norway completed in 2020.

JIM RICHARDS

Director, Nissen Richards Studio

The Future of Music and Performance Venues

The live music industry in the UK has been one of the biggest social, cultural and economic successes over the past decade. The impact of the coronavirus pandemic, however, has been disastrous for all types of venues around the UK, as well as the thousands of people who work and perform within them.

Whilst we await clear guidelines on the reopening of these venues, we need to consider how they can cope with the loss of revenue from the many millions of visitors lost during this period. Many grassroots music venues are already under threat of closure at the time of writing and, though support packages are slowly being announced, we're starting to look at what impact this crisis will have on live music performance and the potential influence on the shaping and adaptation of venues where performance and music are experienced.

I'm an architect, but I'm also a music fan, and, like many others, my enjoyment of attending a gig is shaped by the experience of sharing that experience with others in a crowded space. I don't want to go to a live music event and stand two metres away from my friends – I want to squeeze up against people and enjoy together the tribal experience, the buzz that live show creates. With this in mind, I spoke to Simeon Aldred, Head of Strategy and Founder of experiential pioneers Broadwick Live and production specialists Vibration Group, and Simon Tracey, Group CEO of Broadwick Live and Vibration Group, about how they see the future in this field.

Aldred started by acknowledging they'd experienced their toughest period of trading in 25 years, but did offer some hope: 'When I've been in my darkest moments of despair around the ruination of our entire ticketed cultural industry around the world, I look for signs of hope. I am interested in looking beyond this current crisis to see if there are parallels with other outbreaks in the past, and it appears that during the aftermath of many of these previous pandemics, there has been a number of massive cultural revolutions in direct response to those difficult times.'

Both felt, however, that there would be very little change in the 'architecture' of the venues, and that, while there may be some concern raised at civic level, the real culture players would be doing the opposite of the current situation as soon as possible: 'There will be a desire for a greater relief and the creation of sweatier and darker spaces to allow a closer-knit experience for people who want to act like that.'

Nissen Richards Studio has been working with Broadwick Live and Vibration Group to create a new basement club space, 'Inkwells', planned at Printworks London for 2021, to be located within the basement ink tanks below the former printing presses that once sat within the vast cavernous spaces above. As Aldred explained, 'I hate the expression, the "new norm". In my view, the next 12 to 18 months will be an absolute cultural revolution in dancing and new trends, and this new club space will provide an opportunity for people to do just that. You never know, it could be more famous than Printworks.'

We discussed whether a new cultural revolution would result in changes to how we design and experience those spaces for performance, culture and commerce. Simon Tracey reflected, 'The one thing this pandemic has definitely done is that it's shown people the importance of all of those past experiences. I think we all got used to it and took it for granted, but we miss congregating together. It wasn't until this was taken away from us with social distancing that we suddenly appreciated what we'd had. Live performance and events provide an excellent physical experience, and we do not believe you can create what we do in a virtual space. It's impossible. Lots of people in our industry have tried it and nobody really enjoys it … .'

Aldred adds, 'There are filmmakers and videographers that do it better anyway. If I wanted to watch a band on my computer, I'll watch their pop video as this has been made and curated really beautifully. I don't want to see them perform in their bedroom. I think the issue we're all having as well is it's highly nuanced what we do and the artists don't want to perform either. We're seeing drive-ins popping up around the country for some events but the artists don't want to be performing to a bunch of people in their cars flashing their lights and beeping their horns, so I think everyone is just waiting … because we don't believe this is the "new norm". We would be innovating more if we thought this was forever.'

One thing all agreed on was that the recent drive for a return of a standing culture was welcomed and that the limitations of fixed seating within existing venues would certainly impose restrictions on operations in the future. An increased emphasis on standing and promenade-type events would allow greater fluidity and flexibility for a variety of different events and experiences.

'People want to move around. They don't want to feel fixed. This trend was already happening before the pandemic and was driven to some extent by financial risk, but standing gives you the option to move away, to be flexible – it's why street food is so successful. The price point is key of course but it's also transient, fluid, quick and convenient … people like it,' they commented.

As we saw at the recently opened street-food market as part of the planned programme of arts, music, culture and community events at Mayfield Depot in Manchester, this forms part of a wider ongoing regeneration project that will transform this city-centre location into a modern quarter for innovation and culture. Reflecting on our own previous design experience at

Printworks London, Magazine London (see Figures 2.14 and 2.15) and Exhibition London – all created for Broadwick Live and Vibration Group – as well as our current project for the redevelopment of Clwb Ifor Bach, the iconic grassroots live music venue in Cardiff, it appears that much of what Aldred and Tracey are striving for is still consistent with our own design inspiration: the creation of flexible and fluid spaces that can adapt to create a communal yet visceral experience.

Everything we do from a design perspective needs to reinforce this, even if at times capacities might be limited. The quality of the materials we use to maximise these experiences can go a long way, such as raw metal and timber with exposed concrete and masonry to create a robust industrial aesthetic, complemented with earthy tones, with the infrastructure seamlessly integrated. The manner in which these spaces are then used can be the focus of architects – using modular and adaptable systems to modify scale and their arrangement to create future-facing, flexible and fluid spaces.

Figures 2.14 and 2.15
Robust materials with an industrial feel: Magazine London.

Figure 2.16 View of the new building for the British Museum designed by Sir Robert Smirke in 1823.

DR SUSHMA JANSARI

Tabor Foundation Curator South Asian Collections at the British Museum and Presenter/Producer of The Wonder House podcast

Buildings with a Message – Experimenting with a Rich Mosaic of Objects and Voices

Aspirations

The sudden arrival of the pandemic led to a flurry of activity, followed by a seven-month-long furlough from my curatorial work at the British Museum. Unexpectedly, and for the first time, our movement was curtailed and physical distance from one another encouraged. This is a transformative moment, but it is not clear what the future will hold.

This period of introspection and physical distance from the museum has made me think more carefully about how ideas surrounding connection and change will manifest in the sector in the coming years. There is an opportunity to reshape museums as open, inclusive, multi-vocal spaces that are more easily adaptable, both in terms of their physical environment and purpose.

Outside

Like many others, I spent lockdown and much of my furlough either inside one space – my home – or walking outside. Previously, I moved between these two environments seamlessly. The distinction between inside and outside quickly took on added significance as every moment spent outside became so valuable. I found myself looking carefully at the buildings around me and assessing how I felt when I saw them: Did they feel welcoming and spark curiosity about what lay within? Or, were they intimidating, pushing me away?

Museums and cultural centres are often housed in grand Victorian buildings. Architects like Sir Robert Smirke (1780–1867), who designed the façade and main block of the British Museum, sought to reflect the extraordinary collections housed within (see Figure 2.16). While the latest technology was used in their construction, the exterior designs harked back fashionably to antiquity. Sculptural decoration often expressed current ideas about the progress of civilisation and Britain's place in the world. They are exteriors with a message.

Today, these buildings are an integral part of our built landscape and many of us take them for granted. Others find them daunting to enter and difficult to navigate once inside. This apprehension is not entirely surprising given that they were built to express power and authority – much like cathedrals, temples and mosques. And yet, they are an incredible testament to human ingenuity that link the historic with the contemporary and speak to future aspirations that were prevalent at the time of their construction.

How, then, can we reframe how we think about and engage with these important cultural buildings and, therefore, the institutions and collections housed within? How can we all decode the messages inherent in these buildings? We need to answer these questions because our public cultural institutions and collections are for everyone. If we are all to engage meaningfully with museums, we need to step foot confidently into the buildings that house them in the first place.

Inside

Objects held in museums are testament to the ingenuity and extraordinary creative expression of humanity across time. They often have a complex, multi-faceted history. So, while an object may be exceptional in its artistic rendering of an idea, it may also be associated with some of the worst attributes of our shared history, such as warfare, colonialism, genocide and slavery, the legacies of which are still with us today. Objects can tell this complicated, interconnected story, while displays can harness and reflect changing ideas about their interpretation, relevance and importance.

This object-centred approach is at the heart of my curatorial practice. I work cross-departmentally with scientists and conservators, and collaboratively with different communities, including members of the South Asian diaspora in the UK as well as source communities. The result is a rich mosaic of historical and scientific information and compelling stories that connect antiquity with modernity.

Opportunities to display objects in a multi-layered way, encapsulating a multitude of voices, are often missed because of the way in which our galleries and displays are designed. Museums are full of seemingly endless galleries with never-changing displays, past which streams of glazed-eyed visitors walk. These spaces often look the same, presenting different geographical regions, cultures, periods of time, objects and stories in very similar ways. The design discourages experimentation and telling rich, complex and nuanced stories, while the monotony discourages engagement. We must do better.

Agile design that encourages experimentation will enable us to respond to our changing world in collaboration with our community partners. Technology and the way we interact with the world around us is also rapidly changing and bringing us closer together while also, paradoxically, dividing us as never before. Flexibility in design will provide space for changing digital offers. Most of us obtain and share information with the world through our mobile phones: how can we harness technology and adapt displays to channel this connection to provide a more personally tailored experience? Similarly, 3D printing in galleries encourages us to experience objects through touch and, like countless generations before us, adapt them through use and play.

Figure 2.17 My family exploring the new displays in the South Asia section of the British Museum's Sir Joseph Hotung Gallery of China and South Asia, 2018.

Cost and simplicity are integral to the success of this flexible approach, especially at a time when museum income has been decimated as a result of government measures to deal with COVID-19, including lockdown. The reality is that if a display is expensive or very complicated to change, it will simply become stagnant and gradually obsolete.

Outside to inside

Our world is changing unimaginably fast, and different ideas and approaches to facing the challenges with which we are confronted are swirling around us. Many of the objects held in museums are testament to the fact that humanity has confronted and dealt with many of these problems in different ways over millennia. Museums are uniquely placed to link antiquity to the present day through their collections and, through flexible design, experiment with sharing compelling, multi-vocal stories rooted in rigorous research. Importantly, people need to feel connected to the space and displays – otherwise, none of the magic happens.

JANE SAMUELS

Cultural Inclusion Lead (Engagement), Natural History Museum

COVID-19, Black Lives Matter, and the Changing Face of Museums

On 5 August 2020, London's Natural History Museum opened its doors to the public after 141 days of enforced closure. Not since the Second World War, when the museum closed three times (including on one occasion for over two years), had it experienced such a protracted period of closure.

The killing of George Floyd in Minneapolis, and the subsequent protests of the Black Lives Matter movement around the world, had dramatically thrown inequality and racial injustice into the global spotlight. At the same time, the pandemic both exposed and deepened pre-existing societal inequalities: lower socio-economic groups and black and Asian communities were dying in alarmingly disproportionate numbers, while the elderly and disabled people, confronted by social isolation, felt 'abandoned, forgotten and ignored'.[1]

The Natural History Museum – and many an institution like it – was forced to rethink how to serve its audiences. With the temporary closure

1 Inclusion London, 'Abandoned, Forgotten and Ignored – the Impact of Covid-19 on Disabled People', 24 June 2020, https://www.inclusionlondon.org.uk/disability-in-london/coronavirus-updates-and-information/campaigns-news-during-coronavirus-crisis/abandoned-forgotten-and-ignored-the-impact-of-covid-19-on-disabled-people/.

of schools and public services, the museum immediately repositioned its engagement programme to an online platform, and by August it had laid on more than 40 'Nature Live' events, two 'Dawnosaurs Online' programmes for neurodiverse children, and three virtual 'Family Festivals'.

As museums acclimatise to a universal shift in their approach to public engagement, what is evident moving forward is that the pandemic has prompted the sector to be more adaptable, creative, agile and human-centred. Whereas previously, at the Natural History Museum, intellectual access for blind and other disabled audiences included on-site touch and handling, this resource will need to be temporarily scaled down; instead, a deeper focus will rest with online programming and soundscapes, with large-print information being available online and for single use only. This will also apply to Braille. QR codes as a layer of contactless engagement may also play a growing role and online audio description will continue to thrive as a safe intellectually accessible resource. Gesture recognition technology, involving simple movements to interact with digital devices without touch, may also increase in prevalence. In a climate of social distancing, the once-ubiquitous touchscreens, large group tours and specimen handling stations are, for now, likely to be rarer occurrences.

Building environments that connect people with nature may also feature more widely in an urban society impacted by the constraints of an ongoing pandemic. At the point of lockdown, the Natural History Museum, with its collections of natural diversity and its focus on planetary emergency, was developing an ambitious initiative called the Urban Nature Project. This aimed to transform a five-acre site in South Kensington into a welcoming, accessible and biologically diverse green space in the heart of London. Post lockdown, with social distancing becoming part of the 'new normal' and a deeper awareness of the relationship between nature and wellbeing, the potential value and impact of such a resource has grown even more in relevance.

The collision of Black Lives Matter protests and COVID-19 is unlikely to have been coincidental. Against a backdrop of lockdown, with black and Asian communities being disproportionately killed by the virus, a colossal increase in unemployment, and protracted social isolation, the death of a defenceless man of colour was one social injustice too many. George Floyd's words 'I can't breathe' were heard and felt by a global audience in a way not possible under normal circumstances. Driven by Black Lives Matter, his murder sparked a wave of uncontainable and transformative international demonstrations – an outcome that may be one of the most significant legacies to result from COVID-19.

In the wake of the protests, there were innumerable expressions of global support. UK national museums were amongst these. The significance here lay in the origins of many of these 18th- and 19th-century institutions and their imperialistic foundations. For some museums, such as the Natural History Museum, these contentious narratives are now under review. This will require transparent, difficult and courageous conversations.

Figure 2.18 'Hope' the blue whale during lockdown, March 2020: a symbol of humanity's power to shape a sustainable future.

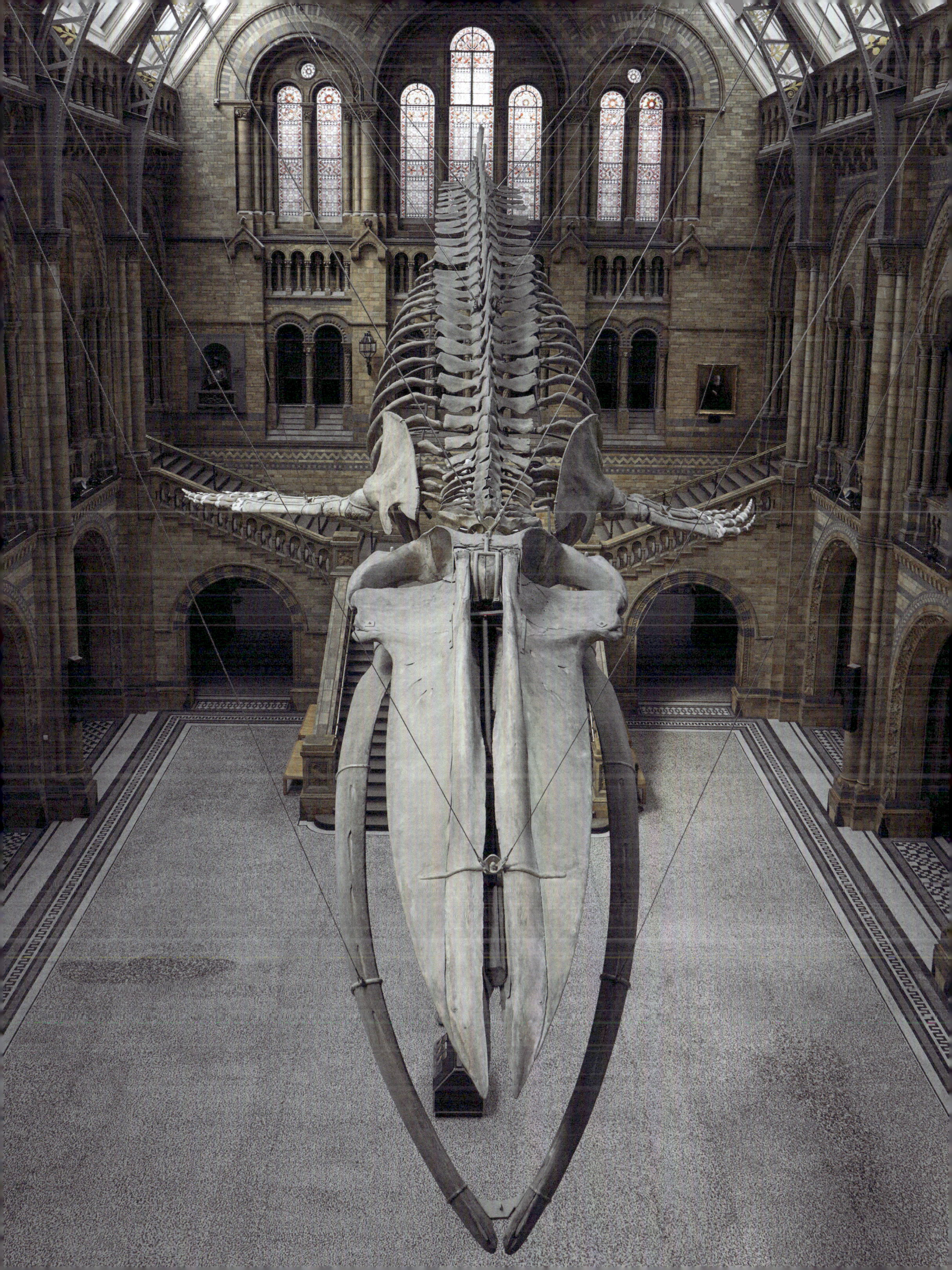

Mistakes are inevitable; but the endgame will be more accessible and inclusive programmes, exhibitions and recruitment strategies with enhanced relevance to and understanding of their diverse public and workforce.

As the Natural History Museum surfaces from lockdown and recalibrates, with a growth in online engagement, a discussion piece around decolonisation and reimagining the future relevance of the Museum, and intensified support to embed equality, diversity and inclusion, the institution, like so much of the world, is exponentially changing. Serendipitously, ahead of recent catastrophic events, the International Council of Museums (ICOM) redefined the term 'museum' as:

> democratising, inclusive and polyphonic spaces for critical dialogue about the pasts and the futures. Acknowledging and addressing the conflicts and challenges of the present, they hold artefacts and specimens in trust for society, safeguard diverse memories for future generations and guarantee equal rights and equal access to heritage for all people. Museums are not for profit. They are participatory and transparent, and work in active partnership with and for diverse communities to collect, preserve, research, interpret, exhibit, and enhance understandings of the world, aiming to contribute to human dignity and social justice, global equality and planetary wellbeing.[2]

Given all that has happened since 17 March 2020, this new ICOM definition resonates powerfully and universally for many museums as they emerge from lockdown. Other than the omnipresent face coverings on Visitor Service staff, and appreciably less crowded galleries, the Natural History Museum may appear to look largely as before; but at its core, because of COVID-19 and the Black Lives Matter network, it has emerged into the 'new normal' as a more reflective, human-centred and creative institution, with accessibility, equality, diversity and inclusion positioned with increasing strategic alignment at its heart more than ever before.

2 G.K. Adams, 'Icom Unveils New Museum Definition', Museums Association website, 31 July 2019, https://www.museumsassociation.org/museums-journal/news/2019/07/31072019-icom-reveals-updated-museum-definition/#.

CHAPTER 3

HOUSING

JULIA PARK

Clare Murray

Richard Harral

JULIA PARK

As an experienced architect and head of housing research at Levitt Bernstein, Julia combines many years of practical design work with a large body of research. A Mayor's Design Advocate and housing policy expert, she has written numerous design guides, reports and publications, often in collaboration. She co-authored the first 'HAPPI report', *Housing Our Ageing Population: Panel for Innovation*, in 2009, and *Age-Friendly Housing: Future Design for Older People* (RIBA Publishing, 2018).

Introduction

For the vast majority of people, their home is the most important building in their life – the one they know best and the place where they spend the most time – yet they rarely have a say in its initial design. Very few have the means to commission a bespoke home, so for the most part, the client is a developer. As architects, we do our best to engage directly with local communities and make the most of the opportunity to work with at least some of the end users when involved with estate regeneration. We leap at the chance to get involved with co-housing projects, but, more often than not, we find ourselves making intensely personal decisions on behalf of individuals, couples and families we will never meet.

Figure 3.1 Co-housing workshop at the New Ground development in Barnet, North London, with its architects Pollard Thomas Edwards.

In many ways this is regrettable, but today's sustainability experts seem to agree that tomorrow's homes need to last at least 200 years. This means that every home is likely to be occupied by perhaps 20 households and 70 individuals; many more if renting continues to increase. Thousands of others will cross each threshold – people of all ages and from many different social and ethnic backgrounds. Despite sharing much in common, their needs and circumstances will vary, and they will all have different ideas about how they want to live. Events, planned and unplanned, will generate different patterns of use, and, unless we are unfortunate

enough to die young, we will all grow old. Even if we could meet the first occupants, we would be wise to look far beyond their immediate needs.

We also have to expect that the tenure of most new homes will change over that long life, and that different types of households will evolve. Long before 2220, we may all be living with robots. An element of generic design is both inevitable and sensible, but generic should never be a byword for boring or an excuse for laziness. Every home can, and should, delight from the start and give successive occupants choices. In the words of Christina Malathouni, architectural historian, architect and lecturer at the University of Liverpool, 'Our homes have to allow us to be who we are, and who we want to be'.[1]

COVID-19 has deepened existing cracks and revealed new weaknesses in many aspects of our lives. Housing is among the most obvious,

1 The Developer, 'Christina Malathouni: Can Flats Be Healthy Homes?', Festival of Place Bytesize, 17 July 2020, https://youtu.be/na1Hkcmw-KY.

Figure 3.2 Designed by Levitt Bernstein, Buccleuch House (2015) in Clapton, North London, reflects the diversity of the local community. Though clearly reading as one, the building, which provides a total of 107 apartments, is split vertically into three parts. Each is tailored to meet a different set of practical and cultural needs: 38 homes for young buyers, 28 for local Orthodox Jewish families for affordable rent, and 41 assisted living apartments for older people.

Figure 3.3 Shawm House (2017) was purpose-built for an ageing couple on land they owned in Northumberland. The project was managed by their son, who became so interested in it that he decided to build it himself. Designed by MawsonKerr Architects to Passivhaus principles, the living accommodation is on the upper floor to take advantage of the spectacular views and sunsets. A space has been set aside for a through-floor lift and the design includes many other age-friendly features.

particularly during lockdown. The shortcomings have not been confined to older stock; some of our newest housing has proved to be much less resilient than we might have hoped. While it would be clumsy to advocate a knee-jerk reaction to an extremely rare event, it is right to see COVID-19 as the catalyst for long-overdue change. Home has never felt more important. As we gear up for a huge reduction in whole-life carbon, we need to re-evaluate our social offer in the context of an ageing population, changing patterns of work, travel, play and leisure; all of this against a backdrop of growing inequality and our over-consumption of 'stuff'.

This undoubtedly requires imagination and innovation; smarter ways of building and greater use of technology in, and around, the home. But it also means relearning some basic lessons. Over the course of 2020 we have all spent more time at home than usual. Anecdotally, while reliable broadband and an ergonomically designed chair have been high on the wish lists of new-found homeworkers, it has generally been the simple attributes – things that we should be able to take for granted in all new homes – that have been found wanting. The benefits of access to green space (particularly private outdoor space), good daylight and views out, ventilation, a controllable indoor ambient temperature and clean air, have all been reinforced.

We have understood that within the home, we need spaces where we can come together to sit, eat and socialise, and places where we can work and relax undisturbed. While many of us had to learn to be more sensitive to those we live with, others have had to find ways to cope with solitude. The contrast between those with gardens and space to rediscover old hobbies or take up new ones, and overcrowded families living above ground without even a balcony, is stark and sobering.

All of this has far-reaching implications for future housing. We have always faced known and unknown challenges, but possibly not on this scale, and not with the same benefit of hindsight. Only dramatic systemic changes will fix the social inequalities laid bare by COVID-19, but architects have a vital role to play. Housing has always been a juggling act. There are still just as many balls to keep in the air, but now much less excuse to drop them.

As part of the 'Home of 2030' initiative, instigated by the Ministry of Housing, Communities and Local Government in early 2020, the Design Council arranged a series of collaborative events to find out what people feel about their current homes and to consider how their lived experience might shape the homes of the future. The investigation included a survey of over 2,000 people, in which participants were asked to consider 20 predetermined principles and select the level of importance of each one. The responses varied by age group but there were many instances where every group felt similarly.

20 principles of the Home of 2030, ranked by importance:		
1	A home that gets the basics right	93%
2	A home that is affordable to run so I can still live a comfortable life	93%
3	A home where I don't have to worry about everything working as it should	90%
4	A home that is simple to fix and maintain without assistance	89%
5	A home with plenty of convenient travel options so that I can get around easily	83%
6	A home that has quality private or shared gardens	81%
7	A home that is in a neighbourhood that has all the amenities that a community of all different ages may need	80%
8	A home that is environmentally friendly and is part of a response to climate change	79%
9	A home that looks attractive and has its own identity	76%
10	A home that makes it easier for me to make more sustainable living choices	76%
11	Having control over what digital technology can do in my home	70%
12	A home that is easy to adapt or extend	66%
13	A home that is my current home, but with improvements	62%
14	Having the opportunity to contribute to the design of my home	60%
15	More choice and freedom over my housing options	59%
16	A home where it is possible for me to work from home	48%
17	A home which is suitable for multiple generations of my family to live in	48%
18	Having regular contact with my neighbours	45%
19	A home that is innovative and different to what people have seen before	33%
20	A home that has spaces and facilities that I can share with my neighbours	25%

Table 1 The 20 principles of the Home of 2030, ranked by importance (% of respondents who chose important or very important). Polling data from Savanta ComRes, England-wide.

Table 1, which comes from the Design Council report titled *A Public Vision for the Home of 2030*, ranks the principles by importance, based on the percentage of respondents who selected 'important' or 'very important' in the England-wide survey which used polling data from Savanta ComRes.[2] Interesting and worth reading in full, but, as with most surveys, it raises as many questions as it answers.

Highs and Lows

Any serious rethink has to start with an honest look at the present. The UK's best new housing is seriously good but there isn't nearly enough of it. Every typology has its strengths and weaknesses, and all face new challenges. Achieving whole-life net zero carbon is probably the area that most needs improvement, but that has far-reaching consequences for many facets of design, from site layout, form, orientation and typology, through to detailed design, specification and construction.

This first section takes a broad look at the current range of mainstream housing typologies and densities. Concentrating on placemaking and general quality of life, and highly critical of most new suburban housing, it also questions whether the long-term impacts of tall, dense buildings have been adequately considered and whether it is time to change tack.

Low-rise suburban housing

One of the most frequent criticisms of new housing is that 'it's all the same wherever you are'. This is generally aimed at suburban housing built speculatively by volume housebuilders for whom success means short-term profit and upsetting as few people as possible. Little has changed since

2 Design Council, *A Public Vision for the Home of 2030*, July 2020, https://www.designcouncil.org.uk/sites/default/files/asset/document/A%20Public%20Vision%20for%20the%20Home%20of%202030.pdf.

the 1980s, including the average density, which still languishes between 30 and 35 dwellings per hectare (dph). Layouts are still designed around the car, house types still spattered across the site at random, and architects still rarely involved. The often-trivial differences are eclipsed by the ubiquitous formula: Poundbury, on a tighter budget.

Buyers bear some responsibility. In consumer surveys, car parking still tends to emerge as the top priority for those seeking a new home. In-curtilage parking is second only to a garage. As parking in the front garden automatically demands an overall distance of at least 20m between street frontages, placemaking is already lost. Detached houses are still associated with 'doing well in life'. Homeowners seem willing to pay a huge premium for the ever-narrower gap between their house and their immediate neighbours'. Building two fully insulated external walls two metres apart, just to claim detached status, feels indefensible given that one party wall is enough to separate two homes.

Listening to what people want has to be weighed against higher-level objectives. With so many different uses vying for scarce land, detached houses must be largely a thing of the past. Developers should be required to focus on brownfield and sloping sites less suitable for commercial food-growing and stay out of flood plains. Better, cheaper public transport, more frequent (electric) bus and tram services, more joined-up cycle routes, less parking space and more local facilities are all crucial to reducing car-dependency and improving placemaking.

Good solutions already exist. Working with enlightened developers, practices such as Proctor & Matthews Architects, Pollard Thomas Edwards, Alison Brooks Architects, Peter Barber Architects, Mikhail Riches and Ash Sakula continue to provide inspiring, contextual solutions to suburban housing, challenging long-held perceptions, such as streets are for cars and roof space is for trussed rafters, and nudging the density up as they do so.

In 1974, Gordon Cullen questioned the approach to suburban housing: 'People live in houses, but where do houses live? If they are homeless all we are left with is the typical, endless, featureless, suburbia.' Almost 50 years later Proctor & Matthews Architects revisited Cullen's rhetorical question in a book titled *Identity and Place: Where Do Houses Live?*[3] It includes 10 principles for placemaking, all of which are evident in their projects:

1. A coherent narrative
2. Spatial hierarchy
3. Boundaries and thresholds
4. Sense of enclosure
5. Massing strategy
6. Townscape markers
7. Spaces for interaction
8. Dwelling typologies
9. Integrated tenure and mixed use
10. Cars, bicycles and refuse.

3 Proctor & Matthews Architects, *Identity and Place: Where Do Houses Live?*, 2018, https://www.proctorandmatthews.com/publication/identity-and-place-where-do-houses-live.

CASE STUDY

INHOLM, NORTHSTOWE, CAMBRIDGE

BY PROCTOR & MATTHEWS ARCHITECTS

Figure 3.4 Inholm site plan showing the wide range of typologies.

Figure 3.5 The distinctive 'Edge House' typology at Inholm.

Inholm is a sustainable, healthy, mixed-tenure, urban neighbourhood of currently 406 homes that sets pioneering townscape design principles for the wider new town of Northstowe, near Cambridge (see Figure 3.4). Initiated by Homes England and masterplanned by Proctor & Matthews Architects for architects collective shedkm, England's most ambitious new town project since Milton Keynes will eventually grow to a community of 10,000 homes.

Taken from the Danish word meaning 'islands in the marshes', Inholm is inspired by the rich archaeology that provides evidence of early fenland settlements on the site. Native villages were typically set on high ground and defined by perimeter landform embankments, ditches and boundaries. The design uses a distinctive, saw-tooth 'Edge House' typology to form a contemporary, inhabited boundary to the settlement and define portal entrances to the neighbourhood (see Figure 3.5).

The protected streetscape (a response to the exposed environment of fenlands) is a permeable hierarchy of shared spaces (streets, mews, squares and pocket parks) which prioritise children's play, walking and cycling. Car parking, bicycle storage and refuse and recycling collection points are carefully integrated into a resilient urban form. The housing comprises clusters of new and established volumetric typologies to offer flexibility and achieve high environmental standards. They respond to the key design concept of establishing a local identity and narrative of place, informed by the rich settlement history of the Northstowe edge of the fenland landscape.

The new neighbourhood will provide a mix of homes and tenures, including family houses for outright sale, homes for first-time buyers, affordable rented apartments and affordable, later-living accommodation, with a mixed-use community focus and civic open space at its heart.

Figure 3.6 A simple model captures the range of possible interventions suggested in the 2015 document *Transforming Suburbia: Supurbia and Semi-permissive*.

What, though, to do about the existing suburbs? *Transforming Suburbia: Supurbia and Semi-permissive*, produced in 2015 by HTA Design, Pollard Thomas Edwards, Savills and Nathaniel Lichfield and Partners, offered 16 ideas for transforming 'Metroland'.[4] There are places where each could work, but the piecemeal approach may mean that the overall housing gain is modest and the physical result untidy. It also runs the risk of making bolder change more difficult. Many pre- and post-war semis were not built with beauty or resilience in mind and are now nearing the end of their useful life. Before embarking on a nationwide retrofitting programme to decarbonise existing homes, we need to be sure that the cost/benefit equation passes the 200-year test and that the retrofitting results in truly zero-carbon homes (with the triple glazing, shading devices and photovoltaic panels that implies); not just forcing insulation into the parts that are easy to reach until the grant runs out. It would also make sense to make these homes more accessible at the same time.

While never to be undertaken lightly, the alternative – systematic demolition and rebuilding – could result in new, well-planned, high-quality homes in walkable neighbourhoods that triple existing densities and provide a wide range of local facilities and employment – the things that cohesive communities are made of. The practical, social and political implications are, of course, immense, but the government needs to think this through very carefully and take a long-term view, not least because we only get one chance at this, and it involves public money.

4 HTA Design, Pollard Thomas Edwards, Savills and Nathaniel Lichfield and Partners, *Transforming Suburbia: Supurbia and Semi-permissive*, 2015, https://www.pollardthomasedwards.co.uk/download/supurbia-semipermissive_v5_LR.pdf.

CASE STUDY

CAUDALE, CAMDEN, LONDON

BY MÆ

Mæ's Caudale housing for the London Borough of Camden comprises eight new family homes. Completed in 2018, it was designed collaboratively with the intended residents and aims to improve quality of life by prioritising generous, well-lit rooms and valuable outdoor space. Apartments are triple and sometimes quadruple aspect, characterised by spatial generosity and planned for the quiet enjoyment of everyday life. Glazing between the kitchen-diner, living room and balcony enables all to connect or be separated, allowing conviviality or privacy. Lifetime Homes standards ensure these homes can be easily adapted to suit changing needs.

A public garden provides new civic space with raised beds for resident allotments, increasing biodiversity and quality of life for residents. Caudale demonstrates how infill sites can enhance existing context, create high-quality homes and change lives:

Figure 3.7 Caudale, viewed from Varndell Street.

> It used to be just a bare patch here with one or two trees [. . .] and now this is on that spot. In the summer you get so much light hitting the patio, it's beautiful. Last summer was great, to be able to invite all my neighbours out here to sit and play FIFA. I mean we didn't even have a balcony in the last place, let alone something this size . . .

→ AMRAN MIHA, RESIDENT

Mid-rise urban housing

The combination of low- and mid-rise apartment buildings and terraced houses continues to serve our towns and cities well. The height-to-width ratio of urban streets generally feels comfortable, and the continuous façades and repeating elements create rhythm, character, enclosure and a sense of place. These places feel more egalitarian and often are – mixed tenure and mixed typologies support diversity and mixed communities.

Car usage tends to be lower, and higher land values often dictate that when parking is required, it is provided as an undercroft. While this contributes to the intimacy of the street, it often results in dead frontages or a wrapping of single-aspect dwellings. A base of two-storey maisonettes is a useful alternative: more front doors, more windows and more family-friendly. The ground floors are necessarily single aspect, but careful planning of unequal floorplates can bring natural light down from above. This is typically achieved by shifting the sitting room to the first floor, where it can open onto a private courtyard at the periphery of the podium that conceals the cars and provides a secure, shared amenity space for all the residents. It works pretty well, but with ground-level space feeling more valuable than ever before, anything that doesn't need to be on or even above ground should surely be underground? Parking is the obvious place to start; in other parts of northern Europe, plant rooms, waste and recycling, bikes, mobility scooters and baby buggies have been relegated to lift-served basements for many years, along within individual storage rooms. Shared laundries and drying rooms also seem to work and become convivial places to meet.

Now is the time to rethink the role of residential, urban streets – design them as social spaces that accommodate play and leisure activities, community events and planting, as well as walking, cycling and vehicular drop-off. Replacing a ground-floor flat with a community-run café shared workspace would reinforce this shift by providing a natural meeting point and offer a good compromise between working from home and commuting to the office.

High-rise city housing

No one could have failed to notice that cities have got noticeably taller, and that this has happened quickly. Average densities have increased accordingly – not only in London and other UK cities, but also in major cities across the world. *Recommendations for Living at Superdensity*, published in 2007, defined 'superdensity' as developments that exceed 150dph, and cautioned about exceeding this admittedly fairly arbitrary, but useful, proxy for 'worryingly big'.[5] Eight years later, 150dph had become the starting point. The authors regrouped and published *Superdensity: The Sequel*, this time coining another new term – 'hyperdensity' – for developments that exceed 350dph.[6]

5 Levitt Bernstein, HTA Design, Pollard Thomas Edwards and PRP Architects with Design for Homes, *Recommendations for Living at Superdensity*, 2007, http://www.superdensity.co.uk/ and http://www.designforhomes.org/wp-content/uploads/2019/09/Superdensity2.pdf.

6 Levitt Bernstein, HTA Design, Pollard Thomas Edwards and PRP Architects with Design for Homes, *Superdensity: The Sequel*, 2015, https://www.levittbernstein.co.uk/site/assets/files/1404/superdensity_thesequel.pdf.

The premise was (and still is) that as density rises above this point, it becomes more difficult to deliver good housing. Houses inevitably give way to flats, buildings get taller and single-aspect dwellings are harder to avoid. The consequences are now well understood: less natural ventilation, fewer windows and the same view from every room, and the near certainty that without mechanical cooling or external shading, some dwellings will overheat, and others will never see the sun. Balconies will be more exposed to wind and rain, so are frequently left off, and the more benign, year-round option of a winter garden considered too expensive.

350dph is now often the starting point. With a single entrance and core often providing access to a hundred or more homes, large residential buildings feel increasingly institutional. Some of the largest, purpose-built 'build to rent' developments seem to be designed more around the needs of the autonomous vacuum cleaners than of the residents. Single entrances tend to mean mono-tenure, heightening concerns about integration and social inequality. And, as we are only too well aware, the fire safety of tall, single-stair residential buildings has been called into question.

COVID-19 has added to mounting concerns that the social and visual impacts arising from the inexorable growth of residential towers need to be questioned. The Greater London Authority's world-renowned high living standards, first set out in the 2010 interim *London Housing Design Guide*,[7] are increasingly compromised by the pressure to deliver numbers.

What do residents feel?

Two recent, concurrent pieces of research provide important insights into the social implications of high-density living in London. The two teams, who were in touch with each other throughout, used a similar range of techniques to gain a first-hand understanding of what residents feel about their home and neighbourhood.

The first, *Living in a Denser London: How Residents See Their Homes*, by LSE London and LSE Cities, looks at life in 11 new schemes (built in the last two to 10 years) and three historical schemes.[8] The second report, produced in-house by the London Borough of Tower Hamlets, comprises a suite of documents, including a pre-engagement report and a draft Supplementary Planning Document, both titled *High Density Living*.[9] These focus on nine new high-density housing developments in the borough. One of the fastest-growing parts of the country, coincidentally or otherwise, Tower Hamlets was particularly hard-hit in the early weeks of COVID-19. It needs almost another 60,000 homes by 2031 in order to house a projected population of around 400,000.

7 Design for London and London Development Agency, *London Housing Design Guide (Interim Edition)*, 2010, https://www.london.gov.uk/sites/default/files/Interim%20London%20Housing%20Design%20Guide.pdf.

8 F. Blanc, K. Scanlon and T. White, *Living in a Denser London: How Residents See Their Homes*, London School of Economics and LSE Cities, March 2020, https://www.lse.ac.uk/cities/Assets/Documents/Research-Reports/2020-LSE-Density-Report-digital.pdf.

9 London Borough of Tower Hamlets, *High Density Living*, 2020, https://democracy.towerhamlets.gov.uk/documents/s161765/HDL%20presentation_Spotlight.pdf.

The findings of both investigations are fascinating – some predictable, others surprising – but all of them timely and important. Across all tenures, many residents reported being happy, but one telling comment stands out: 'there were instances [in the affordable housing blocks] where children questioned why they did not have Christmas decorations when private lobbies did'.

And now a new concern: city-centre residential towers are invariably mixed-use; their active bases – often retail outlets, cafés, bars, restaurants or office space – have made for a much livelier public realm. The future of these ground-floor spaces is now very uncertain. Dare we hope that landlords might transform them into informal workspaces, dance studios, art rooms, crèches, gyms and spaces to make things? Cities are full of imaginative people; could these former shop windows allow us to see their creativity at work?

Figure 3.8 The height and scale of Berkeley Homes' high-rise housing at Woodberry Down in East London – one of the case studies for the LSE report *Living in a Denser London: How Residents See Their Homes* – is typical of much of London's newer housing.

The longer-term impacts of increasing scale and complexity

The fact that density and height are often conflated has just been demonstrated. Density is merely a number, an output rather than an input, and not helped by the fact that different approaches to calculating density produce different results for the same scheme. While it is true that high density does not always mean high-rise, it is also true that above a certain point, additional height is the only way to increase numbers – and that the visual, physical, practical and experiential impacts of a tall building extend far beyond its footprint. A tall building can change the character of an entire neighbourhood and often creates a sterile exclusion zone that effectively pushes future development further away.

We know that service charges tend to be higher in tall buildings, but because lifts and concrete are both relatively new, we have little experience of major high-rise refurbishment. The complete refit of the first phase of Sheffield's Park Hill appears to have been successful, but London's Robin Hood Gardens has gone. As a result of the Grenfell Tower tragedy, the future of thousands of other tall buildings (built and unbuilt) is now uncertain. This implies a collective duty to consider how every tall building we design and build will fare over time. How do we envisage the comprehensive refurbishment of a tall building, home to say 200 leaseholders, would be funded and managed? How run-down or unsafe would it need to become before action was taken; how do you avoid residents spiralling into negative equity or unable to sell; how do you contact individual landlords across the world; and how many flats need to fall vacant before someone forces the remaining residents to leave so the work can proceed? The risk is that when these buildings degrade and can no longer command a market rent, they are sold off to local councils as temporary housing for vulnerable people who deserve better.

Given that all typologies pose challenges, this bleak assessment of high-rise/high-density development may be somewhat unfair. There are far fewer excuses for failing at 30dph than at 900dph, and still few good options for storing bikes or bins in terraced housing. We can, and should, be more creative in our approach to tall buildings and improve the quality of life they offer – forget studio flats, intersperse duplexes and take out pairs of flats to create covered play spaces at multiple levels, for example. But the stakes will remain higher. Without a radical rethink it is difficult to see how tall, dense apartment buildings can provide either the safe haven that lockdown has reminded us home should be, or a clear route to whole-life net zero carbon. And as historians have pointed out, rising density has always resulted in higher land value but never in lower prices.

Choice and Flexibility

Whether for outright sale, shared ownership or market rent, new mainstream housing tends to cater to couples and young families, and, as has been suggested, the range of homes on offer tends to provide little real choice. The growing number of developments aimed at other demographic groups is therefore welcome. Purpose-built 'shared living' offers a new lifestyle model and has proved popular with the restless middle-aged, as well as with young singles, and the housing options for older people continue to expand, albeit not fast enough.

We are starting to see 'choices within choices' whereby purchasers select the basic house type and, on payment of the deposit, are offered options for the internal configuration, not just the colour of the worktop and tiles. Co-housing goes much further, empowering people to take charge of the process and play an active role in the design development. COVID-19 has reinforced the benefits of flexible and adaptable housing that allows us to cope with unexpected events as well as more predictable change.

Initial choice

The RIBA recently estimated that less than 10% of new housing is designed by an architect. This predominantly involves houses rather than flats, where professional designers are usually employed. Countless schemes, such as Accordia in Cambridge, Chimney Pot Park in Salford and Dujardin Mews in the London Borough of Enfield, suggest that employing a professional designer is one of the best ways to increase variety. Add in a menu of options on payment of the deposit (an extra storey and/or a roof terrace, open-plan living or two separate spaces, two large bedrooms or three smaller ones, an en suite or a study) and the market opens up.

Initial choice is also widened by non-mainstream housing. As the book *Age-Friendly Housing: Future Design for Older People* demonstrates,[10] the range of specialised and semi-specialised options for older people has expanded rapidly since the publication of the first *Housing Our Ageing Population: Panel for Innovation* (HAPPI) report in 2009.[11] Providers of extra care and retirement housing will be assessing their models in light of the pandemic, but, enlightened by the European case studies in the HAPPI report, many have already shifted to healthier, homelier solutions. Double-banked corridors are giving way to deck access, flats are being grouped to form clusters and the depressingly large lounge is being reimagined as either a set of smaller spaces or opened to the public. Some have become the local community hub, offering general advice and access to a wide range of facilities – encouraging multi-generational interaction and mutual support networks.

Technically, care homes are not housing. But as growing numbers of people spend many years in residential care, and in light of the devastating

10 J. Park and J. Porteus, *Age-Friendly Housing: Future Design for Older People*, London: RIBA Publishing, 2019.

11 M. Barac and J. Park, *Housing our Ageing Population: Panel for Innovation (HAPPI)*, Homes and Communities Agency, 2009, https://www.housinglin.org.uk/Topics/type/The-Housing-our-Ageing-Population-Panel-for-Innovation-HAPPI-Report-2009/.

impact of COVID-19, it is time to reappraise that model too. The providers that have already moved towards more small clusters of rooms will be aware that the many benefits include improved infection control. The increasing evidence of the remarkable synergy between older people (including those living with advanced dementia) and pre-school children suggests that we should seek to co-locate these uses when we can.[12] And the mutual benefits that appear to accrue from inviting young adults to live alongside older residents (see for instance the Melfield Gardens case study on pages 96–7) – reduced rents in return for companionship and help with everyday activities such as shopping and laundry – should be tested more widely.[13]

The hundreds of thousands of people who currently live in private HMOs (houses in multiple occupation) deserve better. For this huge cohort of mainly young people, lockdown will have been difficult. While HMOs can be a positive and convivial solution, even the best rely on the fact that the sharers will often be out at work by day. Purpose-built shared living works better for some, but the institutional scale that typifies this model is not for everyone and it tends to be expensive. Architects Levitt Bernstein have been exploring the potential for intentional new-build HMOs for two to six people, run on a not-for-profit basis. The large, private (heavily soundproofed) rooms include a shower, tea point and plenty of storage, and the shared spaces comprise a generous living/cooking/eating space, utility room laundry, secure cycle store and garden. It feels like a more civilised way to share space and an approach likely to appeal to groups of friends of all ages.

The housing needs of extended families have also been overlooked, but the enlightened developers who are now offering purpose-built, multi-generational homes (typically comprising a family home connected to a separately accessed 'granny annexe') report record sales. When granny dies, or moves on, the space can be used for Airbnb, a teenager who's had enough of parental advice / younger siblings / regular meals, a live-in carer or friend, a home gym or a home office. The peace of mind, practical benefits and long-term flexibility of this model suggests that demand will only increase as a consequence of COVID-19, and that it should be available in a wider range of tenures. In estate regeneration projects it is common to find two or more generations of the same family; a multi-generational home would provide the perfect solution for some.

Co-housing is also gaining traction. It attracts people of all ages but perhaps older people in particular, especially those who find themselves alone but not by choice. A BBC film of moving-in day at New Ground in Barnet, North London –

12 Channel 4, 'Old People's Home for 4 Year Olds', 25 July 2017, https://www.channel4.com/programmes/old-peoples-home-for-4-year-olds.

13 See for example 'Youths Living with the Elderly – A Finnish Example', Aged Care Guide website, https://www.agedcareguide.com.au/talking-aged-care/youths-living-with-the-elderly-a-finnish-example; 'A Dutch Care Home Experiments With Housing Students With The Old', *The Economist*, 8 August 2019, https://www.economist.com/europe/2019/08/08/a-dutch-care-home-experiments-with-housing-students-with-the-old; E. Gutoskey, 'A Handful of Lucky College Students Live With Senior Citizens In This Minnesota Mansion', 8 November 2019, https://www.mentalfloss.com/article/606981/senior-citizens-and-college-kids-live-together-in-mansion.

the much-celebrated co-housing development for older women, designed by Pollard Thomas Edwards and completed in 2016 (see Figures 3.1 and 3.10) – was watched by over 4.5 million viewers. 400 people applied to live in the 25 (already full) flats within days.

Maria Brenton, the woman who came up with the idea and worked tirelessly to see it through, explains how it fared during lockdown:

> The past four or five months of lockdown due to the COVID-19 pandemic have stress-tested the resilience of this senior co-housing community and it has not been found wanting. Its years of actively developing a sense of community and common purpose have paid off. Mutual support is strong; self-generated activities are many, and older individuals have adapted to WhatsApp and Zoom.

The logistics are complicated – New Ground took nearly 20 years to come to fruition – but the appetite undoubtedly exists, and it is easy to see why architects are keen to engage. As co-housing makes perfect social and economic sense, why do we not make it easier?

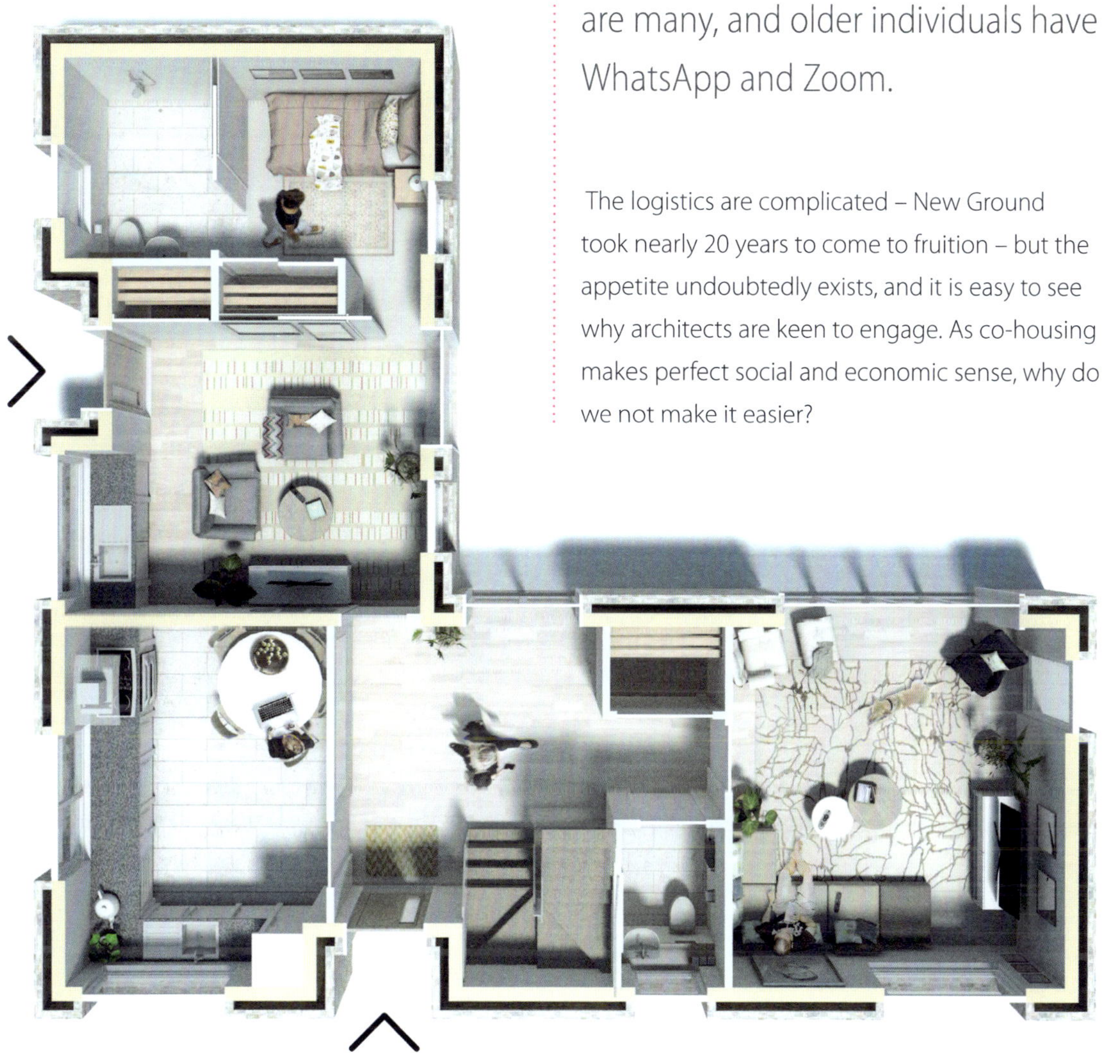

Figure 3.9 The ground-floor plan of a multi-generational corner house designed by Levitt Bernstein.

Figure 3.10 The shared garden enclosed by the homely apartments in New Ground, Barnet.

Flexibility and adaptability

Generous, well-designed and well-proportioned rooms are inherently more flexible. While every designer enjoys the challenge of getting the most out of a tiny space, that often requires the meticulous planning of every millimetre. The result is often rigorous and ingenious – but not usually flexible.

Space is a great enabler; coupled with Category 2 in Volume 1 of the Department for Communities and Local Government's Approved Document M (ADM), the 'nationally described space standard' (NDSS) supports the principle of universal design and the changing patterns of use which are inevitable over two centuries.[14] The minimum room areas allow for a desk in every bedroom. This has been a source of irritation, but the critics have been quieter since the unintentional, global trial of working from home proved so popular that it already feels like a permanent shift, for at

14 Department for Communities and Local Government, *Technical Housing Standards: Nationally Described Space Standard*, March 2015, https://assets.publishing.service.gov.uk/government/uploads/system/uploads/attachment_data/file/524531/160519_Nationally_Described_Space_Standard____Final_Web_version.pdf.

least part of the week. For those fortunate enough to have one, the spare room is the obvious answer; it may not be where you choose to work but it will give you the flexibility to switch things around. Perhaps unsurprisingly, a post-lockdown survey of over 2,000 owners and buyers, conducted by Zoopla, revealed that a home office had become the top priority.[15] Citing benefits for communities, cities and the environment, the 'Workhome Project' advocates for homeworking to be a permanent choice for those who can.[16]

Shared bedrooms can be tough on siblings, especially during a pandemic. In a typical, fully occupied, four-person, two-bedroomed home, the bathroom is the only space that offers reliable solitude. The 2007 version of *Superdensity* advocated that a proportion of four-person dwellings should have three bedrooms (not two) and that no home should have more than two shared bedrooms. It also recommended a dedicated utility room, particularly in flats.[17] Now considered an unaffordable luxury, it is far from clear how we expect people to manage the increasing complexity and quantity of recycling, or to wash and dry laundry and clean the football boots, without one.

Of the many sound pieces of advice, two feel particularly pertinent today. The first is good soundproofing (between rooms as well between dwellings), and the second, a flexible living space; offer the choice of an open-plan living/cooking/eating space or two separate spaces at the start and ensure that both arrangements are interchangeable over time. Logic dictates that the way to do this is to start with at least two windows and design the two-room layout before paring back to the open-plan alternative, ensure that the dividing wall is not loadbearing and install sprinklers if either arrangement requires them for fire safety reasons. A sliding wall offers a useful compromise and is a good example of how flexible design can effect instant change. Smart lighting, mobile storage, foldaway desks and modular furniture can also transform spaces with minimal effort but are usually best left to the occupants.

Good design goes further – it anticipates and pre-enables foreseeable life-changing events. COVID-19 gave us no warning, but people have always grown old. Notwithstanding the many benefits and safeguards afforded by specialised housing and care homes, 93% of us still choose to remain in our own home.[18] This is despite the fact that many will struggle to manage because only 7% of UK housing stock has the most basic accessibility features – the bare minimum to make a home 'visitable' by a disabled person.[19]

15 A. Dixon, 'Revealed: How Lockdown Has Changed Homehunters' Priorities', Zoopla website, 2 July 2020, https://www.zoopla.co.uk/discover/property-news/revealed-how-lockdown-has-changed-home-priorities/.

16 Workhome Project, 'Our Mission', 2020, https://www.workhomeproject.org/.

17 Levitt Bernstein et al., *Recommendations for Living at Superdensity.*

18 Foresight and Government Office for Science, *Future of an Ageing Population*, 2016, https://assets.publishing.service.gov.uk/government/uploads/system/uploads/attachment_data/file/816458/future-of-an-ageing-population.pdf.

19 Department for Communities and Local Government, *English Housing Survey: Adaptations and Accessibility Report, 2014–15*, 2016, https://assets.publishing.service.gov.uk/government/uploads/system/uploads/attachment_data/file/539541/Adaptations_and_Accessibility_Report.pdf.

Figure 3.11 Thoughtfully designed by PRP, the winter gardens at Pilgrim Gardens assisted living in Evington, Leicester (completed in 2013) extend the living space of their older residents. Sliding glass partitions allow the residents to use the space as either a sheltered winter garden or an open balcony on warmer days.

Numerous attempts to persuade the government to join up policies in housing, health and social care have gone unheeded. In a blog titled 'COVID, Housing Rights and Social Justice', James Bullion, President of the Association of Directors of Adult Social Services (ADASS), writes powerfully about the devasting impact the virus has had on adult social care and the people who rely on it. Reflecting on the fact that COVID-19 has exposed the underlying social inequalities that disproportionately affect older and disabled people and those from black, Asian or minority ethnic (BAME) communities, he went on to say: 'Every decision about care is also a decision about housing. Recent events really bring it home, that things like housing adaptations, equipment and technology are incredibly important in people, and help to avoid having to go into residential or institutional settings.'[20]

The 200-year home makes a compelling case for universal design. No one has minded the shift to wider internal doors and yet it needed legislation to achieve it. While a new 900mm door set costs little more than an 800mm one, retrofitting is hugely expensive and disruptive, requiring not just the fitting of new doors, new frames and (probably) new lintels, but also cutting back the walls and skirting boards, redecorating and replacing the floor coverings. Next time you curse ADM, remind yourself what it is trying to do and why.

20 J. Bullion, 'COVID-19, Housing Rights and Social Justice', Housing LIN website, 13 July 2020, https://www.housinglin.org.uk/blogs/COVID-19-Housing-Rights-and-Social-Justice/.

Figure 3.12 This diagrammatic 'one-bed-plus' apartment layout, designed by Levitt Bernstein, can be configured in five different ways. It offers initial choice and future choice; as the 'wet areas' (the kitchen and shower room) remain the same in all options, the variations can be achieved very easily. It is intended for older people but would be suitable for people of any age.

In a BBC Radio 4 piece aired in July 2020, actors Mat Fraser and Liz Carr asked, 'What if everyone was disabled?' Mat described hiding in 'the disability closet' until his thirties. He and Liz agreed that 'if design doesn't work for you, you feel less valued; without step-free access you're excluded; you don't exist. You find yourself grateful when you are let in'.[21] They answered their own question by concluding that if everyone were disabled, the world would be a very different place. Mat accused architects of being 'terribly conservative'. A little unfair because decisions tend to be driven by cost and efficiency whereby clients expect designers to do the minimum required 'to pass'. We are now hard-wired to plan a flat with as few soil stacks as possible; ideally just one stack for every two flats. Undeniably efficient but may mean that the kitchen and/or the bathroom can never be moved, or another one added. What would it cost to specify a couple of extra soil stacks, connect them to the drainage system and cap them off?

None of this implies that aspiring to stay put in the same home for the whole of our lives is a worthy ambition. It simply reflects the fact that while we aim to buy or rent the best-fitting home

21 M. Fraser, 'What If Everyone Was Disabled?', BBC Radio 4, 16 July 2020, https://www.bbc.co.uk/programmes/m000kx1l.

we can find and afford at the time, and in the location we need it, we all value the opportunity to make it our own. We know, too, that our lives will change in ways we cannot always anticipate; our homes need to flex accordingly. Pre-enabled adaptations often remain invisible. Although this is in many ways a benefit, the danger is that even the initial residents may be unaware of the pre-trimmed hole in the floor, pre-installed floor-drain beneath the bath or steel in the floor that allows the wall to come out. Planning and building control records may help to identify these features, but that relies on knowing where to look. It would be sensible to list them in marketing literature and require as-built drawings to be in title deeds.

The role of assistive technology

Technology has revolutionised the way we communicate, shop and conduct business and permeates many aspects of our home life; it carries significant risks but has provided a social lifeline during lockdown. Assistive technology is already changing the lives of older people and those living with dementia or a disability. This rapidly advancing field already offers these and other features:

- communication aids (from single-message buttons, to electronic word boards and devices controlled by eye movement)
- panic buttons and bogus caller alerts
- GPS devices
- voice-controlled assistants and smart speakers
- falls detection and bed and chair occupancy sensors
- devices that detect and prevent flooding when taps have been running
- automatic doors, curtain openers and environmental controls.

Bespoke packages tailor the devices to suit individual need. Most simply connect to a central wireless hub. As competition is fierce, and new systems are constantly emerging, commissioners are holding back. It would be good to pool research and resources to make the best system universal and available on a not-for-profit basis.

CLARE MURRAY

Head of Sustainability, Levitt Bernstein

Addressing the Climate Emergency

From a climate-change perspective, retrofitting existing homes is infinitely better than building new ones. But life is rarely that simple. We need more housing and we have to decide where it should go, what form it should take and what we are prepared to sacrifice in the process. As has been suggested earlier in this chapter, there may be places where demolition would be a better solution – areas with significant potential for densification and where better placemaking and more appealing, more accessible housing would improve lives and reinvigorate local communities. This would require careful thought and must be an informed and targeted approach. What is clear is that wherever we build new housing, it must achieve net zero operational carbon and use materials from a circular economy.

Defining zero carbon

For many years the industry lacked a meaningful definition of zero carbon – with the focus being on cutting red tape and stemming complaints of complexity and cost increase from housebuilders. But climate change doesn't care for half-hearted definitions or clever ways of counting carbon. A definition of zero carbon must mean zero – not offsetting with payments, feel-good tree planting or reducing as far as we can today, in the hope we can fix it tomorrow. We can no longer afford to build homes that will need retrofitting 10 to 20 years after they are complete, when we have so many targets and solutions and so much guidance to hand now.

At the end of 2019, a definition of net zero operational carbon was developed by a group of industry experts. The London Energy Transformation Initiative (LETI), UK Green Building Council and Better Buildings Partnership, with the support of the RIBA, CIBSE and Good Homes Alliance, developed a set of simple net zero operational carbon targets.[22] Across one page they set out 10 key requirements for new buildings – the first to use an EUI metric to significantly reduce energy demand rather than focus solely on carbon emissions. The document aligns with the RIBA 2030 Climate Challenge targets.[23]

For the first time, the operational energy target is based on the true energy consumption of a building and seeks to balance that with the renewable capacity of the UK electrical grid. The zero carbon definition targets an energy use intensity (EUI) metric for total energy consumed in a given building over a year. As opposed to carbon emissions, which mean very little to residents, the EUI is an indicator of a building's performance in use. Having set the bar for net zero operational carbon, the next step is to set targets for embodied carbon, based on a better understanding of the materials we use. London Energy Transformation Initiative's (LETI) *Climate Emergency Design Guide* provides guidance on how to meet these climate-change targets.[24]

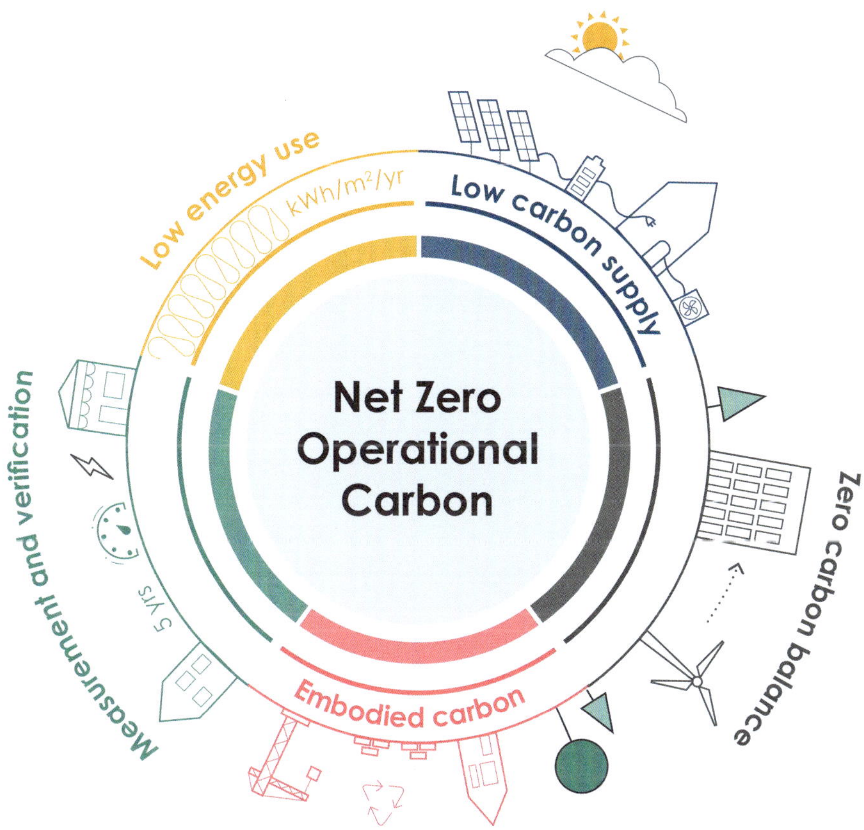

Figure 3.13 A simple set of targets for a new definition of net zero operational carbon.

22 London Energy Transformation Initiative, *Net Zero Operational Carbon: One Pager*, December 2019, https://www.leti.london/one-pager.

23 https://www.architecture.com/about/policy/climate-action/2030-climate-challenge.

24 London Energy Transformation Initiative, *Climate Emergency Design Guide*, January 2020, https://www.leti.london/cedg.

CASE STUDY

MELFIELD GARDENS, LEWISHAM, LONDON

BY LEVITT BERNSTEIN

Exemplifying many of the key elements discussed in this chapter, Melfield Gardens is a highly sustainable, inter-generational, affordable housing scheme on a constrained urban site. Designed by Levitt Bernstein for Phoenix Community Housing, it will provide 30 flexible flats for existing residents aged 55 and above (currently under-occupying family homes in the borough), and two four-bedroom flats for eight postgraduate students from Goldsmiths, University of London.

In return for being 'good neighbours', the students will be charged a lower rent. Each will spend a few hours each week with the older residents, offering company or helping with simple domestic tasks, and will be encouraged to participate in the cultural and recreational activities that will take place in the communal spaces. As well as learning from this innovative social pilot, the client was keen to achieve Passivhaus standards. This fabric-first approach demands design rigour and excellent teamwork. The architectural team is working closely with sustainability experts Etude, who will continue to guide first principles through to detailing and technical specification and undertake thermal and daylight modelling at key stages.

The site straddles a private road which gives access to an existing residential building, and is a well-used, but quiet, pedestrian route to Beckenham Hill Station. The scheme is split into two subtly cranked buildings that partially enclose a central green space which will retain the public route. The new residents will access their homes from this space, and the shared entrance cores, external decks and front doors will overlook it, increasing the sense of community. A shared 'garden room' sits at the foot of the western building, wrapping around into the protected garden for residents and their visitors.

The east/west orientation of the site is not ideal for Passivhaus (north/south is preferable), so it was essential to optimise the 'form factor' by keeping the massing simple. The size and placement of the triple-glazed windows have been carefully considered in relation to orientation, and shutters will be used to prevent overheating on the west-facing façades. Brick banding, slight recesses, ribs and columns will add expression to the façades without adversely impacting the wall build-ups. Balconies are cantilevered, and the access decks supported on the outer face, as well as from the floor slabs, to minimise the steel connections needed.

To make the new Category 2 homes as attractive as possible to the older residents, the flexible 'one-bedroom-plus' model has been adopted. This incorporates an additional 'study room'; large enough for a desk, shelves and a single bed, and with a pocket door to allow it to become part of the main living space or remain separate. Due to the high thermal performance of the building envelope, each home will only need one small electric radiator. Individual MVHR (mechanical ventilation with heat recovery) units will be housed within the envelope but accessed from the decks to allow the equipment to be maintained without disturbing the residents. To meet the exacting energy standards, these cupboards will need high-performance doors, and shower trays will need to include wastewater heat recovery systems – two more examples of the many steps that need to be taken.

Figure 3.14 Early concept sketch for Melfield Gardens.

As the client explains, the development also has wider benefits:

> ‘By rehousing under-occupiers, larger family sized homes can be released, helping those in overcrowded conditions and temporary accommodation. A similar approach was adopted with our Hazelhurst Court extra care scheme and led to 39 more households being rehoused from Lewisham’s housing waiting list, including 12 homeless households, and 16 overcrowded households.
>
> ···➝ PHOENIX COMMUNITY HOUSING, 2020

Figure 3.15 The route through the centre of the Melfield Gardens development.

Why we must consider operational and embodied carbon

Operational carbon refers to the carbon emitted as a result of a building's day-to-day energy consumption. This is quite different from embodied carbon which arises from the manufacture, transport and erection of building materials used during construction. While operational carbon emissions can vary over the lifetime of the building, the majority of embodied carbon emissions occur during the construction and deconstruction. Historically, operational emissions have far outweighed the embodied emissions. However, as the energy efficiency of buildings improves, the impact of embodied carbon becomes increasingly important. We are still only scratching the surface of the embodied carbon wrapped up in our buildings, but we must work to reduce the amount and types of carbon-intensive materials we specify. Updates to fire regulations are not making this easy, with timber effectively no longer considered safe in external walls over three storeys.

Demonstrating performance

The solutions for sustainable design have been extensively discussed and largely resolved, but challenges remain in their implementation. Often the greatest opportunities lie in quiet and integrated sustainable design that is effortless in operation and demonstratable on completion. Bolt-on or complex 'eco-bling' and technology are not necessary to make a truly sustainable home. The most effective measures are integrated into the design from the outset – gifting residents with a sustainable lifestyle by default. Meeting the net zero operational carbon target starts by making the building design and fabric as efficient as possible. Through good design, orientation, form and window proportions we can significantly reduce the energy intensity of a building. Passivhaus design and certification – utilising efficient building envelopes and verifying performance on completion to minimise the energy demand and consumption needed for heating – is one way of achieving this. Similarly, roof design must be driven by optimising the potential for photovoltaics (PV) to maximise on-site energy generation.

The technical requirements of Passivhaus and good housing design are often seen as competing forces. However, Goldsmith Street in Norwich (2018; see Figure 3.16), by Mikhail Riches with Cathy Hawley, puts Passivhaus at the centre of the design concept – setting the bar for all future homes and proving that sustainability doesn't need to be complex, rely on technological fixes or compromise design quality.

Future-proofing

As a result of climate change and improvements in fabric efficiency, new homes must strike a balance between keeping occupants warm in winter and cool in summer. Overheating has become more prevalent in new homes and this is particularly concerning for older people who are generally less able to moderate their body temperature. Good thermal comfort is rarely achieved by chance but can be created with careful consideration, optimum conditions and

Figure 3.16 Goldsmith Street in Norwich (2018), by Mikhail Riches with Cathy Hawley – putting Passivhaus at the heart of the design concept.

adjustable environments. The external shutters and awnings that are already common across southern Europe should become regular features in the UK too, if we are to avoid energy-intensive mechanical cooling. We also know that when occupants are able to control their internal environment, they are found to have higher levels of satisfaction, even if this means opening a window when external noise levels might be considered too high.

Connecting people and nature

Good daylight, natural ventilation and access to high-quality external landscaped spaces are central to our health and overall wellbeing. Creating high-quality green spaces for people and wildlife can simultaneously address the collapse of ecosystems in urban environments and increase biodiversity and habitat provision, while giving people purpose and pleasure – opportunities to enjoy their natural surroundings and meet with one another. Green spaces also offer natural processes for improving air quality, reducing local air temperatures and rainwater run-off.

Understanding performance

Only when we regularly monitor and learn from the homes and spaces we design and build, will we discover whether they perform as we intended. The most effective evaluation takes place throughout the design process and continues for many years after completion. Wherever possible we should engage with residents as well as clients and contractors during the pre-planning stages, and with end-users at handover and beyond. Monitoring conditions and spot-checking energy consumption is part of this but building performance should also strive to understand users' needs and lifestyles over time. Resident questionnaires provide invaluable insights which should inform subsequent briefs and design priorities. We should never assume that homes are meeting residents' needs just because they are lived in.

JULIA PARK

Rethinking Procurement in a Post-Pandemic World

Improving a product often requires improving the process. Procurement in the post-COVID-19 world must, in the government's words, be about 'building back better'. The key to this is shifting from an industry that focuses on discharging transactional obligations, to one that sets out to deliver high-performing buildings in a reliable and predictable way. Among other things, this means stepping away from traditional Design and Build and other procurement routes predicated on lowest-cost bidding and moving to models that achieve better long-term value: social value as well as financial.

The 'cost-suppression model' and the management-speak that characterises it, ultimately result in an industry that is not only working in a counter-productive way – socially, environmentally and economically – but is also dangerous. The Grenfell tragedy and the inequalities exposed by COVID-19 suggest that we are fast approaching that point. The implication is that clients need to radically change the way they commission, and that the industry needs to radically change the way it works.

What does this mean? Firstly, more integrated supply chains particularly in relation to design. Single-stage Design and Build must give way to a process that allows design teams and construction managers, contractors and key suppliers to work together prior to planning. Many forms of modern methods of construction (MMC) require a detailed understanding of the process and dimensional rigour; the system supplier needs to be on board from the start if costly redesign is to be avoided. Secondly, everyone needs to be more realistic about how much good buildings cost, and how long they take to achieve. Designing for a 200-year life makes whole-life cost much more relevant than initial cost. 'How long will it last?' is a better question than 'How long will it take to build?'

What does this imply for architects? The seismic shifts we need are clearly not something the profession can achieve alone, and to be frank, in the current political climate, a top-down shift to long-term value feels a long way off. But that doesn't make us powerless and certainly doesn't make us voiceless. Supported by the RIBA, architects can, and should, continue to lobby for systemic change while re-evaluating their own approach and practices now. It goes without saying that 'suicidal fee bids' are unhelpful and counterproductive, and that it is vital to keep abreast of planning policy, regulations and best practice and maintain comprehensive records. We should have a clear and deliverable brief for every project (compile it ourselves if necessary), keep it up-to-date and confirm changes with the client throughout the process. We must improve our understanding of building services and cost-in-use and design in a way that facilitates maintenance, repair, replacement and, ultimately, demolition.

These issues are particularly important to public-sector clients, but we should take every opportunity to nudge all clients towards more sustainable outcomes and a whole-life approach to procurement.

Our immediate priority is to understand how to achieve net-zero-carbon homes and encourage our clients to be early adopters. Given the importance of orientation and form, most projects will require specialist advice and modelling from the start. That implies earlier appointments, even closer teamwork and an element of humility. We need to avoid wilful decisions that compromise environmental performance; complicated sections, cantilevers and large, unshaded windows all make zero carbon more difficult to achieve. Good design matters more than ever, but 'good' must evolve.

RICHARD HARRAL

Technical Director of the Chartered Association of Building Engineers (CABE), shares his thoughts on ethical practice

Acting with Integrity

'Ethics' sounds esoteric and can often be viewed as something that – whilst clearly important – is for philosophical debate by academics; a subject for theory rather than practice. This view, subconsciously held by many building professionals, could not be further from the truth. Ethical frameworks are essential to good decision-making. They allow us to differentiate between what is right and what is wrong. They create space to debate how best to balance commercial imperatives with wider societal needs. Perhaps most importantly, ethical frameworks allow us to exercise sound judgement where guidance, regulation and past experience aren't sufficient to tell us what to do.

We desperately need to create space for ethical debate. Clients and employers need to put ethics at the heart of their strategic thinking to ensure that what they are doing is not just legal but is also right. Policies need to ensure that employees at all levels are empowered to challenge decisions and actions to ensure there is genuine agency and encouragement for individuals to act. This requires strong and visible leadership. Leaders need to stand up and talk about the ethical beliefs they value – and require the managers and team leaders in their organisation to do the same.

Given a moment to pause, and space to think beyond our own immediate needs, we are all capable of making better decisions. No magic is required to integrate ethics into our professional behaviours once they are embraced in our strategies and backed up with leadership and agency. And there is no great mystery as to what those beliefs should be; we simply need to ensure that we treat others – including wider society, our communities and our environment – in the way we would want to be treated ourselves.

COVID-19 and climate change have exposed the fragility of a world we have taken for granted for far too long. Designers are necessarily decision-makers; it goes to the heart of what we do. We can't always get it right, but we can ensure that we always act in good faith and have the necessary knowledge and skills to do our job well. We need to embrace continuing professional development (CPD) as a genuine learning experience and feel able to question those with whom we work.

Housing architects need to be at the centre of the building recovery if better homes are to form part of COVID-19's legacy. That may mean being more honest with ourselves and with our clients, ultimately having the moral courage to turn down a commission. Our work is unlikely to get easier, but it may become more rewarding. Getting the politicians to understand the scale and rate of change required may be the most difficult task of all – and why we need to speak with one voice.

CHAPTER 4

RETAIL AND HOSPITALITY

ADAM SCOTT

ADAM SCOTT

Adam is the creative force and founder of FreeState, the pioneering experience masterplanning agency. Based in London but working globally, Adam and his team advise some of the world's most innovative brand builders and city makers. Adam is co-author of *The Experience Book*, published in 2021 by Black Dog Press.

> What got you here, won't get you there.
>
> ···➔ MARSHAL GOLDSMITH, WRITER[1]

Introduction: A Stark Optimism

Testifying before Congress in July 2020, Amazon's Jeff Bezos defended the company in familiar vein. Amazon's success, he argues, is based on speed, availability and cost. 'The only real constant in retail is customers' desire for lower prices, better selection, and convenience.'[2] This is Bezos's shtick, and has been from the beginning. Customers don't want to have to wait. They don't want less to choose from. And they don't want non-competitive prices. Always have done – always will. Amazon gives people what they want. In doing so, it has become one of the world's most valuable companies, and Bezos that world's richest human being.

Beyond Bezos

I share the above as a means of setting the terms of reference for this chapter. First, we need to tacitly accept a defeat. Certain sectors excepted, physical retail cannot compete with the internet on Bezos's terms. What was true pre-COVID-19 is even more so amid the pandemic. Lockdown saw all but non-essential stores closed, forcing traditional physical businesses onto e-commerce platforms, into government-assisted comas or to file for bankruptcy. Meanwhile, people that once never dreamed of shopping online have got to grips with user interfaces, dealt with trust issues, and are increasingly enamoured by everything Bezos speaks of. The result: today e-commerce accounts for 27.5% of the British retail pie,[3] a 6% rise on last year.[4] Predicted to increase that share to a whopping 32% by 2024, it's more of the same for the foreseeable future.[5]

1 M. Goldsmith, *What Got You Here, Won't Get You There*, New York: Hyperion, 2007.

2 Opening testimony to Congress, 29 July 2020, https://cnb.cx/34wckzj.

3 B. Fisher, 'UK Ecommerce 2020', 15 June 2020, *eMarketer*, https://bit.ly/34vJ7EO.

4 Office for National Statistics, 'Internet Sales as a Percentage of Total Sales (Ratio) (%)', 18 September 2020, https://bit.ly/2GB9CjY.

5 B. Fisher, 'UK Ecommerce 2020', 15 June 2020, *eMarketer*, https://www.emarketer.com/content/uk-ecommerce-2020.

Figure 4.1 Amazon, giving people what they want.

Second and therefore, when I talk here about retail and hospitality, I'm talking about nearly everything Bezos is not. In doing so, I borrow an old philosophical trick, and define something by that which it is not. Let us begin. It is not the user interface. It's not the insight afforded by digital user experience data. It's not the future customer journey as determined by the often too generic science of analytics. It's not the ease of consuming the world from the comfort of your home, actual or mobile. And perhaps most importantly, it's not mistaking people for customers, a label that – when used exclusively – has the effect of reducing relationships to the narrowest form of transaction.

On the contrary, the world of retail and hospitality that ought to be the object of the architect and designer's interest is the one that compels us to trade Bezos's constants – lower prices, mind-boggling choice, convenience – for something else entirely. That something is a genuine understanding of the wants and needs of people as social, curious and creative beings. It's the thought of a place composed less of what is generally labelled mixed use, and more of a rich campus-like mix of activities, a blur of traditional retail, hospitality, workplace, entertainment and, less obviously, healthcare, education and experience-based pop-ups. Much further away than the touch of a button, generally requiring a healthy dollop of one's time, and not necessarily led by price, it's the space that confounds Bezos's mantra. It's our theatre and it's our memory-making machine. It's the experience of loving being out. It's about the joy of being together, in the street, alive.

Shot in the foot

Unfortunately, while fine examples abound, the ever-relevant rich mix of activities that ought to comprise what it means to be out – shopping, eating, meeting, playing, working, entertaining, learning, enjoying – is an unevenly applied typology. It's all too easy to blame the digital revolution for this. Fact is, we are our own worst enemies when it comes to designing and building for retail and hospitality, and in several ways. In the first instance, architecture continues to fall for the buildings it is yet to design. By which I mean, we are a product-led discipline and our process – design brief, masterplan, build – is predicated on the engineered outcome. All too often, the research involved in deciding the direction of that process is either ceded to the client, non-specific, or inadequate to the task at hand. Meaning, we are ill-prepared for understanding what it is people want and need, a lack of preparation compounded by systemic bias. Ergo, we are ignoring Jan Gehl's oft-quoted dictum: 'first life, then spaces, then buildings – the other way around never works'.[6] We need to fall in love with the life it is our honour to enable.

6 J. Gehl, *Life Between Buildings: Using Public Space*, translated by J. Koch, New York: Van Nostrand Reinhold, 1987, p 23.

This predication for irrelevance is underwritten by an overwhelmingly sales-model approach to commercial property development. As is the case across multiple sectors, it's a model beholden to its shareholders, to a philosophy most famously espoused by the economist Milton Friedman, and which dictates that a business's singular objective is to make its investors a profit. Here, the meaning of 'commercially astute' is the property as asset, ideally bought and sold in a deregulated market, its value determined not by the services it provides, but rather by its potential income, based on either annual gross rents or net operating income. The result: high streets and town centres owned by multiple and (often) absent landlords; investor-conscious rent practices resulting in grossly overvalued spaces; a tenant typology that has little or no investment in the wider local community and is the opposite of what we mean by a rich mix of activities; a daily, weekly and seasonal programme bereft of imagination and theatre; and the complete absence of opportunity for pop-ups, start-ups and independents. Rewarding the few at the expense of the many, we are speculating on much more than the value of commercial property.

In all of this, as alluded to by London First's *Planning Manifesto for High Streets and Town Centres* (2020),[7] planning law and the context in which it is enacted has not always played the part you imagine it might or could. Enlightened authorities apart, the planning and development

7 London First, *Planning Manifesto for High Streets and Town Centres*, January 2020, https://bit.ly/3iLSOnL.

of high streets and town centres has been hamstrung by poor leadership, turgid visions and the inability to align planning, licensing and regeneration. The rigidity of Use Classes Orders and their application has been the bane of the creative developer's vision. Few policies exist for the meanwhile use of sites awaiting development or demolition. Ditto that for dealing with vacant units. Owing to a historic decline in the likes of in-house Compulsory Purchase Order teams, local authorities often lack the intellectual capital, skill set and powers with which to go about reclaiming fragmented high streets and town centres. Finally, the means of rewarding success through upgraded statuses benefits centres capable of attracting visitors

Figure 4.2 Shuttered shops in Edinburgh. Big or small, many a town centre has suffered general decline, a situation compounded by the present crisis.

while doing little to halt the decline of those that can't. Ironic that planning permission – the chief mechanism designed to protect our streets and centres from the diluting effects of competing interests – is often bound by law or convention from protecting our streets and centres from the diluting effects of competing interests. We are shooting ourselves in the foot, endlessly.

A not-so-blind optimism

It's a stark picture, made especially so by the current crisis. However, it's only stark if we continue to insist on competing on online terms; if we fail to take advantage of the opportunities presented by the crisis; if we can't get our act together on what it means to create sustainably – socially, financially, environmentally; and if we don't start answering people's needs for a genuinely different form of retail, a category not entirely based on the sale of physical goods, and much more on the experience of being out. A raft of tough conditions, I know, the meeting of which will no doubt require a coming together of every moving part of the ecosystem that constitutes the retail-and-hospitality built environment. Even so, I'm confident, and not least because we already have a blueprint – the campus as high street – for moving forward. Inspired, this chapter explores how. It's the project for the decade. Let's jump in.

Bring Back the Agora

> The high street needs to go back to the birthplace of retail: the agora in Ancient Greece.
>
> ···→ ROSS BAILEY, RETAIL ENTREPRENEUR[8]

A story for the times. In 2011, Stockton-on-Tees Borough Council published a prospectus for the regeneration of a high street in seemingly terminal decline. Vacancies pockmarked the streets, footfall was low, and potential investors were sprinting for the hills. The prospectus outlines a simple vision for the future of the Stockton high street – one based not on the purchase of physical goods, but rather on the experience of visiting a very different kind of market town. Building on its past and on the fact that it is the 30-year home to an enormously successful international arts festival, it aimed to turn the town into a place of perpetual festival. Strategic highlights: real support for independent businesses, including a retail advice service and a low-rent, short-lease test bed for start-ups; a well-thought-through, staggered and still-ongoing restoration of the public realm, particularly with a view to growing a nascent night-time economy; and a clutch of incentives designed to attract business, including vacancy-occupation grants,

8 Interview with the author, July 2020.

a substantial two-year rates discount, and a shopfront support scheme. Five years later and Stockton's on the move, its now 50-plus pubs, bars and restaurants, its arts centre and reclaimed theatre, and its socially minded public realm combining to create the start of that envisaged perpetual festival. All this for real clarity of (shared) purpose, a super-progressive interpretation of licensing laws, and an ongoing comprehensive regeneration programme that includes provision for improved, affordable housing. By hook or by crook, Stockton is busy reinventing the high street as the agora of old – a public place, where we gather as much to meet and share as we do to buy and sell.

Seeing clearly

The aforementioned London First *Planning Manifesto for High Streets and Town Centres* argues that masterplans fail as town-centre (re)development management strategies 'because they are too prescriptive, take too long to consult on and adopt as policy, and are not flexible enough to react [and] adapt to changing markets.'[9] Instead, it champions a town-centre management strategy supported by an effective delivery plan. The development and managing of such a framework requires the nous and capability of an empowered and empowering stakeholder-focused team, one as at home with unlocking private and public purses as it is with planning *and* licensing as it is with the needs and wants of business as it is with liaising with a multitude of public service departments. Ideally, as is true of Stockton-on-Tees, that would be a Business Improvement District team, appointed to work a strategy that 'strike[s] the right local balance between economic growth, social benefit and residential amenity'.

For architects, the key takeaways are reasonably clear. Effective high-street and town-centre (re)development is led by what might be loosely called an experience masterplan. It's a strategy informed by a relevant and constantly replenished evidence-base, which in the case of Stockton began in earnest in 2005, and resulted in a number of foundational and ongoing studies into town-centre use needs. The result is its ever-evolving media-neutral Local Development Framework – that is, the entire portfolio of its planning documents, as spearheaded by the *Core Strategy* (2010). By media-neutral, I simply mean that a life-first framework for successful retail and hospitality placemaking has no favourites. It's as much concerned with technology as it is with content as it is with in-built redundancy as it is with new architecture as it is with activation and operations. In this respect, Stockton's built-form guidance is part of a framework that includes policies on regeneration, environment and licensing. It sits cheek-by-jowl with design briefs on the likes of sustainability and shop frontage design. Here, standard principles for urban design – identity, community, permeability, legibility, connectivity, quality, security, vitality – are rooted in a very local understanding of what will make for an experience-led high street. If Stockton

9 London First, *Planning Manifesto for High Streets and Town Centres*, p 3.

Borough Council were a brand, then we would be describing its approach as holistic and integrated, its personality as creatively rebellious, its purpose as shared and abundantly clear, its understanding of its audience as almost pitch perfect.

The Emperor's New Clothes

Stockton town centre's journey from dying high street to the super-vibrant marketplace of experiences that the likes of retail space agency Appear Here's founder and chief executive Ross Bailey advocates, is far from over. Long and fraught with difficulties, it's a battle waged not only on its own terms, but also with historic regional economic hardship. While marked by a high birth rate of businesses, the borough lacks big industry employers. Meaning, the wider business-size picture is largely micro to small, with significant numbers of die-offs, all of which makes for unsteady times and reduced levels of expendable income. As a result, Stockton's supply of retail continues to outstrip demand, vacancies continue to blight the street, and even big-box chains continue to shut up shop. Whatever the extent of its creative rebelliousness, Stockton-on-Tees Borough Council has and continues to face forces that constantly threaten to scupper its plans.

One of these is the fact that ownership of the town centre is fragmented. This is the unfortunate norm, the national picture, and it's where local authority promises to take back the high street can flounder on the rocks of property law. Compulsory Purchase Orders (CPOs) must prove a compelling case for public interest, and can be prohibitively expensive and super drawn out. They do happen, but usually as part and parcel of large public projects, often transport. Which is not to say that Stockton is a complete stranger to the CPO. Just that notices are few and far between, the council forced to bide its time, pouncing when key properties and land become available. If difficult for Stockton, imagine Westminster City Council's dealings with Oxford Street, veritable graveyard of upgrade plans, the last being London Mayor Sadiq Khan's hopes for pedestrianising the street. Oxford Street is a special case, of course. It lives off its historic reputation, its ease of access (with Crossrail to come) and its proximity to the likes of Marylebone and Soho. Still, whatever its extraordinary capacity for survival, just think where it would be if owned – as in the case of Regent Street – by a single enabling owner, one with a long view of what it takes to create a high street that is as socially useful as it is commercially viable.

The impact of the fragmented high street and town centre is far reaching. Protected by the law and incentivised by income-potential valuation practices, commercial property owners are largely shareholder facing. As food hall pioneer Market Halls founder Andy Pratt says, 'the sole aim of property ownership is to grow the value of the portfolio, which is judged on the basis of rent plus multiplier, which is why everyone pushes up the rent – to grow valuation.'[10] The result: cookie-cutter streets occupied by same-old-same-old chains, their small-margin-many-store business models making them the only tenants capable

10 Interview with the author, July 2020.

of turning a decent profit. Seen this way, the rent review is more a speculator's financial instrument than it is a rationally indexed mechanism, and has resulted in what Pratt calls an emperor-in-new-clothes approach to commercial property valuation: it's unsustainable – we know it and we're pretending we don't.

Upsetting emperors

Hans Christian Andersen's *The Emperor's New Clothes* ends with a boy – unencumbered by pride, vanity or fear – blurting out exactly what everyone knows and has pretended not to know: the Emperor is not wearing any clothes. If I may be allowed to push Pratt's analogy to its final conclusion, the boy is everything that the fragmented high street is not, and the moment he speaks is the day lockdown is announced and all but essential shops are closed. COVID-19 has decimated the high street, and while it is showing signs of recovery, it's an uneven recovery, and is especially poor in cities and towns heavily reliant on commuter spend. At the time of writing, and despite government announcements encouraging a return, just over a third of the UK workforce is actually travelling to work. Meanwhile, footfall as an average across the country is down a third. The market's wearing a brave face, but the impact of Brexit, the current relative lack of activity, and first- and second-quarter poor rent collection rates – especially in retail and leisure – will have a marked effect on confidence going forward. The boy has spoken and the Emperor is, indeed, butt naked.

Sadiq Khan has called the above an existential crisis. And yet, for every giant crisis, a giant opportunity. The fault lines inherent in the disjointed and unevolved high street and town centre are laid bare: streets based entirely on age-old sales models resulting in streets full of age-old middle-market big-box chains; landlords and tenants with little or no long-term social investment in place and community; offline retail competing on online retail's terms, birthing a race to a bottom called empty and vacant. Laid bare, it's do or die, and if we're going to do, then we need a set of mechanisms designed to move us from a shareholder to a stakeholder model for the high street. First, ensure that the regeneration of any high street is framed by a vision that is inherently flexible, commercially astute and socially useful. To paraphrase Sustainability Manager for Frasers Property (Australia) Rory Martin, developers need to adopt a joined-up 'complete neighbourhood' approach,[11] whereby teams are representative of all stakeholders, work with the community to investigate, design, activate and manage the project, and are contractually invested in its long-term success.

Second, and aiming to give the above real teeth, as recommended by the London First manifesto, it means empowering local authorities to act on behalf of all. Most obviously, that would be greater investment in CPO know-how and powers. It's also the introduction of Compulsory Selling Orders, currently being considered

11 Interview with the author, July 2020.

Figure 4.3 Burwood Brickworks neighbourhood shopping centre (2019), designed by NH Architects. Developed by Frasers Property, it has helped complete the neighbourhood.

in Scotland, whereby vacant properties are sold – compelling case proven – on the open market. It's Investment Orders with the power to make property owners invest in vacant or derelict properties. It's the wholesale use of discharge-of-conditions criteria binding landlords to agreements vis-à-vis managing vacancies. It's ensuring a much richer mix of leaseholds, designed to both fill vacancies in the short term and encourage a richer mix of tenants and experiential retail types in the long term.

Third, it means an old-new type of owner – one that genuinely operates a triple-bottom-line approach, and therefore understands that being socially useful is one and the same as being commercially astute. Key to this is a move away from a base rent to a turnover model. An anathema to those developers for whom the raison d'être of any project is simply flipping product valued on potential income, turnover models see landlords peg rent to the takings of their tenants. As an approach, it underpins the extraordinary success of Bicester Village Fashion Outlet, owned by Value Retail. It's Andy Pratt's model for Food Halls. It's British Land's promise for Canada Water, which is set to create London's first high street in over a century. Highly invested in tenant success, it's a model that makes for a different calibre of landlord – present, creative, enabling.

Towards a new type

As Stockton-on-Tees Borough Council's epic journey continues to demonstrate, anyone in the business of reinventing the high street faces an uphill struggle. The alternative, however, is what we've just had, at the height of lockdown. In this respect, however terrible, COVID-19 is a gift. It is a worst-case scenario made real. It's what many a British high street has been facing for the last 20 years. As such, it's an opportunity to return to the marketplace of old, to the sensibility of the market trader, to a place of experience, of culture and of commerce. It's the loss, says property consultants CBRE's Nigel Costain, of the squeezed middle (the Pret A Manger and Victoria's Secrets of this world) and the resulting flight to, at one end, the rare, the niche and the pop-up, and at the other, the familiarly local. It's the vision and the everyday follow through, as stewarded by the local authority – planning, licensing and regeneration policies aligned. It's understanding that retail and hospitality is the churn and very liveness of our public spaces. It's knowing that the high street is the catalyst and support for the making of the sorts of places people want to live, work and play in. Bring back the agora. It's that important.

Falling in Love with Life

> I want to understand the meaning of your experience, to walk in your shoes, to feel things as you feel them, to explain things as you explain them.
>
> → JAMES P. SPRADLEY, ANTHROPOLOGIST[12]

I know I will be accused of mythologising the role of the developer in the regeneration of London's King's Cross, but it is well known that as part of its investigation phase the Argent then chief executive Roger Madelin met with 7,500 local people at 353 meetings, to which he travelled on his bicycle (see Figure 4.4). I am not party to the field notes Madelin made as a result of the experience, but I'm certain they helped form the basis of Argent's 'human city' thinking, as published in the first edition of its

12 J.P. Spradley, *The Ethnographic Interview*, New York: Holt, Rinehart and Winston, 1979, p 34.

Figure 4.4 Argent chief executive Roger Madelin in King's Cross.

Principles for a Human City (2000), and which in editions two and three evolved to wrap its arms around landowner, policy-maker, heritage watchdog and designer.[13] The final edition was taken back to the public. The investigation phase would be given further heft by a clutch of feasibility studies, and finish in 2004. Based on this, the development plan was drawn up in 2006, and allowed for enough room to adapt a fifth of the site to redesign, depending on evolving needs and wants. Planning permits staggered across the next two years, and ground was broken in 2007, the subsequent development overseen by Argent, London & Continental Railways and Exel.

13 Argent St George with London & Continental Railways and Exel, *Principles for a Human City*, third (revised) edition, 2001, https://bit.ly/2GGpPEu.

Towards designing for the human

King's Cross isn't perfect. It's had its own fair share of controversies. As a retail venture, Coal Drops Yard needs a deep rethink. In terms of our focus, its large mixed-use scheme lies somewhere across and beyond the remit of this chapter. However, it is rightly lauded as an extraordinary success, and I dramatise the story of the head of one of the world's leading developers cycling about a run-down piece of London to listen to the wants and needs of thousands of people as a means of illustrating the deep and enduring importance of any (re)development's investigation phase. Informing the vision, guidelines and framework for any given (re)development, the investigation phase ought to precede the design brief by a country mile, be alive-and-well throughout the development, and continue to guide its ongoing activation and operation.

That it does not can't simply be explained away by the fact that the investigation phase is not what architects are generally hired to do. Equally, nor can its absence be excused on the basis that we often employ user-profile and scenario data to inform our design – that data is largely quantitative, and giving it a face and a life does not make it the face and the life we are designing for. When you've got a hammer, everything looks like a nail. If you only ask end-product questions you will only get end-product solutions. Seen this way, any investigation is biased towards making the most efficient, cost-effective and safe end product. As an approach, it largely obeys a set of universal and highly rational principles, champions the task of getting things done and rests its case on the final product doing what it says it does on the tin.

All of which can result in great buildings, but less often in always-relevant ones, and in some cases ends – to invert Argent's vision for King's Cross Central – in contributing to the making of an inhuman high street or town centre. It's not that function-led design isn't right. It's just that it needs to be better informed by the life it seeks to serve. Much more human-centred design approaches argue that if we are to ensure relevance, then our processes need to take account of our likes and dislikes, and therefore of the conscious and subconscious cognitive makeups that govern our behaviour, form our rituals and create our myths. In other words, when designing for truly interesting retail and hospitality, don't just look at footfall, dwell time and sales data as supplied by a prospective big-box tenant. Begin instead with understanding what makes people tick. Dig into the past, the now and the future of place, its people, their social mores and their patterns of behaviour. Find out what entertains us. Discover our theatre. Know our story. Be an ethnographer.

Bring on the ethnographer

Today, one of the leading proponents of the architect as ethnographer is Atelier Bow Wow's Momoyo Kaijima. As she writes in the exhibition notes for 'Architectural Ethnography' – the Japanese Pavilion's display at the 16th Venice Architecture Biennale (2018) – ethnology's key research tool is fieldwork, which when used as part of the investigation phase in architecture translates as a stakeholder-wide case study, and is communicated largely in a range of drawings, from the small, simple and abstract to the large, complex and representative. The key here is that design is understood in relation to people and to time. It adapts to social and economic factors, serving as an 'index for the observation of urban life'. It is a pattern language, and often communicates technique, information about materials or processes for making. It is interested in our tools, our objects, our private spaces. It is habit fascinated. It loves daily life and how that life has changed over time. Its focus is all encompassing, arguing that 'the relationship between architecture and human life is not defined by a continuous physical space', but rather through our experiences. In short, form and function must follow a genuine grasp of the relations between people and their experiences, as understood by the observing designer.

As a means of illustrating how such thinking translates into planning and designing for relevant retail and hospitality, two quick examples, one old, the other current. First, the retail and leisure strategy for Shibuya (Tokyo) in the 1970s was hugely influenced by the likes of Wajiro Kon's 'Modernology' (1930), which advocates fixed-point fieldwork surveys of people – with their possessions, fashions, belongings and houses – in relation to placemaking. As writer and thinker Izumi Kuroishi says, it asserts that we see urban space as essentially theatrical, that we constantly describe it through our movements, and that its structure is designed to integrate our needs and wants as social, sensual and symbolic beings.[14]

14 W. Kon and K. Yoshida, *Modernologio (Kōgengaku)*, Tokyo: Shun'yodo, 1930.

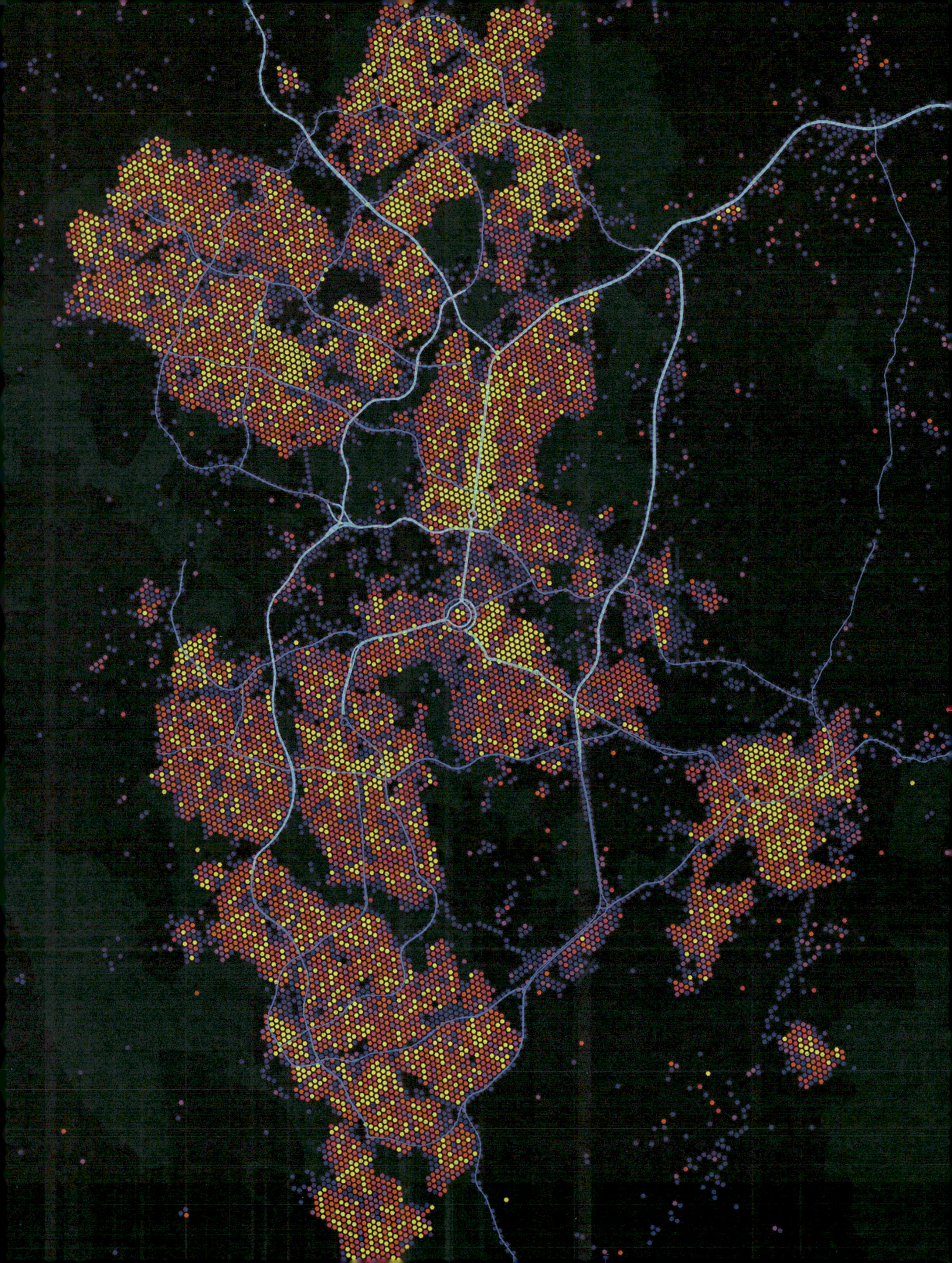

This all sat well with an approach that believed the department store a site for commerce *and* culture. As a result, the Shibuya department store played home to a heterogeneous collection of smaller stores, to streets, to squares and to art. It hosted rolling event-laden programmes. It commissioned graphics and other marketing collateral from young outlier artists. And it understood itself as a complement to Shibuya's wider identity. As a result, for a time, before it lost its way in the 1980s, Shibuya was a one-of-a-kind destination, an extraordinary melding of the old and the new, of small and big, of culture and commerce.

What is true of the influence of fieldwork carried out in 1970s Shibuya is even more so of work currently being carried out by the Australian National University. The university has conducted – through data analysts Place Intelligence – a year-long, city-wide survey of the comings and goings of its students and staff in order to better understand what it is about its campus that fails to attract and involve as it should, and which therefore has serious consequences for attracting future students, staff and partners. Unlike a Tokyo or a London, Canberra – a relatively new city – is a closed system, and therefore perfectly positioned for becoming a smart city, all of which has a bearing on how the investigation has been carried out. Even so, while the method of gathering it may have differed, analysed data sourced through the tracking of subjects via mobile phones is the digitalised form of the observational drawings that Kaijima speaks of. Well scraped for factual and sentiment insight, it has provided the university with information on the rituals and myths of individuals and groups; it has given it the means with which to analyse the motivators behind people's own timetables; and it has

Figure 4.5 A heat map of activity patterns in Canberra is shown at metropolitan scale created from mobile device signals to inform urban strategy, design and placemaking.

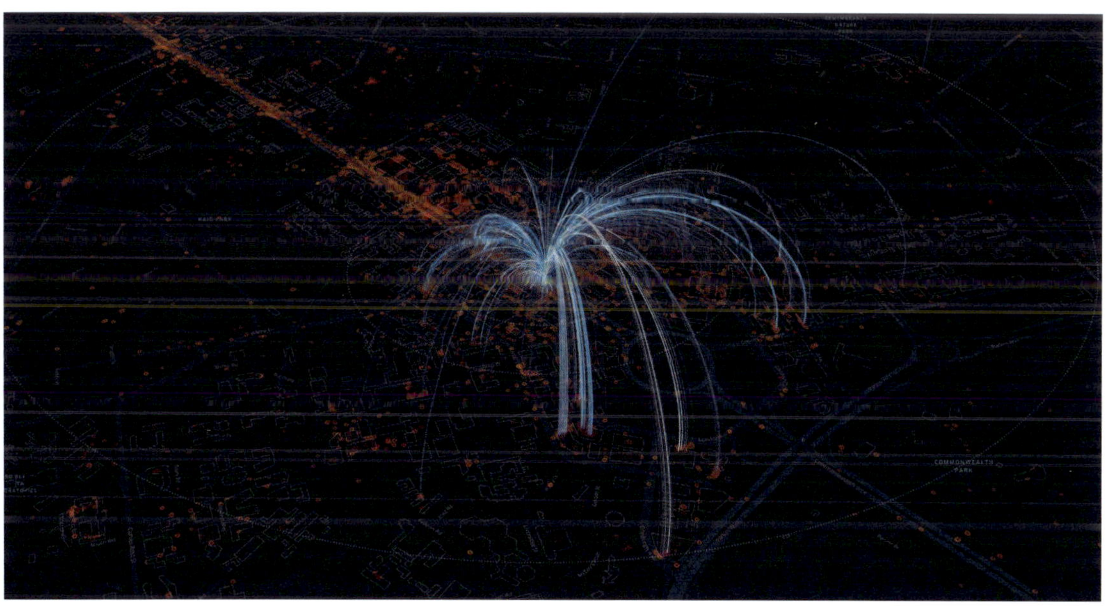

Figure 4.6 Mapping patterns of movement in Canberra to and from a light-rail station blends mobile device signal data with point-of-interest information to reveal user behaviours over time.

mapped types and popularity of destinations across the city (see Figures 4.5 and 4.6). Findings include the fact that there is an exodus from campus at 12.30 pm every day, and that one of the seemingly counterintuitive reasons for the mass exit is the opportunity to spend time working in less obviously work-orientated environments. The insight will have a significant bearing on the university's vision for its students' and staff's on-campus experience, for how it repurposes whatever levels of redundancy are built into the shell-and-core, and for how the new campus retail, leisure and hospitality offer contextually fits with the city as whole. In the same way that the department store revolution did for Shibuya, so the university seeks to complement and enrich Canberra as a whole. What's good for the goose is good for the gander – so to speak.

Cutting-edge empathy

Crucially, the investigation phase is both the foundation and a constant. We would need a lot more time and space than we have here to evaluate how 1980s Shibuya went wrong, but I'm betting all I have on the fact that planning and operations lost its feel for a super-heterogeneous identity, as mediated by the experiences of those it ostensibly served. In contrast, Argent's masterplan for King's Cross built an unusual degree of flexibility into the design. As is true of every project, it expected change – and if true of something as relatively slow-moving as the physical build, then it is especially true when planning for retail and hospitality. 'Retail,' argues Argent's Joint Managing Partner Nick Searl, 'moves at 1000 miles per hour.'[15] The framework for developments including retail and hospitality has to run on what he calls a 'cutting-edge empathy', whereby masterplan and activation and operation plans are alert to the need for constantly standing in the shoes of their occupiers, customers and visitors. Meaning, it's vital that the investigation phase – ethnologist and analyst and the data they provide – continues to inform design during and after the project's delivery. This way, the vision for a project such as that which was imagined by Roger Madelin and his fieldwork all those years ago has the capacity for creating a sense of permanence while at the same time remaining absolutely relevant. It's exactly this that will continue to inform King's Cross's ongoing and COVID-recovery retail and hospitality strategies. We need to keep on falling in love.

15 Interview with the author, July 2020.

Always Meanwhile

> A building properly conceived is several layers of longevity of built components.
>
> → FRANK DUFFY, ARCHITECT[16]

In June 2020, the UK government announced its 'strategy to rebuild Britain and fuel economic recovery across the UK'.[17] Part promise to 'tackle this country's great unresolved challenges of the last three decades' and part COVID-19 emergency response, *A New Deal for Britain* (2020) trumpets itself as a deregulatory initiative. Long on headlines but short on detail, its ideas for a complete overhaul of the English planning system are expanded on in a recently published white paper *Planning for the Future* (2020), which proposes – in the name of beauty – to zone land as areas of 'growth', 'renewal' and 'protection'.[18] Part of the reform includes a fundamental change in the Use Classes Order, and the extension of permitted development rights, allowing for a range of building types – shops, offices, warehouse and industrial buildings – to be converted to residential use. Rolled out over the next five years, to the tune of £640 billion, the new deal is headed up by the somewhat unoriginally named infrastructure delivery taskforce Project Speed, and echoes previous pledges to cut red tape. 'Build back better, build back greener, build back faster' is its mantra.

While everyone welcomes action and agrees current planning law requires reform, the government's proposals to rip up the planning rule book threaten to upend the intervention and build Britain back less than better. Key concerns: the frankly alarming lack of understanding with regards to the level of joined-up central, regional and local planning required for the delivery of really decent zonal land-use development; the basis for its notions of beauty and the design codes for achieving that beauty; the reneging on promises to achieve sustainability objectives through a greener retrofit programme; and the extension of permitted development rights and the increased erosion of Section 106 agreements, both of which have variously and largely ended in schemes as far away from the government's promise of 'good quality, attractive and affordable' as it is possible to get. Equally, the claim that the English planning system slows or halts development doesn't hold water, with research showing 90% of planning requests permitted, and the bottleneck to be found not at planning stage, but rather at the point of delivery, with developers releasing stock into markets predicated on favourable absorption rates.

16 Quoted in S. Brand, *How Buildings Learn: What Happens After They're Built*, New York: Viking, 1994, Chapter 2.

17 Prime Minister's Office, 10 Downing Street, 'PM: A New Deal for Britain', press release, 30 June 2020, https://bit.ly/36FwmKw.

18 Ministry of Housing, Communities and Local Government, *Planning for the Future*, white paper, August 2020, https://bit.ly/2SyDKir.

Class Es anyone?

My apologies for straying so far from the remit of this chapter. Think of it as a sobering caveat to this section's otherwise unbridled enthusiasm for the high street and town centre operating in an *always meanwhile* state. Traditionally, a meanwhile-state strategy is the name given for the temporary and imaginative use of land earmarked for development. At its best, it's a space for prototyping ideas for the eventual development, involving stakeholders in that idea-making, and better landing and knitting the scheme into the wider neighbourhood. Often it sees buildings set for demolition temporarily utilised in ways – markets, hubs, campuses – its original designers could only have dreamt

Figure 4.7 London's Old Street Station, super-curated by Appear Here: theatre and memory-making machine par excellence.

of. Bastardising Frank Duffy's theory that the building's components – fixed, non-fixed and programmatic – are better understood as layers of temporality, and therefore always in various states of flux, we argue for the high street as being in an always meanwhile state. As an example, I tend to cite Melbourne's laneways, where streets metamorphose – as carless street-vendor paradise or live music event or traditional independent retail space – as ceaselessly as the programme will allow. However, for something closer to home, the ever-morphing market that has sprung up on the entrance floor to Old Street tube station (see Figure 4.7) is exactly this: super-curated by Appear Here, it is the high street as always meanwhile.

That it remains a rare type comes down – at least in part – to the law and the interpretation of that law: namely, as planning consultant David Morris says, 'thou shalt not lose A1 shops.'[19] However, the want and need for greater flexibility has reached something of a fever pitch. With online retail increasingly owning much of the category, being out and about needs to be defined by so much more than Mission Search and Find. It's not simply about cheaper prices, extraordinary choice and absolute convenience. It's not a search engine plus retail dashboard plus shopping cart. On the contrary, it is the immersive and multisensory experience that marks what it means to journey through – and help create – the theatre of public space, our high streets and town centres. Alert to this, many a landlord, developer, architect and tenant has wanted nothing more than to be given the opportunity to break out of use class siloes. Battered by COVID-19, government has listened. The change in the categorising of use classes – mainly via the shapeshifting enabler Class E – is that opportunity. Able to hop, as architecture firm Gort Scott's Fiona Scott intimates, much more easily from use class to use class, and to mix those classes across rolling – daily, weekly, seasonal – programmes in single properties, it provides the legal framework for the making of the experiential high street.[20] Save the very serious concern around conversion to residential, it's just the ticket.

Making it elastic

Making the always meanwhile work requires more than permission. The entire ecosystem – plan, design, build, activate and manage – needs to be flexible, at every level, from large to small. Here, if I may borrow a retail yardstick, extra-large is the elasticity granted by the change in the Use Classes Order. Large is the elasticity of a framework that creates and fosters a permanent sense of identity and, at the same time, is ever alive to the need for staying relevant. Medium is the elasticity of adaptive reuse and built-in flexibility of the architecture. Small is the elasticity of the play of its many moving parts, the content, its rolling programme. Together, they constitute a new-old typology of the high street, one born of our curiosity, of our need to socialise with our whole bodies, and of our desire to create as much as consume. Always meanwhile, it's the high street as agora, a campus grounded in experience. Let's dig into what exactly this means.

19 Interview with the author, August 2020.

20 Interview with the author, July 2020.

Figure 4.8 Chippendale Street, Sydney – a high street re-imagined.

Figure 4.9 The future of a successfully stitched-together Olympia, London – new development by YOO Capital and design by Heatherwick Studio.

An elastic framework

When landlords, developers and tenants speak of the retail and hospitality sector as moving from a sales to a service model, my fervent hope is that they don't mean service in the commoditised and generic sense. Rather, in keeping with B. Joseph Pine and James H. Gilmore's 'experience economy,'[21] they understand it as a dynamic, personalised and relevant experience-based model. 'We create a big platform,' says Roger Madelin (now of British Land), 'and encourage a mix of many tenants, partnerships and associations to activate the framework, and then we help amplify that activation. We don't over-curate – facilitation is the key.'[22] Inherently elastic, it's a framework for the always meanwhile, as exemplified by YOO Capital's ambitions for the new development at London's Olympia (see Figure 4.9), due for completion in 2023. Taking its cue from a traditional Olympia tradeshow-and-conference programme that changes every three days, the wider mixed-use development is as open platform as it gets. As YOO Capital managing director Lloyd Lee says, it really is about co-creation. 'Share the pen around. Be a co-authored platform. Let the tenants write their own stories.'[23]

21 B.J. Pine II and J.H. Gilmore, 'Welcome to the Experience Economy', *Harvard Business Review*, July–August 1998, https://bit.ly/36DB8rJ.

22 Interview with the author, July 2020.

23 Interview with the author, August 2020.

Figure 4.10 Bikini Berlin, Germany's first concept mall, combines well-established boutiques with start-ups and pop ups to fantastic effect. The development, by Bayerische Hausbau, was completed in 2013.

Flexible architecture

The last generation of retail and hospitality architecture has found itself shackled by the push for high efficiency, by siloed leaseholds and by a commissioning regime that is more an old boys' club than a meritocracy. The result, says architecture, design and planning practice ACME's Friedrich Ludewig, is architecture as 'highly specialised dinosaur – it cannot evolve, and dies with the first breath of volcanic dust'.[24]

This is especially true of anything built since the mid-1980s one-trick ponies that at only 35 years old end up at the knacker's yard, their apparent lack of inbuilt flexibility their downfall. Truth is, in the name of social and environmental sustainability, we're just not looking hard enough. Arguably, even the most unpromising of buildings possesses an alternative future, as Market Hall's exciting adaption of the former British Home Stores building on Oxford Street more than proves. Even so, if we are to facilitate an always meanwhile high street, then it's critical that we adopt a two-pronged design

24 Interview with the author, July 2020.

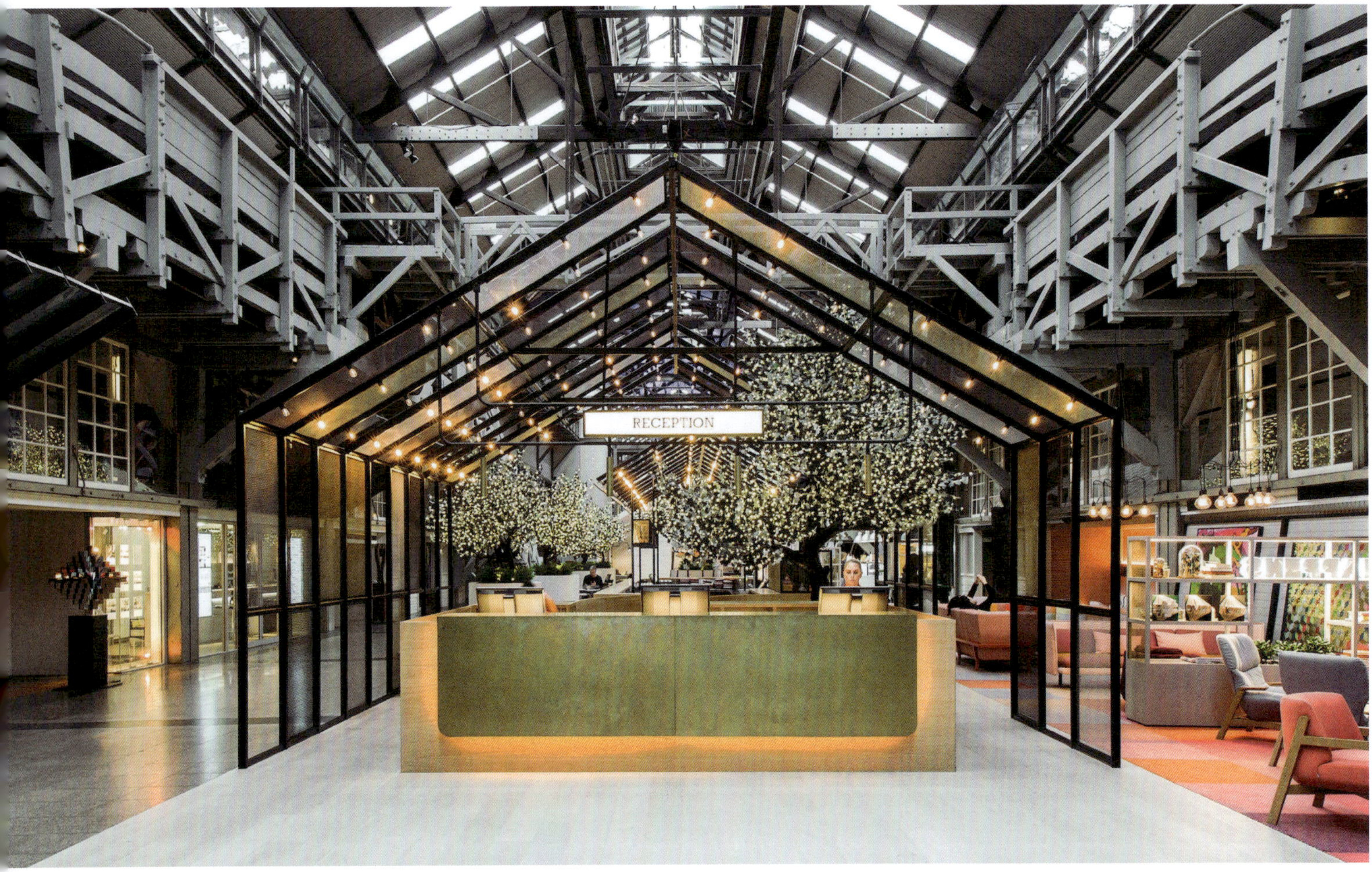

Figure 4.11 Ovolo Woolloomooloo Hotel, Sydney, designed by Hassell. A 100-year-old wharf beautifully adapted in 2015.

Figure 4.12 Hammerson commissioned ACME to create a 21st-century extension of the existing Victorian arcades that helped make Leeds famous. It opened in 2015.

strategy: the socially responsible adaptive reuse of old buildings; and an 'intentional redundancy' imperative when it comes to new architecture, a flexibility informed in planning by extensive possible-scenario modelling, rendering schemes production-ready for a range of future uses. 'We need,' says developer Hammerson's Mark Bourgeois, 'a more dynamic architecture, an architecture that can be as agile and flexible as possible – over a shorter period of time.'[25]

25 Interview with the author, July 2020.

None of this is new, just relatively rare. Bikini Berlin (Bayerische Hausbau, 2013; see Figure 4.10), Shanghai's Tianzifang (an ongoing public/private project begun in 1998) and Sydney's Ovolo Woolloomooloo (Hassell, 2015; see Figure 4.11) are super-fine examples of adaptive reuse. Meanwhile, for inbuilt-redundancy new build, let the lyrical hutzpah of Cedric Price's Fun Palace (1961) be your enduring guide (see Figure 4.13).

AMAZING
CHOCOLATE
WORKSHOP

Figure 4.13 Cedric Price's unrealised Fun Palace (1961) was designed as a giant interactive machine, highly adaptable to the shifting cultural and social conditions of its time.

Moving content is king

Critically, everything we have spoken about begins and ends with the activation of a given development. This is the place of (trans)action. It's the proof of concept. It's the key performance indicator. It's the only game in town. It's where we – the people – buy in to the experience. Ideally, the elasticity of the law, the framework and the architecture is determined and continually determined by the experience, the fast-moving content, this always meanwhile state. This is the domain of the impresario, the maker, the storyteller. It's the work of the theatre designers, the art director, the event manager, the live producer. It's where the art installation hoarding informs the market stall informs the pop-up restaurant informs the maker festival informs the seasonal enterprise scheme informs the modular neighbourhood centre. This is the designer as maker of the prototype. It's about the care for the small and the live, for the fast-moving content, at multiple scales. It's what Vitruvius meant – if

I may be so bold – when he defined the third pillar of 'good building' as *venustas* or delight.[26] If we are to design for the always meanwhile, it's essential that we understand that that delight is the content. It's how, for example, Melbourne gets its laneways and Beijing its hutongs. It's about the inhabiting of our campus-like high streets with ever-meaningful prototypes.

The other c-word

Innovative businesses are by necessity fascinated by the soft edges of their discipline and sector. From our perspective, that soft edge means going above and beyond what we would normally consider the remit of the architect. It means going beyond the BIM manager, the visualiser, the engineer, the M&E consultant, the quantity surveyor, the project manager. These are the experts, and we know our beans, and we have our Gantt charts. However, whatever the extent of our expertise, we are only the sum of our experience, and therein lies the bias – professionally, culturally and socially. By going beyond, I mean the putting together of a diverse and transdisciplinary team capable of wrapping its arms around the ramifications of the intervention. It's participatory design, actively involving all stakeholders in a process to help ensure the end result better meets their needs and wants. In other words, designing for the always meanwhile ecosystem demands that architecture embrace all things people, programme and place. Not to be mistaken for the other c-word, that thorny, duplicitous and much-trotted-out trope 'collaboration', it means being genuinely and empathically co-creative.

Figure 4.14 Looking beyond the RIBA Plan of Work.

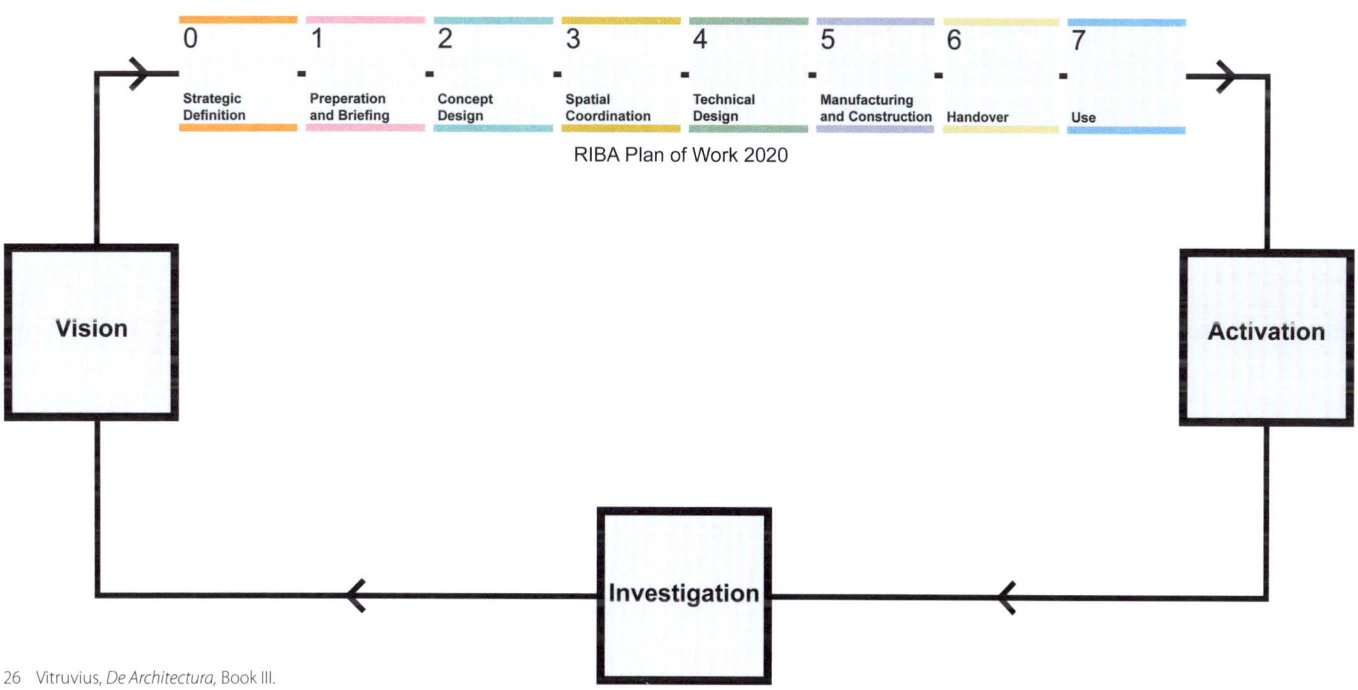

26 Vitruvius, *De Architectura*, Book III.

A Manifesto for the High Street as Co-created Campus

Towns and buildings will not be able to become alive, unless they are made by all the people in society

→ SARA ISHIKAWA, ARCHITECT[27]

As journalist Oliver Burkeman says, there's never been a better time to be a futurist.[28] Whatever the field, whatever the expertise, certain uncertainty is what we know. Meaning, crystal balls up and down the country are happily dispensing the vaguest of prophecies: it's all change. Stunned by the day's exceptional circumstances, we are in agreement. Unless a modeller of the behaviour of viruses and the climate, anything more detailed from our speculators of the tomorrow is no longer to be trusted. Of course, telling the future doesn't have to be this way. The future doesn't exist until it does. When thinking about architecture and the retail and hospitality sector – in the next five, 10 or 100 years – rather than speculate as to how things will be, much better, in the words of political scientist Mark Lilla, to 'ask only what we want to happen, and how to make it happen, given the constraints of the moment'.[29]

In which spirit, and given everything we've learned, a good old-fashioned manifesto for the high street, working title the less-than-catchy 'A Manifesto for the High Street as Co-created Campus'. We've touched on the campus as adapted model for the high street throughout the chapter. The word 'campus' was first used in its modern sense in 1774, to describe the college grounds of Princeton University. It is derived from the Latin for 'field', and I like that kampe in Greek is 'a bend'. Derivatives in other modern languages have it as 'a corner', 'curved' and 'to bend'. The truly great campus is a programme-driven field of delight. It's a corner of great cultural exchange. It's a festival, a stage set, a place of many moving parts. The pop-up, the food truck, the installation, the local, the independent – these are its types. It's porous, inviting, a place of conversation. It's where we choose to drink, eat, explore, meet, create. It fosters friendships, movements, future businesses. It's messy around the edges. Wayfinding curves. It's a latter-day agora crossed with an MIT-type innovation hub. In terms of the emphasis on places on co-created rolling programmes and ever-adaptable spaces, it's a memory-making machine. It bends with the times – and to what comes next. It's the open platform made real. It's where we need to be heading in the high street.

27 C. Alexander, S. Ishikawa and M. Silverstein, *A Pattern Language: Towns, Buildings, Construction*, New York: Oxford University Press, p x.

28 O. Burkeman, 'Life in a Post-Coronavirus World: Will It Feel So Very Different?', *The Guardian*, 19 June 2020, https://bit.ly/36GYYCT.

29 M. Lilla, 'Opinion: No One Knows What's Going to Happen', *New York Times*, 22 May 2020, https://nyti.ms/3iCzs48.

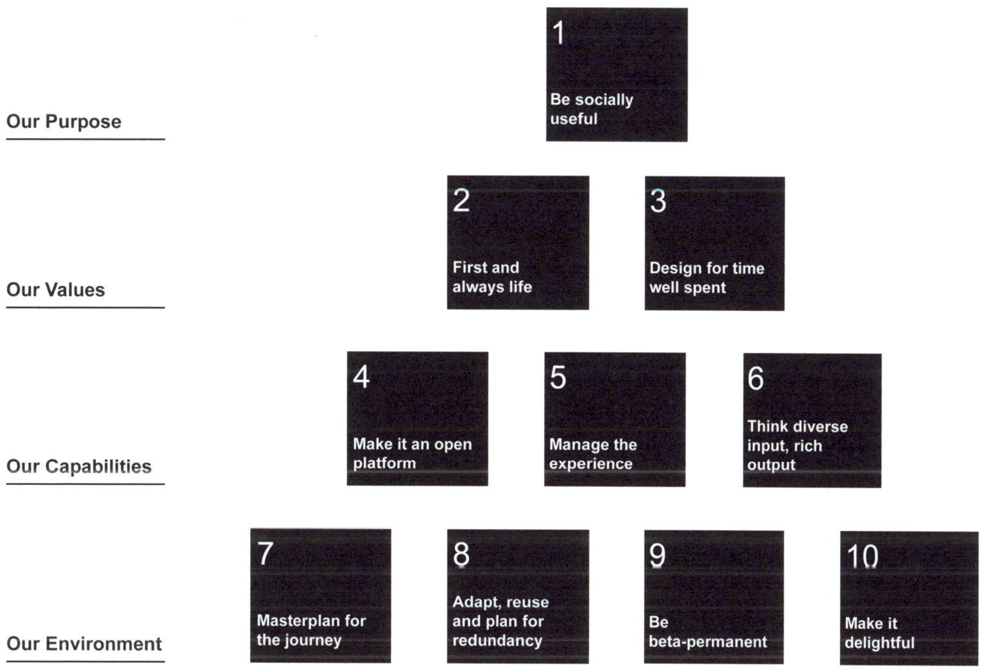

Figure 4.15 10 Principles for the co-created campus.

A set of simple principles (see Figure 4.15), the manifesto is both vision and guide. As such, it is framed by our purpose, our values, our capabilities and our environments. As well as this, each principle references a point of post-pandemic design. Here it is, a manifesto for what we want to happen, and how to make it happen, given the constraints of whatever moment we find ourselves in.

1. Be socially useful

Have a higher purpose and know that that purpose is one and the same as being commercially astute. This is our North Star. Without it, we are nothing. It trumps reputation, depth of portfolio, short-term shareholder concerns. It guides investment, investigation, plans, design, build, activation and management. It balances purpose with profit. It's B Corp for the high street. Take the long view. Be socially useful.

Post-pandemic design

Ensure that measuring social sustainability is a critical success factor added to all your Return Briefs. Work with developers that are not exclusively concerned with high absorption and rental rates and flipping product.

2. First and always life

Begin with life. Form may follow function, but both are meaningless unless guided by our rituals and our myths. Design for the local and the locale. Be open-minded ethnographers and open-sourced curators. Involve the people you serve. Stand in their shoes. Become their stories; then tell them – beautifully, with care.

Post-pandemic design

Before picking up the pen, make time for more human-centred research up front – and follow through with a detailed and ongoing process of post-occupancy evaluation.

3. Design for time well spent

Design for the service model. Know that real dwell time is not to be confused with the metrics of engagement and footfall. It is the *quality* of time spent that counts. Create a high street of great experiences. Ensure that it encourages a participation for the common good. Be guided by models – the turnover model, for example – that share in the risk and reward of the experience-led campus-like high street.

Post-pandemic design

Make the effort to storyboard your findings. There's nothing like simple step-by-step storyboards – based on ethnographic research – illustrating how we go from attraction to involvement to belonging.

4. Make it an open platform

Involve all stakeholders in the planning, design, activation and management of the high street. Programme the various – daily, weekly, seasonal, physical, virtual – campus touchpoints through the lens of multiple and evolving types of use. Encourage facilitation rather than over-curation. Catalyse the small, the start-up, the local, the independent. Be a conscious experience masterplanner.

Post-pandemic design

Throughout the process, look to enable and host live experience workshops with key stakeholders.

5. Manage the experience

Know thy theatre. Plan for both back and front of house to have the people, the wherewithal, the skill set and the tools with which to create, facilitate and host the experience that is the high street. Invest in visionary, stakeholder-focused town-centre management teams, and give them sharp teeth – effective compulsory purchase/sale and vacancy management orders. Ensure landlord buy-in and tenant success.

Post-pandemic design

Make a point of identifying, recruiting and on-boarding activation team members from the outset – that is, the moment you enter the bidding process.

6. Think diverse input, rich output

Champion the importance of diversity and silo-busting at every level. Create diverse transdisciplinary design teams that reflect the stakeholders they serve. Think diverse process-input equals rich product-output – a virtuous circle, inspiring ongoing curiosity, debate and activism.

Post-pandemic design

Having properly understood your end user, ensure that the design team reflects that diversity of need and want. If you don't have it, buy it in.

7. Masterplan for the journey

Consistently celebrate the importance of the narrative journey and how a rich-mix of the long and the short, the big and the small, inspires a step-by-step wander to wonder. Ensure that curiosity is piqued with each turn. Seed sites with the installation, the pop-up, the start-up and the upstart. Attract, involve and create a sense of belonging. Know that the purchase funnel is the journey, played out in space, on campus. Design with the sensibility of a Harry Selfridge.

Post-pandemic design

Ensure that space is made for the short term, the small, the continuously evolving and the exceedingly generous. Hardwire them into the masterplanning so that they can't be cost-engineered out over the design and procurement processes.

8. Adapt, reuse, and plan for redundancy

Make places and spaces flex with the ever-changing wants and needs of the tenants and their experience-hungry audiences. Be the eternally flexible co-created campus. Fall in love with the patina of adaptive reuse. Design generously, for now, next and after we're gone. Give your buildings the versatility of the Victorian warehouse.

Post-pandemic design

Push for 'experience-ready' versatility, with multiple concepts for multiple scenarios.

9. Be beta-permanent

Learn from out-of-sector beta playbooks. Substitute build-and-they-will-come mantras for a much more fluid beta-plan approach to retail, one that takes a leaf out of the Silicon Valley book of the product in seemingly perpetual field test.

The beta plan is the never-perfect plan. It's rough and ready. It begins with making designers out of users. It involves people – customers, drinkers, diners, lovers, gawpers, travellers – in its constant making, and because it does, it learns – always and fast. Be beta-permanent.

Post-pandemic design

Make 28-day event licences and other similar relaxation of permission and licensing opportunities the norm. Design for the next experience.

10. Make it delightful

Make the most of the really real. Remember that it is the ever-morphing crowd of experiencing individuals that describes our high street. Design for delight. Encourage curiosity, sociability and creativity. Let the Andy Pratts and Ross Baileys of this world have their way.

Post-pandemic design

Collaborate with the content providers wherever possible. Set up practice on the high street.

Beta it and they will come

In keeping with our 'always meanwhile' mantra, the above is neither fixed nor finished. It's a manifesto in progress, and always will be. Indeed, if you forget everything shared in this chapter, the one and singular takeaway is this: In thinking better about the quality of the experience, we are then much more likely to attract and involve people, and in attracting and involving, so the high street as hybrid campus evolves to further attract and involve. Build it and they might come, perhaps once, possibly twice. Beta it and they will come – again and again and again.

Figure 4.16 Argent's King's Cross, 2019: the co-created campus in action.

CHAPTER 5

HEALTHCARE

SUMITA SINGHA

SUMITA SINGHA

Sumita is an award-winning architect, academic and author and has served on various RIBA committees for over 25 years. Since 2013, she has worked as a non-executive director of Moorfields Eye Hospital NHS Foundation Trust. She is the author of many books, including *Future Healthcare Design* (RIBA Publishing, 2020).

Introduction

Despite scientific advances and healthcare being written in as 'a fundamental right of every human' in the World Health Organization's constitution 75 years ago, the COVID-19 pandemic has shown how difficult it is to provide universal good healthcare. The pandemic has clearly revealed the fault lines in each nation's healthcare provision. The transmission of diseases today is fast and almost unstoppable in our connected world – and therefore, solutions need to embrace both the new and the tried and tested. The health sector contributes almost 10% of global GDP,[1] and therefore is an important determinant of global economic strategy. Currently, it is estimated that the COVID-19 pandemic is costing the world economy £375 billion per month,[2] and until a reliable vaccine is found, it will continue to impact with its worst effects trickling down to the most vulnerable.

1 Katie Puckett, 'The Future of Healthcare', *The Possible*, April 2020, https://www.the-possible.com/the-future-of-healthcare/.

2 'World At One', BBC Radio 4, 14 September 2020, https://www.bbc.co.uk/sounds/play/m000mkhn.

The WHO's constitution also says that it is the State's duty to provide the underlying determinants of health, such as safe and potable water, sanitation, food, housing, health-related information and education, and gender equality. Healthcare is not just about provision of hospitals, equipment, medicine or medical staff but linked to the design of cities, infrastructure, buildings and the environment. The underlying determinants of health are where architects, planners and engineers, along with the public, can have major influences. Thus, in a way all architects work in healthcare, whether directly or indirectly.

In Table 5.1, the best possible scenario is the goal of 'health for all' which will prevent people from entering hospitals, instead being able to remain healthy and mobile in their own homes for as long as possible. The demand for healthy cities and places is being driven increasingly by pandemics, pollution and environmental degradation. While in some ways, 'health for all' and healthy cities are connected, they also have divergences. 'Health for all' is a global vision and applies to everyone – whether they are living in a urban or rural environment, whether they are settled or migrants/refugees, whatever their income, gender, age and background.

Goals	Drivers	Enablers
Health for all (or how to keep people out of hospitals) – a global vision	• Lack of space • Lack of upkeep of existing facilities • Lack of equipment • Lack of staff • Health trends • Social and community care • Remote consultation • Environmental pollution	• Policy-makers • Healthcare think-tanks and charities • Government • Scientists and researchers • AI and technology • Appropriate housing and IT facilities • Public health education • Strict enforcement of environmental policies
Healthy cities and places (local and national)	• Environment- or lifestyle- related diseases such as asthma, cancer, obesity, etc. • Health trends • Rise in mental health problems • Public pressure • Environmental pollution	• Self-care • Public health education • City planning including transport, infrastructure, building design and proximity to services • Good housing design and secure IT • Green public spaces • Community facilities • Combating the environmental crisis with good design and specification
Acute care, A&E, specialist care including mental health (targeted care)	• Comorbidities • Emergency care • Traffic-related accidents • External or domestic accidents • Crime • Frequency of zoonotic diseases • Rise of mental health issues	• Specialist clinical care availability • Temporary facilities • Self-isolation spaces in homes
General hospitals, testing, GP surgeries, community healthcare, palliative care/hospices, care homes (general care)	• Recuperation • Follow-ups / routine care • Palliative care • Public demand • Ageing population	• Walkability or cyclability • Based on '15-minute city' (where amenities are within 15 minutes' reach by walking or cycling) • Opening hours • Facilities

Table 5.1 Healthcare goals, enablers and drivers.
Note that some of the drivers are also enablers.

Because it includes the global connections and inequalities in delivery of healthcare, along with economics, environment, politics and placemaking, 'health for all' is a more wicked problem than the design of healthy cities which is more localised. That is because health systems are complex adaptive systems – not linear ones – and even one small change affects the whole system.

The need for acute and emergency care will remain everywhere – people will have accidents or get seriously ill. Not every person is born equal in health and every person, no matter how healthy or wealthy, will fall ill during the course of their lives. By having the vision of 'health for all' and healthy cities, it is possible to limit the numbers of people entering hospitals for chronic illnesses and even accidents. Finally, there is need for places for recuperation, follow-up care and testing which can be delivered anywhere – including homes, and temporary or permanent general healthcare facilities. With comorbidities and an ageing population, palliative care and care homes will always be needed. In the US, it has been estimated that chronic diseases account for 75% of the nation's total healthcare expenditure.[3] The number of people over 60 is expected to increase to 18.5 million in 2025, while by 2050 and globally, there will be more than one billion people over 70.[4] Existing homes will need to be redesigned to be fit for purpose as 'lifetime homes'.

The care home crisis during COVID-19 in several countries demonstrated that older people were affected disproportionately. The pandemic has also affected men more than women; but generally, women, children and older people suffer more from health inequalities. Vulnerable people – mostly women, children and older people – are also affected during war and famine – from injuries, lack of medication and food – as they are left behind in inhospitable places. But in a war situation, hospitals themselves become the targets. In Aden, Yemen, for example, with a civil war going on and a cholera epidemic, only one doctor, a woman, was left in a hospital that was barely equipped to cope with the influx of COVID-19 patients and other casualties. Thus, peace has been recognised by the United Nations as a prerequisite for health.

Learning from History and Others

Can we learn from history and from other countries? Unlike the cholera epidemic in early 19th-century London, where closing a single water pump enabled the disease to stop, airborne diseases are much more difficult to control. During the Influenza pandemic of 1918 which came towards the end of a devastating World War, 50–100 million people were estimated to have died. In 2020, despite the lack of a vaccine, the world population being much larger, cities much denser and the popularity of travel and tourism, we are in a better position than in 1918, thanks to better healthcare facilities and advances in medical care. However, one needless death is one too many. City design and housing conditions always have been important, whether for cholera, tuberculosis or COVID-19.

The disproportionate deaths of minority ethnic populations in the UK and US during pandemic, arising from living in poor-quality, crowded housing in polluted areas, point to the inequities embedded in planning and design. In the US, the areas which were 'redlined' or divested from

3 'Six Ways Healthcare Will Move Into Our Homes', Philips website, 23 June 2020, https://www.philips.com/a-w/about/news/archive/blogs/innovation-matters/2020/20200623-six-ways-healthcare-will-move-into-our-homes.html.

4 J. Vass, *Agenda for Later Life 2015: A Great Place to Grow Older*, Age UK, 2015, pp 5 and 15, https://www.ageuk.org.uk/Documents/EN-GB/For-professionals/Policy/agenda_for_later_life_2015_full_report.pdf?dtrk=true.

investment in the 1930s–60s were also places where people from minority ethnic backgrounds lived. These areas lacked green spaces which help to bring down external temperatures. While temperatures in different neighbourhoods within the same city can vary as much as 20°F (6–7°C), researchers found a 12°F to 13°F difference between formerly redlined and non-redlined neighbourhoods.[5] Such 'heat islands' saw a spike in COVID-19 cases,[6] besides deaths from heat made worse by the climate crisis. Architects and planners can get involved in redesigning these urban areas to contain and prevent future pandemics.

Not surprisingly, the countries that have managed to stop new cases or have very few cases are mostly places where there is good healthcare and are usually low-density countries (for example, Scotland and New Zealand). But there are also countries with high densities such as South Korea and Taiwan, where rigorously enforced contact tracing has helped to curb the spread of the disease. Even a poor nation such as Vietnam, which had its second spike in August 2020, was able to halt the transmission of COVID-19 by quarantining, contact tracing and testing. But these measures also need to have buy-in from the citizens and the acceptance of curtailment of freedom which people in Western nations are reluctant to accept. So, there is a cultural dimension to healthcare measures which needs to be recognised.

Figure 5.1 The lack of suitable open spaces in modern housing estates where younger people can socialise and play can be important for both physical and mental health. This park in West London closed during COVID-19 for a couple of months before it was reopened after public outcry. The local authority hadn't appreciated that a significant number of people live in flats, especially from low-income groups, who had no access to private gardens.

Quarantining or isolation of infectious patients is a tried and tested method throughout history when vaccination or medications are not available – the flu pandemic of 1918 lasted about 36 months without the development of a vaccine. However, homes have to be spacious enough for such measures to work. Multi-generational living (which is becoming popular in the UK and other Western nations) or a group of people (such as students who are flat-sharing or in a social bubble) is fundamentally not a bad idea, but there must be enough space to isolate. That is why COVID-19 spread in crowded migrant construction labour dormitories in wealthy countries such as Singapore and UAE. While Table 5.1 does not remove the need for hospitals entirely, classification and diversification of healthcare facilities and a chain of connected healthy cities, buildings and homes can become tools for 'health for all'.

5 N. Lakhani, '"Heat Islands": Racist Housing Policies in US Linked to Deadly Heatwave Exposure', *The Guardian*, 13 January 2020, https://www.theguardian.com/society/2020/jan/13/racist-housing-policies-us-deadly-heatwaves-exposure-study.

6 C. Kim, 'New Study Finds Formerly Redlined Neighborhoods Are More At Risk For COVID-19', WBUR website, 14 September 2020, https://www.wbur.org/hereandnow/2020/09/14/redlined-neighborhoods-coronavirus-study

Figure 5.2 Paintings that patients can take to put up in their room to personalise it, at Oslo University Hospital, Rikshospitalet. Such simple acts of empowerment can help in the healing process.

The ability to make choices is an important determinant of 'health for all' because it is linked to the self-esteem of the individual. That choice also depends upon trust in the safety of the overall system. The more people have confidence in the system, the more they will use it. This is important in Western individualistic societies where choice and empowerment go together.[7] The success of track-and-trace technology depends upon the honesty of the person reporting and also on the belief that the information will be used securely.

7 J. Woodall, G. Raine, J. South and L. Warwick-Booth, 'Empowerment & Health and Well-Being: Evidence Review', project report, Centre for Health Promotion Research, Leeds Metropolitan University, 2010, p 14.

Safety is also a major concern of those who return to work and use public transport and spaces. Public health education can enable people to be better informed in order to make healthy lifestyle choices and in the face of conspiracy theories.

Technology 2025

Technology has already catalysed remote working and conferencing quite naturally during COVID-19. Remote clinical consultation will remain in place for some time to come and may become quite commonplace. In December 2019, NHS Digital reported that just 15% of 23 million

Figure 5.3 Fully digitised remote cardiology unit at Chiba-Nishi General Hospital, Chiba, Japan.

primary-care appointments during the month were carried out remotely. Just three months later, NHS Digital reported that nearly 50% of medical consultations took place remotely, using Attend Anywhere, a platform that supports video consultations in outpatient settings.[8] During an airborne pandemic, it may be safer, quicker and more comfortable to do some of the diagnostics and monitoring remotely than being in the same space as the patient. Many companies are developing sophisticated remote examination instruments for eyes, nose and teeth due to health risks from the close contact needed to examine these. 'Virtual clinics' where diagnostics are carried out by nurses or technicians, followed by telephone call if something serious is found, were used and tested during the COVID-19 pandemic by Moorfields Eye Hospital in London. Patient feedback found this to be very successful – and patients said that they preferred these clinics as they were quicker and safer.

8 B. Collins, 'What Is Covid-19 Revealing About Innovation In The NHS?', The King's Fund website, 3 August 2020, https://www.kingsfund.org.uk/blog/2020/08/covid-19-innovation-nhs.

Looking to 2025 and beyond, predictive analytics of patient groups, using data from connected health technology, will help healthcare providers proactively. Artificial intelligence can be used to make sense of the data from multiple sources such as hospital-based electronic medical records, medical alert services and auto-alerts. This kind of care could help older people or those at risk (such as those 'shielding'), and those unable to go out due to severe disability. Remote screening and monitoring of people suspected of being infected helps to fence off critical care and prevent unnecessary visits to GPs and hospitals. Remote health monitoring in the home is equally valuable after patients return from hospital care. Another group set to benefit from at-home medical technology are people with chronic diseases and comorbidities. On the 'health for all' aspect, technology that tracks health and lifestyle data, such as weight, blood pressure or oral hygiene, can be further embedded into the home environment, via a smart mirror in the bathroom or mobile interfaces that display insights. Artificial intelligence can be used to answer straightforward queries to many health- or clinic-related questions. It has been used by banks and airlines but not so much by healthcare providers.

The ability to control one's environment in a hospital room, in the home, in the place of work is also part of empowering a patient. Technology will continue to help those who can access such technology. In Alder Hey hospital in Liverpool, for example, child patients can use a special app to personalise their room's environment and find their way around the building – this happened after a child asked for such an app to be developed. However, technology is neither smart nor intelligent by itself – it depends on the user and also on how secure it is. But technology can be empowering. For home telemedicine and remote consultation to be successful, secure and good-quality internet access will be needed. People will also need to become familiar with the technology and learn to use it effectively.

Pandemics, Diseases and Health 2025

Viruses that jump from animals to humans cause 'zoonotic' diseases. Such diseases have been known for a long time but now they are arriving at a frequency of four to six years. The Democratic Republic of Congo has had 11 Ebola virus outbreaks since the 1970s, but six have occurred in the past decade. Coronavirus infections are also emerging more frequently: from SARS, to MERS, and now COVID-19. Not all zoonotic diseases become pandemics, but environmental degradation is causing more frequent recurrence of such diseases. The degradation of the natural environment such as clearing of forests, increased livestock farming and wild-animal trading, dense urbanisation and global travel have all made it easier to transmit zoonotic diseases now than in the past. As humans encroach on land used for animals or eat wild animals, viruses can jump from animals to humans via a secondary host. We may well see another new zoonotic pandemic in 2025 or earlier.

Another important thing to note is that the previous zoonotic diseases such as HIV, Ebola, MERS etc. are still around – they haven't been eliminated, while new ones such as COVID-19 are being added. So, it is vital that environmental concerns are taken seriously. Besides zoonotic diseases, there are 10 killer diseases that have accounted for millions of deaths globally. In 2018, the WHO identified the top 10 causes of death – of which ischaemic heart disease and stroke have remained the two leading ones globally in the last 15 years.[9] The burden of disease has multiplied and that is why, despite scientific advances, there is a situation of moving medical goalposts.

Ways in which zoonotic diseases can be eliminated or minimised lie within the gift of the urban planner. Land use, zoning, biodiversity, urban density and planning – these are important not only to limit zoonotic disease spread but for ensuring the 'health for all' agenda. Environmental planning and land use should be seen not only as preventative mechanisms but also as forces for good with improved biodiversity, public amenities and the reduction of carbon dioxide. It is also important to note that not all zoonotic infections spread via air. So there always will be an element of surprise in what is needed; and healthcare facilities – and those who design them – will have to be prepared for such emergencies by enabling more adaptive design.

Most zoonotic pandemics have become a characteristic of the Anthropocene era and global warming when animals are coming out earlier from hibernation. Healthcare and emergency workers are the first responders during any crisis generated by the changing environment (such as the recent wildfires in Australia and the US, and floods in many parts of the world). Climate change as that cause of mortality is not acknowledged on death certificates at present. Scientists warn that if greenhouse gas emissions continue to rise on the current trajectory, the world has little hope of limiting global warming to 1.5°C, or even 2°C. If the world warms beyond that, tens of millions of people could be exposed to shortages of drinking water, dangerous heat waves and coastal flooding from rising sea levels.

The climate crisis is exacerbating the already badly resourced health systems of poor countries while creating more homeless, stateless and migrating people. Some of the poorest people in the world are the most vulnerable as they are without health information, tools and resources to protect themselves. And while the coronavirus pandemic led to a large temporary drop in carbon dioxide emissions as transportation – including air travel – and industry ground to a halt, there are signs methane emissions have not dropped nearly as much, and now the carbon dioxide emissions are back to the previous levels. Global methane emissions (which are much more destructive than carbon dioxide) are actually up 9% from the early 2000s, according to the latest findings, and human activity is responsible for more than half of those emissions. Carbon dioxide emissions are also coming back to pre-COVID-19 levels, so climate crisis issues remain current.

9 World Health Organization, 'The Top 10 Causes of Death', 24 May 2018, https://www.who.int/news-room/fact-sheets/detail/the-top-10-causes-of-death.

Healthcare's Own Environmental Crisis

Healthcare's own climate footprint is equivalent to 4.4% of global net emissions,[10] which may seem small compared to the building industry's 40%. After the oil crisis of 1973, healthcare buildings also started looking at energy efficiency. The NHS, like many other global healthcare providers, has sustainability written into its constitution. The European Commission has legislated for 'near to zero energy use' in public buildings.[11] The US also recognises the value of sustainable healthcare within its 2030 Challenge launched in 2006.[12] However, hospitals are enormous energy users due to the very nature of their business. Operating theatres, organ and medicine storage and laboratories in a hospital require to be air-conditioned spaces, and are consequently high-energy.

The US, China and the EU are the top healthcare carbon dioxide emitters – comprising more than half the world's total healthcare climate footprint (56%).

10 J. Karliner, S. Slotterback, R. Boyd, B. Ashby and K. Steele, *Healthcare's Climate Footprint: How the Health Sector Contributes to the Global Climate Crisis and Opportunities for Action*, Climate-smart health care series, Green Paper Number One, London: Health Care Without Harm in association with Arup, September 2019, https://noharm-global.org/sites/default/files/documents-files/5961/HealthCaresClimateFootprint_092319.pdf.

11 Y. Saheb, S. Shnapp and D. Paci, *From Nearly-Zero Energy Buildings To Net-Zero Energy Districts*, Luxembourg: Publications Office of the European Union, 2019, p 4.

12 R. Guenther and G. Vittori, *Sustainable Healthcare Architecture*, Hoboken, NJ: Wiley, 2013, p 8.

A report from Arup revealed the following statistics:

- The top 10 healthcare emitters make up 75% of the global healthcare climate footprint.
- The US health sector, the world's number one emitter in both absolute and per-capita terms, produces 57 times more emissions per person than does India.
- While India has the seventh-largest absolute health-sector climate footprint, it has the lowest health-related emissions per capita of all 43 nations considered in detail in this study.
- China's health sector produces six times more greenhouse gases per person than India's does. But China's health system also emits one-seventh the greenhouse gases per capita as that of the US, one-third that of Korea and just under one-half per capita that of the EU.[13]

Given the lack of funding for healthcare and that many countries want their healthcare estates to be as energy-efficient as possible, it is still sensible and right to move towards low-energy buildings. There appears to be a correlation between a country's health-sector climate footprint and a country's health spending. Generally, the higher the spending, the higher the per-capita healthcare emissions. In other words, better healthcare usually means higher carbon dioxide emissions. Robin Guenther, principal of architects Perkins&Will, says that biomedical campuses such

13 Arup, *Cities Alive: Towards a Walking World*, 2016, https://www.arup.com/perspectives/publications/research/section/cities-alive-towards-a-walking-world.

Figure 5.4 St Mary's Hospital, Newport, Isle of Wight, designed by ABK Architects, 1990.

as the one in Texas, Houston (the largest in the world) are one of the biggest energy guzzlers in the US.[14] With different measurements being used in different countries and types of hospitals, any kind of benchmarking and consequent standardised guidance for energy saving is not possible. So how can the healthcare sector reduce its operational carbon dioxide emissions without reducing its quality of care?

One way is through reducing operational energy needs – by maximising the use of daylight and other passive design features. When St Mary's Hospital opened on the Isle of Wight (see Figure 5.4) in 1990, 80% of the space benefited from daylighting using a cruciform plan. It has been shown to need 50% less energy than conventional hospital design.[15] Wansbeck Hospital in Ashington, Northumbria has also demonstrated an impressive 60% reduction in energy and received a green building award in 2003.[16] Another way could be to use energy suppliers who are in the process of turning to 'green energy' or already supply this.[17] Coronavirus and the climate crisis have had unusual benefits: when the UK went into its first lockdown, electricity demands from offices came down too, and when power plants were taken off the network, the four coal-fired plants were among the first. As medicine moves towards digitalisation, energy, technology and internet

14 R. Guenther, 'Why Hospitals Are Making Us Sick', TEDMED Talk, 2014, https://www.tedmed.com/talks/show?id=293069.

15 N. Baker and K. Steemers, *Energy and Environment in Architecture: A Technical Design Guide*, London: Taylor & Francis, 2003, pp 130–35.

16 R.G. Kensett, *The Changing Scene of Health Care and Technology: Proceedings of the 11th International Congress of Hospital Engineering*, London: Taylor & Francis, 1990, p 34.

17 The National Grid Electricity System Operator (ESO) in the UK announced in 2019 that it will be able to fully operate the UK's electricity system with zero carbon by 2025.

providers can also reduce their own carbon footprints. DeepMmind Technologies, a UK-based artificial intelligence company, which works with healthcare providers, intends to use 100% percent renewable energy by 2030. They've built their own super-efficient servers at Google (which also wants to be using only green energy by 2030), invented more efficient ways to cool the data centres and invested heavily in green energy sources.

Another method is the use of decentralised power where CHP (combined heat and power) systems (see Figure 5.5) or local green power production, including solar and wind generation, could be used. Currently CHP is used in thousands of healthcare facilities around the world including hospitals, health clubs and nursing homes. Deventer Ziekenhuis, a teaching hospital in Deventer, Netherlands, completed in 2008, was the first hospital to use aquifer-based thermal storage retrieval systems of heat pumps and ventilation, and heat and moisture recovery units.[18] Like the Oslo University Hospital (see Figures 5.2, 5.7 and 5.15), its design influenced generations of European hospital designs. Adaptive interior design, whole-life design, rainwater harvesting and maximising of natural ventilation (including openable windows) and lighting were other ways that this hospital demonstrated the best of low-energy and patient-centred design.

Healthcare facilities can become off-grid where power supply is erratic or it is situated in a remote location. Nav Jivan healthcare facility in Jharkand, India, faced many operational challenges that are common for rural hospitals in poor countries, especially due to erratic electrical supply and voltage fluctuations. It installed a 10-kilowatt peak (kWp) solar photovoltaic system in January 2020, and now is able run without interruptions. Even in colder countries with less sunlight hours, solar cells can supplement conventional electricity. Many hospitals in the US also use roof-mounted solar panels on roofs where space is limited. Wind and tidal energy are other sources that can be harnessed depending on the location of the facility. Thermal and geo heat pumps for cooling and heating are also extremely dependable and are used in healthcare facilities, as demonstrated in the Khoo Teck Puat Hospital in Singapore (see boxed-out section on Khoo Teck Puat Hospital later in the chapter).

Figure 5.5 The third-generation CHP gas engine at Great Ormond Street Hospital for children, used for providing heating and lighting.

18 R. Guenther and G. Vittori, *Sustainable Healthcare Architecture*, Hoboken, NJ: Wiley, 2013, pp 257–62.

One of the scarcest resources in the world that is needed in large quantities in hospital and healthcare facilities is clean water. Handwashing has been recommended as the single most important practice to control hospital-acquired infection. Hand hygiene has become particularly important during the COVID-19 pandemic. Washbasins should be designed and sited to encourage healthcare workers to practise hand hygiene before and after every patient care activity. 'No-touch' sensor-operated water taps could be better for hygiene as well as saving water. An innovative water-saving programme at Guy's and St Thomas' NHS Foundation Trust in London has reduced the Trust's water consumption by nearly 20% and helped to provide access to clean and safe drinking water to some of the poorest people in the world: a percentage of the resulting saving of £120,000 went to the charity WaterAid to provide safe water and sanitation in Nepal. Great Ormond Street hospital also has introduced rainwater and grey-water recycling. However, in poor countries, lack of clean water means that not enough is around for drinking, let alone for handwashing.

Healthcare facilities generate much solid waste such as contaminated plastic. The COVID-19 pandemic has increased the amount of throwaway plastic as used in personal protective equipment (PPE), in healthcare facilities as well as by the public. These have included facemasks and gloves which are biohazards and have washed up on beaches and rivers. In poor countries like India, waste workers are often sorting such waste without PPE themselves. Architectural firms such as Foster + Partners designed reusable masks, for example, at the start of the COVID-19 crisis,[19] but the healthcare workers, more used to throwaway culture, did not recognise this. Reduction of the use of throwaway plastic will cut environmental pollution as well as costs.[20]

Zoning Spaces and Resources

Louis Kahn categorised spaces into two categories of the 'served and servant'.[21] The servant spaces are uninhabited spaces with technical or mechanical functions and support the more human-centred 'served' spaces. So, toilets, storage and kitchens are servant spaces in a home, while in an office setting spaces needed for mechanical services such as lifts as well as toilets and kitchen can be termed servant spaces. Served spaces are spaces inhabited by people such as bedrooms, auditoriums, classrooms and exhibition spaces. These are crude differentiations. But in a healthcare setting, often the servant spaces need to be near the served space – for example, the 'hot zones' of operating theatres and intensive care units, with their array of advanced medical resources and equipment near the patient. These servant pipes and channels spread vertically as well horizontally through the building.

Thinking of a building like a human body in which fluids flow can be useful in hospital design

19 T. Ravenscroft, 'Foster + Partners Designs Reusable Open-Source Face Shield', *Dezeen*, 6 April 2020, https://www.dezeen.com/2020/04/06/foster-partners-reusable-open-source-face-shield/

20 J. Parkinson, 'Coronavirus: Disposable Masks "Causing Enormous Plastic Waste"', BBC News website, 13 September, https://www.bbc.co.uk/news/uk-politics-54057799.

21 Louis Kahn spoke of this concept in a film recording made at the International Design Conference of Aspen (IDCA), Colorado, US, on 6 June 1972: https://www.youtube.com/watch?v=ZaUtcKqdL5E. Since then the concept has been written about by many.

for maintaining hygiene. We take in food, water and air through various channels, and waste is secreted separately – thus the human body keeps its own hygiene. In a building, there is inanimate matter like air, water, and energy that moves through the structure. There are also the animate, the people who move through spaces. At each point where these types of elements meet, there is a possibility for infection.[22] The basic concept in hospital hygiene is to move from 'green' or clean to dirty or infectious 'red' zones and then safely dispose of all biohazard materials. Circulation should be planned for easy movement of staff from one clean area to another without passing through infectious or dirty zones. In a healthcare setting, the biohazard is also the human who can spread disease, particularly airborne ones.

Four main types of areas – operating theatres; research and laboratory spaces; outpatient and waiting areas; inpatient areas such as wards, single rooms and recovery areas – are connected via circulation systems of corridors, lifts and stairs. These circulatory areas have air which moves through the space and can contain virus in aerosol form. Further, the shape and sizes of spaces also influence the convection currents which can spread the airborne virus, and even people passing each other in the circulation spaces can create air currents that spread the virus.[23] Lifts are also enclosed spaces where airborne virus can spread.[24] A continuous flow of clean air inside a room, or filtering and cleaning it, can disperse and dilute any infectious airborne virus amounts.

The most difficult aspect to control in a hospital environment is air, which needs to be progressively filtered and cleaned until it becomes the cleanest in the operating theatres where human organs are exposed to it. Air comes in from the outside when external and internal doors or windows open, and from vents and cracks in the structure. The choice of air-conditioning systems that are energy-efficient as well as having effective virus filters is important in hospitals. During the COVID-19 pandemic, surgeons in Singapore were forced to work in sweltering heat because the air-conditioning system had to be switched off as it could recycle air with virus in it.[25] Also, seasonal adjustments have to be made. The ventilation system needs to supply 10 litres of air changes per second. But this has to be achieved in colder weather without causing discomfort to people or creating heat loss (and therefore increasing energy costs).

Given that space in hospitals is often restricted and that many don't have spare corridors, it is not easy to ensure that infectious or vulnerable inpatients moving on trolley beds are kept separate from outpatients walking or in wheelchairs or lifts, and

22 D. Shukman, 'Covid-19: Five Ways to Avoid Catching the Virus Indoors', BBC News website, 27 August 2020, https://www.bbc.co.uk/news/explainers-53917432.

23 N. Mingotti, R. Wood, C. Noakes and A.W. Woods, 'The Mixing of Airborne Contaminants by the Repeated Passage of People Along a Corridor', *Journal of Fluid Mechanics*, 903, July 2020, A52.

24 C. van Rijn, G. Aernout Somsen, L. Hofstra, G. Dahhan, R.A. Bem, S. Kooij and D. Bonn, 'Reducing Aerosol Transmission of SARS-CoV-2 in Hospital Elevators', *Indoor Air*, 23 September 2020, https://onlinelibrary.wiley.com/doi/10.1111/ina.12744.

25 D. Shukman, 'Climate Change: Summers Could Become "Too Hot for Humans"', BBC News website, 16 July 2020, https://www.bbc.co.uk/news/science-environment-53415298.

from waste pathways. In Cotugno Hospital in Italy, the use of airlocks and compartmentalisation, disinfection machines that cleaned people as they walked through, and protected corridors, ensured deaths of clinicians were avoided during COVID-19.[26] In future, design of hospitals will have to take into account separated corridors for such functions – therefore they will need to be larger or have alternative means of access. Wards and rooms can have double access during an infectious outbreak. Some patients prefer single rooms, while others prefer wards. Single bedrooms depend upon availability of enough staff and equipment. Staff shortages – nursing, doctors and administrative – plus lack of space, not to mention lack of funding, will make single-roomed hospitals difficult to build and maintain. Wards are noisy and lack privacy but provide the reassurance of being noticed in case of problems. But a well-designed space, whether in a single bedroom or in a ward, will help with healing and getting out of the hospital faster.

Complicated plans or tower structures can also be difficult to modify or use during a pandemic. They make ventilation and access difficult. In particular, vertical connections such as lifts which are small enclosed spaces need restricted access to decrease the numbers of people using them. The height of a hospital building can be crucial during pandemic and emergencies, not to mention fire risks if unsafe cladding materials have been used. In a tall tower hospital in London which is dependent upon lifts, many clinics had to be brought down to the ground floor for outpatient use during the COVID-19 period. Courtyard forms are not only space-efficient but also enable views, cross-ventilation and light from two sides. Many of the Victorian designs were courtyard hospitals. Thus, future hospitals may well move away from tall sealed towers to more open, low-height structures. This also cuts down on lift use which is expensive.

It is not just air that can move through buildings in an uncontrolled way: people do too. Hospital-acquired infections happen through surfaces touched by human hands. Cleaning takes a lot of effort and expense, and generates more waste. Keeping surfaces easy to clean while being aesthetically pleasing can be achieved if surface materials such as tiles are used (see Figure 5.6). Copper has

Figure 5.6 Tilework in the University College London hospital building, designed by Alfred Waterhouse in the 19th century. Tiles are easy to clean, long-lasting and more environmentally friendly than plastic. The floor patterns can be useful for wayfinding too.

26 S. Ramsay, 'Coronavirus: The Italian COVID-19 Hospital Where No Medics Have Been Infected', Sky News website, 1 April 2020, https://news.sky.com/story/coronavirus-the-italian-covid-19-hospital-where-no-medics-have-been-infected-11966344.

Figure 5.7 Intuitive wayfinding in Oslo University Hospital, Rikshospitalet (by Medplan Arkitekter Norway – now renamed RATIO Arkitekter – 1997), through design (street), artwork, bridges, light and colours. Note also the skylights to bring in light to the main thoroughfare in a country where there is poor daylight for six months of the year.

antimicrobial properties but is expensive, so it might be worth using it for high-touch elements such as door handles. Circulation lines on the floor, putting up too many signs and floor plans/maps are all things that are not understood or followed by people (note the way people ignored arrows on the floor in supermarkets during the pandemic). Design for wayfinding and circulation should be intuitive (see Figure 5.7). Zoning of areas through use of colour, placing of artworks, use of staff or volunteers, and referencing of internal landmarks such as restaurants work better than other methods.

Hospital Design in Times of Scarcity

As the world population grows, it is more important to use resources wisely and carefully. The first action should be reducing, followed by reusing and finally recycling. This is also important as we enter uncharted territories with an economic recession of unknown proportions. In such a period, along with priority being given for COVID-19 testing and treatment, money for building new hospitals will be restricted. But it was already insufficient to begin with. Multiple lockdowns and quarantines impact unfairly on those with low incomes and ironically, those living in poor housing. A long-term view of health and prevention of disease might be more prudent. Promotion of healthy housing, cities and people can seem a slow process but in the long term they could turn out to be the most economical and permanent solutions.

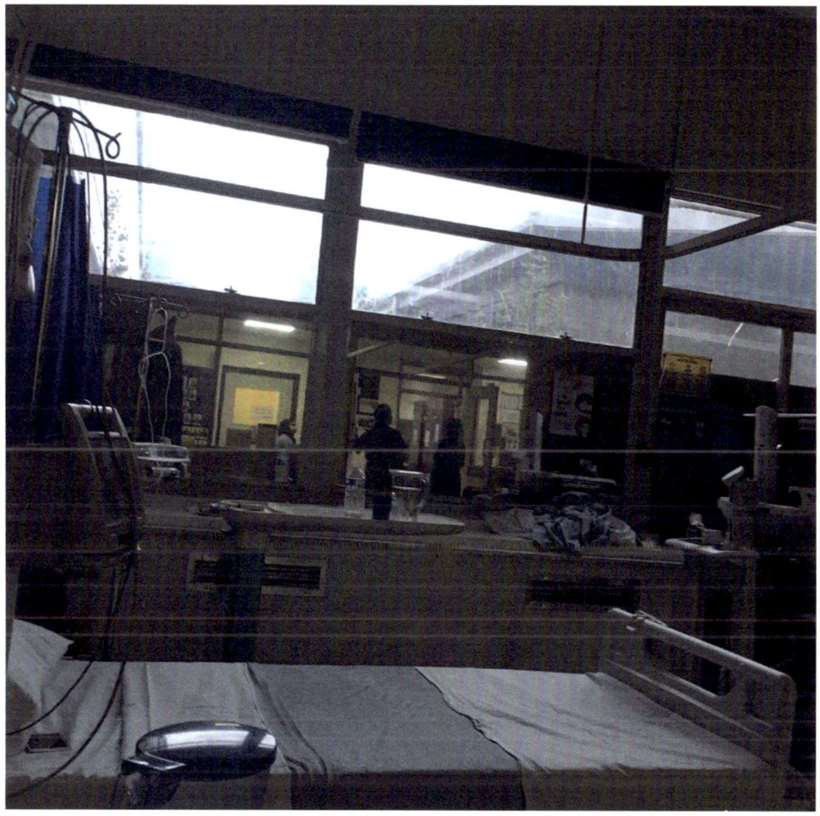

Figure 5.8 An acute care unit on the ground floor of Charing Cross Hospital, London, built in 1973. Most healthcare estates all over the world have typically been developed piecemeal over many decades. Some open spaces have been filled in without consideration to the ward inside – affecting light and views.

Most hospitals in the UK generally fall under bad retrofit and patchwork extensions which are difficult to maintain and are less energy-efficient. During the financial year 2018–19, the total costs of running the NHS estate were £9.5 billion, while the total cost to eradicate backlog maintenance (that is, the amount needed to restore a building to a certain state based on assessed risk criteria – but not including planned maintenance work) was £6.5 billion.[27] It is costly and disruptive to build from scratch, especially for healthcare.

27 NHS Digital, 'Estates Returns Information Collection Summary page and dataset for ERIC 2018/19', 17 October 2019, https://digital.nhs.uk/data-and-information/publications/statistical/estates-returns-information-collection/england-2018-19.

For both new-builds and redevelopments, it is important to plan for the future of different zones and how they connect with each other in a coherent masterplan. Efficient planning of spaces based on time and motion studies devised during the early days of the NHS went out of the window with hasty and piecemeal additions as demand for space grew. During the COVID-19 emergency, in the UK existing facilities such as stadiums, hotels and exhibition centres served as the Nightingale temporary hospitals (known in China as Fangcang hospitals or 'square-cabin hospitals'). There is an irony as well as impracticality in selling excess space for generating revenue (as recommended in the Robert Naylor review 2017)[28] and then putting up and taking down temporary hospitals with additional costs, including environmental – this points to the lack of an overall strategy for healthcare estates for a pandemic situation. Most of these temporary hospitals in the UK are now in 'furlough' for possible future use or being dismantled, and were not really used much during the first wave of the pandemic.

Long-term plans for hospital development keeping in mind future demographic changes are pragmatic solutions. Oslo University Hospital developed a 20-year masterplan for its future development in consultation with staff and public. Although it can take a long time to develop such a plan, it can be better than a piecemeal development or shutting down parts of a hospital during construction. Keeping aside space is also important for future needs. Reuse and reorganisation of internal spaces could be another solution instead of building new but this must be built into the original design. Aravind Eye Hospitals in India keep aside as much as 20% of space in the building for future use. When not needed, this extra space is used for patient overflow, conferences or exhibitions. Adaptive design such as that used in the Deventer Ziekenhuis hospital in the Netherlands is another way of reorganising internal space without demolition. Internal reorganisation is also being brought forward by technological developments, such as the increasing use of digital patient notes that removes the need for paper storage, and short recovery periods for specialisms such as ophthalmology so that inpatient wards are no longer needed.

Retrofitting of existing hospitals solves some of the funding problems, as well as carbon dioxide emission arising from demolition and building anew. The NHS has signed up to become the world's first carbon-net-zero national health system, with a new Net Zero Carbon Hospital Standard, available from spring 2021, to be applied across the 40 new hospitals that form part of the UK Government's Health Infrastructure Plan. However, this means that the remaining NHS estates will also need to be retrofitted to comply with this direction because the 40 new hospitals will form less than one-fifth of the NHS estates.

The 6.13 billion square metres of new buildings that are constructed annually give rise to approximately 3,729 million metric tons of

28 Robert Naylor, *NHS Property and Estates: Why the Estate Matters for Patients*, March 2017, UK Department of Health, https://assets.publishing.service.gov.uk/government/uploads/system/uploads/attachment_data/file/607725/Naylor_review.pdf.

carbon dioxide.[29] In the next 30 years, embodied and operational carbon emissions will become almost equal in new builds. While we can reduce operational carbon emissions by using energy-efficient systems and clean energy, embodied carbon emissions are locked in the materials. The embodied carbon emissions of building products and construction represent a significant portion of global emissions of around 11%. Concrete, iron and steel produce around 9% of annual global greenhouse gas emissions. Concrete remains the primary material used in many large healthcare projects but it cannot be recycled to its original state and requires a lot of energy to manufacture, mix and transport. Both concrete and cement use a non-renewable resource: sand. So, it would be more 'carbon-efficient' to repair and retrofit a concrete building, rather than demolishing and building anew. Use of metals – steel, aluminium etc. – which can be recycled easily, with only 5% of carbon dioxide emissions during recycling, are another option (see Umeda Hospital box later in this section).

Hospitals also contain hybrid materials such as polymer-based parts and e-waste which can make recycling difficult. A new system, 'White ReCapture', is being developed by Swedish architects White Arkitekter to sell reusable or recycled materials from hospitals. The first live project involves the assessment of an existing hospital in Stockholm, based on 'as-built' scans. Anything that can be easily reused or refitted elsewhere such as doors, glass partition walls and ceiling tiles can be sold on an online marketplace being developed by the Swedish Environmental Research Institute. However, for this system to work, the design needs whole-life thinking right from the start. Many construction materials, such as the high-grade plastic commonly used in healthcare, cannot be recycled or reused. Also, in this system users are allowed to generate their own carbon values for any building elements that do not have a manufacturer's Environmental Product Declaration (EPD), by treating them as hybrid materials which may leave this methodology to misuse and more waste creation. Further, since in 2020 construction is still the

Figure 5.9 Demolition waste from a private clinic, Central London. Many hybrid materials as shown here such as electric wires, tempered glass and plastic waste cannot be reused.

29 'New Buildings: Embodied Carbon', Architecture 2030 website, 2019, https://architecture2030.org/new-buildings-embodied/.

second least digitised sector in the world, digital applications could be difficult to introduce universally. But this is a good start in rethinking reuse of materials from a hospital.

Carbon sequestration is the long-term removal and capture of carbon dioxide from the atmosphere. Wood is a living building material which can sequester carbon dioxide during its growth and it remains in the wood when it is being used. Timber can be used for big-span and high-rise construction as cross-laminated timber (CLT). In the past, use of timber in hospitals has been difficult due to concern over hygiene, but new treatments have made timber use possible for healthcare buildings (see Umeda Hospital box opposite). The medical centre in Taverny, near Paris, by MAAJ Architectes (completed in 2020), not only uses wood but the design is based around a courtyard. Fire safety was managed by the inclusion of wooden ladders that reach down to the courtyard space. The wood fibre boards used internally were also useful for their acoustical properties.[30]

Carbon sequestration can also be achieved by passive means such as designing buildings incorporating vegetation and gardens – biophilic designs – as proposed by Professor Roger Ulrich in the 1990s. Such schemes have the advantage of having therapeutic views and practical engagement for patients and staff as well as attracting community participation (see Khoo Teck Puat Hospital box below). Gardening has been shown to lower stress hormones. However, these solutions have to be according to climate and context. A high-rise housing estate in Chengdu, China, which incorporated biophilic ideas (similar to those used by Stefano Boeri for the new Policlinico (multi-speciality hospital) and high-rise housing in Milan),[31] now lies vacant as mosquitos and plants have taken over. In contrast, in Singapore – which also has a hot and humid city like Chengdu – strict maintenance controls over the vegetation are in place in public buildings and these avoid problems associated with vegetation, as seen in the Khoo Teck Puat Hospital.

30 A. Munter, 'Wellness Encouraged by Nature', *Wood Magazine*, 2, 2020, pp 11–14, https://www.swedishwood.com/publications/wood-magazine/2020-2/wellness-encouraged-by-nature/.

31 S. Singha, *Future Healthcare Design*, London: RIBA Publishing, 2020, p 145.

CASE STUDY

UMEDA HOSPITAL, YAMAGUCHI, JAPAN

SMALL INNER-CITY CHILDREN'S HOSPITAL CONSTRUCTED OF METAL AND TIMBER

Client: Umeda Hospital Medical Corporation, Chairman Dr Kaoru Umeda

Architects: Kengo Kuma & Associates

Structural Engineer: YSE Structural Engineers Co.

Services Engineer: P.T. Morimura & Associates

Signage: Nippon Design Center

General contractor: Obayashi Corporation

Gross internal area: 1,985sqm within site area of 2,400sqm

Completion year: 2015

Kengo Kuma & Associates (KKA) buildings are often characterised by natural materials that include bamboo and timber.[32] Over the past few years, KKA has completed a number of healthcare buildings that have been designed for doctors and patients and that depart from the typical white walls of a hospital. Hospitals can seem cold and institutional to a visitor, creating a stressful and daunting experience. In KKA's Umeda Hospital, the aim has been to change this, and create a hospital that can feel like another home for both parents and children. With a maximum height of about 20m, it is built of a steel-framed structure, including the roof which is galvanised steel plate. KKA has also created a playful design that incorporates an origami-like folded roof and child-sized openings in the timber walls (see Figure 5.10), taking account of how a child may experience the building. Part of the exterior is made of *yakisugi* – cedar shingles with a charred surface. The interior uses *yamatobari* – a traditional method of Japanese cladding – with a board-and-batten wall system (see Figure 5.11), adding warmth and texture to the environment. The rhythm of the *yamatobari* walls also creates a more relaxed atmosphere for parents and children who may experience anxiety while waiting for their diagnosis and treatment.

Figures 5.10 and 5.11
Timber use in Umeda Hospital, especially the *yamatobari*, or folded timber panels. The hospital uses an efficient modular system made of steel for the main structure.

32 N.R. Pollock, 'Umeda Hospital by Kengo Kuma and Associates', *Architectural Record*, 1 July 2016, https://www.architecturalrecord.com/articles/11764-umeda-hospital-by-kengo-kuma-and-associates.

CASE STUDY

KHOO TECK PUAT HOSPITAL, SINGAPORE

LARGE HOSPITAL DEMONSTRATING BIOPHILIA AND ENERGY-EFFICIENCY

Client: Ministry of Health, Singapore

Architects: CPG Consultants

Structural and MEP: CPG Consultants

Landscaping: CPG Consultants

Contractor: Hyundai Engineering and Construction Co.

Design consultant: RMJM Hillier

Gross internal area: 108,676sqm within 3.4 hectares

Completion year: 2010

Located next to Yishun pond, Khoo Teck Puat Hospital is one of the most energy-efficient hospitals in Singapore, often called a 'city in a garden'. While the hospital is constructed of concrete, the key feature of the hospital are the roof gardens that provide green respite and moderate the heat-island effect. There is a terraced garden at the podium roof where treated exhaust air from the operating theatres is used to lower the ambient temperature. Passive design features include the use of operable jalousie windows to optimise daylight while minimising glare, and the orientation of the subsidised ward tower to the prevailing wind directions to optimise natural ventilation and reduce air-conditioning load. Solar vacuum tubes and heat pumps are used to produce hot water for the hospital's needs. In 2009, Khoo Teck Puat was awarded the Green Mark Platinum rating by the Building and Construction Authority (BCA) of Singapore.

Figures 5.12 and 5.13: Community gardens at Khoo Teck Puat Hospital in Singapore. These gardens are tended by patients, staff and the local community. Some produce is harvested and eaten in the hospital.

CASE STUDY

BLOSSOM COURT, ST ANN'S HOSPITAL, TOTTENHAM, LONDON

MENTAL HEALTH UNIT DEMONSTRATING BIOPHILIA AND ENERGY-EFFICIENCY

Client: Barnet Enfield and Haringey Mental Health NHS Trust

Architect: Medical Architecture

Services Engineer: Hulley & Kirkwood

Structure and Civil Engineer: Perega

Landscape: PLACE Design + Planning

Contractor: Integrated Health Projects

Gross internal area: 4,300sqm within a site of 4 hectares

Completion year: 2020

Sustainability: BREEAM 'Excellent'

Accommodating four mental health wards over two storeys, this new building is organised around two private courtyards which fill the interior with daylight and provide an intuitive focal point for wayfinding. Patients can directly access the courtyards from each ward. This autonomy reduces pressures on staff, removing a potential source of conflict, while encouraging physical health. The building is designed to encourage wellbeing. Generous-sized windows provide a connection to the mature surrounding landscape. Acoustic ceilings and natural materials help create a calming environment. The bedroom corridor features a colonnade with seating between, encouraging patients to stop and contemplate, or socialise with others.

By Ruairi Reeves, Director, Medical Architecture

Figure 5.14 Internal court at St Ann's Hospital's Blossom Court, with patterned brick. The pattern was carefully designed to provide texture and interest without climbing opportunities.

Mental Health

Dementia and other mental health issues are becoming the world's biggest health problems as people live longer. Even until the early 2000s, cruel methods of treating mental health problems including lobotomy were being used without proper consent for vulnerable adults. During the COVID-19 pandemic, the Office for National Statistics reported that the number of people suffering from depression doubled from the year before, to one in five.[33] People dying of dementia were steadily increasing year on year in England and Wales, with dementia becoming UK's biggest killer.[34] In May 2020, the data showed that dementia, including Alzheimer's disease, was the most common main pre-existing condition in deaths involving COVID-19 in March and April 2020.[35]

In care homes with dementia patients, the poignant and painful deaths of people opened up the debate about how internal layouts and views to the outside could have helped in reducing stress and helping families to connect with their loved ones. Design can be an important element in treating or minimising harm arising from mental health issues. Biophilia and the introduction of different kinds of sensory spaces in a healthcare setting can help both adults and younger people. Morag Myerscough used colour and patterns to transform wards within the new Sheffield Children's Hospital in 2017, transforming them into 'uplifting' spaces by use of colour and patterns.[36] At Belfast City Hospital's Acute Mental Health Inpatient Centre, a period of six months after its opening in summer 2019 recorded a 22% reduction in behavioural incidents with mental health patients.[37] A clean simple design with spaces for relaxing outdoors, water features, artwork or views to nature can help with stress and anxiety.

The Walkable Healthy City

The connection between disease spread and the planning and infrastructure of the modern city was exposed when COVID-19 virus was found in the sewage systems in Spain in the summer of 2020. The WHO Regional Office for Europe convened a Pan-European Commission on Health and Sustainable Development to put health at the top of the political agenda within the Sustainable 3Development Goals. For holistic health systems, it is important to 'think globally and act locally', as in systems thinking. Sir Peng Tee Khaw, renowned ophthalmologist at Moorfields Eye Hospital, referring to the new eye hospital being designed in Central London, has said: 'The way I see it, there is no point in building a new hospital in London, if it's not going to be used to improve lives in the whole country and

33 Office for National Statistics, 'Coronavirus and Depression in Adults, Great Britain: June 2020', 18 August 2020, https://www.ons.gov.uk/peoplepopulationandcommunity/wellbeing/articles/coronavirusanddepressioninadultsgreatbritain/june2020.

34 Office for National Statistics, 'Deaths Registered in England and Wales: 2018', 6 August 2019, https://www.ons.gov.uk/peoplepopulationandcommunity/birthsdeathsandmarriages/deaths/bulletins/deathsregistrationsummarytables/2018.

35 Alheimer's Society, 'The UK's Biggest Killer: Why Are Deaths From Dementia On The Rise?', 26 May 2020, https://www.alzheimers.org.uk/blog/research-dementia-UK-biggest-killer-on-the-rise.

36 Singha, *Future Healthcare Design*, pp 140–43.

37 'RUUA Awards: Northern Ireland Shortlist', *RIBA Journal*, 127 (6), June 2020, p 51.

all around the world. Global thinking is important in every aspect of our lives, from climate change to ophthalmology.'[38]

The role of decentralised health systems in the UK was examined in the 2020 report of the cross-party Health Devolution Commission. But the report's aim of connecting health with the economy is probably the most revolutionary point in the document.[39] Showing that health improvement equals improvement in the economy provides another incentive to put more money and effort behind it. Research from professional services firm PwC (formerly PricewaterhouseCoopers) has put an economic value on this post-pandemic vision.[40] As stated in their document, 'the high street can't recover through the retail sector alone: business, communities and local and central government need to come together and create liveable vibrant places where people want to live, work and visit.' In other words, we need a joined-up vision of healthcare, economics and placemaking.

38 'Thinking Globally: Sitting Down With … Sir Peng Tee Khaw, Consultant Ophthalmic Surgeon at Moorfields Eye Hospital', *The Ophthalmologist*, 26 July 2019, https://theophthalmologist.com/subspecialties/thinking-globally?utm_source=Sir%20Peng%20Tee%20Khaw%20on%20thinking%20globally:%20a%20throwback%20to%20our%202019%20Moorfields%20takeover%20issue&utm_medium=email&utm_campaign=Two%20Column%20Teaser&utm_content=Headline&iitt=VuU9RM4lhMPshFWsbdi3adEWbdeZbdLWEkU.Ey41hdJLRfXcbdiA.

39 P. Hope and S. Barwick, *Building Back Health and Prosperity: Report of the Health Devolution Commission*, Manchester: DevoConnect, August 2020 https://healthdevolution.org.uk/wp-content/uploads/2020/08/DEVO-Report-of-the-Health-Devolution-Commission-Final.pdf.

40 PwC, 'Return to the High Streets: Lessons from the Reopening of Town and City Centres', undated, https://www.pwc.co.uk/industries/government-public-sector/local-government/insights/return-to-high-street-reopening-of-town-and-city-centres.html.

The vision that is emerging is not of a low-density solution but a vibrant place for local use – businesses, homes, high streets, cafés, schools and open spaces for local communities – all within walking or cycling distance. Research found that even through the pandemic, local demand has been resilient, with fewer people willing to travel more than 5km to visit high streets and a reluctance to commute for work.[41] For footfall to return to normal levels, city centres can replace the long-distance visitors and tourists with local people, making them walkable healthy cities. This ties in with urban sociologist Ray Oldenburg's theory that communal spaces such as streets, pubs, cafés, post offices and other 'third places' are the heart of a community's social vitality and the foundation of a functioning democracy.[42]

The idea that cities must be organised as a series of connected villages rather than one urban mass unites many different visions and ideas.[43] From Victorian developers to estate agents, the idea of villages inside a city has been a very attractive one. Jeff Speck's book *Walkable City: How Downtown Can Save America, One Step at a Time*, was one of the first published, in 2012.[44] It was a bestseller for the next two years but

41 PwC, 'Return to the High Streets: Lessons from the Reopening of Town and City Centres', undated, https://www.pwc.co.uk/industries/government-public-sector/local-government/insights/return-to-high-street-reopening-of-town-and-city-centres.html.

42 R. Oldenburg, *Celebrating the Third Place: Inspiring Stories About the 'Great Good Places' at the Heart of Our Communities*, Boston, MA: Da Capo Press, 2002, p 2.

43 Arup, 'Cities Alive – Towards a Walking World', https://www.arup.com/perspectives/cities-alive-towards-a-walking-world.https://www.arup.com/perspectives/cities-alive-towards-a-walking-world.

44 Jeff Speck, *Walkable City: How Downtown Can Save America, One Step at a Time*, New York: Farrar, Straus & Giroux, 2012.

the US has yet to adopt his ideas more widely due to its car-dominant culture. European cities have been more amenable to the idea. Professor Carlos Moreno's '15-minute city' concept is being adopted in Paris.[45] Copenhagen in Denmark and Utrecht in the Netherlands also use walkability and cyclability for future planning. Melbourne has also developed 20-minute neighbourhoods where shops, schools, parks and doctors are all within a 20-minute walk, bike ride or journey on public transport.

Even before the COVID-19 pandemic, lower respiratory infections were among the leading causes of death across all income groups. The COVID-19 virus affects the lungs first, and therefore good lung health is the solution to reduce hospital admission for COVID-19. The improvement of air quality in city centres by cutting car use is vital to this aim. Coincidentally, road injuries killed 1.4 million people globally in 2016, about three-quarters (74%) of whom were men and boys.[46] Therefore, by restricting traffic and encouraging cycling and walking through better street design and planning, air pollution and road injuries can be decreased while good health can be increased.

Actual access to healthcare contributes towards the empowerment of the citizen. But such empowerment can be difficult to achieve due to the way healthcare is organised. For example, the UK has its sustainability and transformation partnerships (STPs) which define geographic boundaries of healthcare provision. In the future, these are to be replaced with integrated care systems (ICSs) which will involve healthcare, social care, policing, mental health etc. While this is good, the geographic divisions make patient choice or actual accessibility difficult because healthcare and other facilities are not distributed evenly. The system exists on paper only. Instead, the user should become the focus, enabling someone to easily walk or go by public transport to the nearest available healthcare facility, as for schools or doctors. The walkable healthy city should put the user at its heart who can walk or cycle within 15 minutes to larger health and other community facilities.

Walkable cities also need open and green spaces. Trees and plants are any city's living air-purification systems and can be designed into the city. Existing green areas can be retained, as shown in the case of planning of New Delhi in the 1920s. Rather than removing an existing wooded and hilly area which would have been expensive and disruptive, it was retained as the 'lungs of the city'.[47] In Japan, people practice *shinrin-yoku* – 'forest bathing', which enables them to connect with nature and feel calm.[48] This is now embraced in many Western nations with 'certified forest

45 K. Willsher, 'Paris Mayor Unveils "15-Minute City" Plan in Re-election Campaign', *The Guardian*, 7 February 2020, https://www.theguardian.com/world/2020/feb/07/paris-mayor-unveils-15-minute-city-plan-in-re-election-campaign.

46 World Health Organization, 'The Top 10 Causes of Death', 24 May 2018, https://www.who.int/news-room/fact-sheets/detail/the-top-10-causes-of-death.

47 K.P. Agrawal, *Delhi – 'A Role Model' Of Urban India: Part 1*, New Delhi: Educreation Publishing, 2016, p 2.

48 S. Fitzgerald, 'What Is "Forest Bathing" – And How Does It Help?', *National Geographic*, 21 October 2019, https://www.nationalgeographic.co.uk/environment-and-conservation/2019/10/what-forest-bathing-and-how-does-it-help.

Figure 5.15 An adventure playground for children and teenagers at Oslo University Hospital, Rikshospitalet. Open spaces are good for the physical and mental healing of children who are in hospital. Even if they can't physically participate, just being outside is good for them.

therapy guides'. With large umbrellas and physical distancing, suitable accessible open spaces can be a safe way to enjoy communal gatherings, 'walk-in' cinemas and theatres, even in inclement weather. In South Korea, people can book beach spaces and they are temperature checked before visiting. So far, all indications are that these outings have not resulted in pandemic spikes.

The work commute is the one thing that is more difficult to replace, but the pandemic has proved that people can work from home and are in fact more efficient and organised when they do so. With the rise in digital technology, work can be now done anywhere, and this has benefits for both employees and employers. In 2020, the investment firm Schroders told its 2,500 British staff that they could work from home permanently if they chose to – so long as they worked the hours set out in their contracts. Such flexibility has other benefits, such as reduction in commuting time, with less stress and better quality of life. So, this way of working could continue into 2025 and beyond. However, remote working is dependent on having adequate space to work from, secure IT and ergonomic furniture. Working locally or flexibly, or from home also reduces road traffic, congestion on public transport and, by extension, disease transmission.

In the end, 'health for all' that includes walkable healthy cities is where each country should aim to get to. Globally a vision of ending the environmental and climate crisis will aid in the provision of 'health for all', while local and transnational initiatives will help immediate crisis. The 2020 victory over the wild polio virus that once paralysed 75,000 children on the African continent annually gives hope that such collaborative work can be successful, even in the poorest nations and even during a pandemic. The international collaboration on the pandemic also provides a blueprint for the future – lessons learnt and good ideas. By engaging with people on design of services, improving biodiversity and land use, using technology effectively, and using natural resources wisely, there have already been significant improvements in hospital design and cities. In five years' time, the world will know much more and work much better. For architects and planners, the COVID-19 pandemic can become a catalyst for the provision of good healthcare facilities as well as healthy cities and a healthy planet.

CHAPTER 6

SCHOOLS

HELEN TAYLOR

HELEN TAYLOR

Recently made a Fellow of RIBA, Helen is Director of Practice at collaborative international design practice Scott Brownrigg. Specialising in education design for more than 20 years, she co-authored *Urban Schools: Designing for High Density* (RIBA Publishing, 2020), and is currently an Honorary Research Fellow at Oxford Brookes University.

Introduction

At the time of writing a group of students in the UK have got organised and proposed a Climate Education Act.[1] 'Teach the Future' is a 'campaign by secondary and tertiary education students to repurpose the UK education system around the climate emergency and ecological crisis'. If they succeed, the design of schools will be forced to change and a zero-carbon school will become the norm. In the meantime, architects are not waiting. Whilst supporting school re-opening post pandemic by generating short-term practical suggestions for space planning to meet current government guidelines, they are also imagining how school design could recover, develop and change positively as a result of the global pandemic, and to fit with the need to respond to climate change within the next five years.

The global pandemic of the COVID-19 virus will have some outcomes that we might be able to predict, and many that we cannot even begin to guess. What is clear is that it will change the way in which education happens, even after we return to 'normal' conditions. It has given us – as students, teachers and parents – a chance to live-test a remote digital learning environment; to see its opportunities and limitations, and to establish that broadband internet is now a core utility we all need access to. It has made it clear how vital the experience of the physical school environment and real interaction with others is to children's social development and mental health. It has also revealed how much society relies on children going to school in order to co-ordinate their safeguarding as well as enable parents to work.[2] The social and economic support role that schools play has been recognised across the board and led to a resurgence of the demand for community schools, community access, and dedicated community space in every school.

While for some, home learning has provided a level of freedom and independence that they have relished, for others – particularly those with disadvantaged backgrounds, living in poor-quality housing or neighbourhoods, or with additional educational needs – it has led to serious concern about social equality, setting back

1 https://www.teachthefuture.uk/?source=actnow.

2 F.M. Reimers and A. Schleicher, 'A Framework to Guide an Education Response to the COVID-19 Pandemic of 2020', Organisation for Economic Co-operation and Development, 2020, https://read.oecd-ilibrary.org/view/?ref=126_126988-t63lxosohs&title=A-framework-to-guide-an-education-response-to-the-Covid-19-Pandemic-of-2020.

children's learning and even endangering their physical and mental health.[3] For some, school is a significantly better environment than home. Whilst the pandemic continues, and we don't know if it will ever completely go away,[4] parents in lower income brackets are unfortunately reportedly more concerned about safety and are less likely to send their children back to school. Understandably, many head teachers are currently more focused on risk assessments than on blue-sky thinking about post-pandemic school design.[5]

So what do schools need for a resilient future? They all want to be able to continue delivering the best possible diverse and inclusive education and opportunities to young people in an environment that is functional, safe and comfortable for pupils, staff and visitors. Physical and digital space, flexibility and adaptability, access to outside, hygiene, welfare and wellbeing are high on the agenda and difficult to achieve in many current school buildings. Community integration and access, ease of operation, overheating, and energy costs – and their effect on the school environment and opportunities for learning – were high on the list of demands pre-pandemic and will soon rise up the priority list again.

3 A. Andrew, S. Cattan, M.Costa Dias, C. Farquharson, L. Kraftman, S. Krutikova, A. Phimister and A. Sevilla, 'Learning During the Lockdown: Real-Time Data on Children's Experiences During Home Learning', Institute for Fiscal Studies website, 18 May 2020, https://www.ifs.org.uk/publications/14848.

4 D. Knowles, 'How and When Will This Pandemic End? We Asked a Virologist', World Economic Forum website, 6 April 2020, https://www.weforum.org/agenda/2020/04/how-and-when-will-this-pandemic-end-we-asked-a-virologist/.

5 Star Academies, 'Reopening Schools Toolkit', 2020, https://www.reopeningschools.org/.

Outdoor learning has become a hotter topic than ever – addressing internal space restrictions and funding constraints, and meeting the demand for schools to embed the natural and the built environment into the curriculum to enrich children's learning and life experiences.

Architecture and design have an important role in supporting basic hygiene, health and safety. Space standards, access and security, water and sanitary systems, heating and cooling, acoustics, light, ventilation and air quality all have a demonstrable impact on our comfort, and sometimes on our ability to lead a productive life.

Schools want an environment where learning can take place in comfort and calm. Where people – students, staff, visitors – are able to focus and where no aspects of the building impact negatively or intrude. Educators want inclusive schools that meet the needs of everyone. Some of that is invisible or sensory – light, airflow, acoustics or movement around the building. Designs must also consider the needs of the most vulnerable children in schools. The ability of mainstream schools to provide an environment that can support a range of needs is a vital element for inclusion and wellbeing.

To stimulate this conversation, a number of practices, and students of architecture, have offered design ideas for schools captured in this chapter under three main sections:

- Redesigning the School
- Expanding School Space
- Blurring the Edges of School.

From innovative solutions to providing cost-effective additional space, to rethinking the design of school buildings themselves; from dispersing and embedding education across the urban environment, to creating an inclusive, fun and engaging 'Learnscape' – these ideas could provide better flexibility for today and resilience for the future.

Redesigning the School

The 'open-air' schools of the 1930s – built for the TB pandemic – were inspired by 19th-century sanatoria and the 'outward-bound' ideas of the Scout movement. Their designs included bi-folding doors and retractable roofs to maximise access to fresh air and sunshine. Children were outside whatever the weather. These were lauded at the time for the positive impact they made on some children,[6] but fell out of fashion when better post-war housing and healthcare reduced some of the issues they were set up to address. Their existence is a clear acknowledgement that schools are not just for passing on knowledge.

Jump forward to the 21st century where 'Nature Deficit Disorder' has become a recognised condition for children lacking exposure to nature.[7] Improving connection to nature through biophilic design has been shown to increase rates of learning by 20–25%, as well as boosting test results, concentration levels and attendance, and reducing the impacts of ADHD.[8] We clearly need to safeguard green infrastructure within schools. Early Years in Scotland have introduced a mandatory 20% external learning and play allocation within their funding-area metric. Does access to outdoors need to be mandated as it is in Scotland or Sweden or as 'learning through movement' is in Denmark? Or would extending the curriculum to outside for all ages be enough?

The COVID-19 pandemic has led to calls for Ofsted to start assessing pupils' wellbeing.[9] Wellbeing is a sensory and physical experience – conscious and unconscious. Research shows we spend 90% of our time indoors[10] – so school design matters for wellbeing because the built environment affects how we feel, what we do, our ability to perform tasks, and our health – even more so for developing children or anyone with sensory or physical impairment. The WELL Building Standard – a relatively new industry assessment system – focuses on air, water, nourishment, light, fitness, comfort and mind.[11] 'Good Health and Wellbeing' is one of the established United Nations Sustainable Development Goals,[12] while

6 B. Cathcart, 'In 1930s Britain, Thousands of Sickly Children Were Sent to Open-Air Schools – Even in the Harshest Depths of Winter', *The Independent (Indy/Life)*, 23 January 2005, https://www.independent.co.uk/life-style/health-and-families/health-news/schools-out-487619.html.

7 M. St-Esprit McKivigan, '"Nature Deficit Disorder" Is Really a Thing', *The New York Times*, 23 June 2020, https://www.nytimes.com/2020/06/23/parenting/nature-health-benefits-coronavirus-outdoors.html.

8 'Biophilic Design – Connecting With Nature to Improve Health & Wellbeing', Oliver Heath Design website, https://www.oliverheath.com/biophilic-design-connecting-nature-improve-health-well/.

9 C. Lough, 'Ofsted "Must Focus on Wellbeing" After Covid Closures', 3 June 2020, TES website, https://www.tes.com/news/ofsted-must-focus-wellbeing-after-covid-closures.

10 T. Roberts, 'We Spend 90% of Our Time Indoors. Says Who?', Building Green website, 15 December 2016, https://www.buildinggreen.com/blog/we-spend-90-our-time-indoors-says-who.

11 https://standard.wellcertified.com/well.

12 https://www.un.org/sustainabledevelopment/health/.

the World Health Organization (WHO) defines health as a state of complete physical, mental and social wellbeing and not merely the absence of disease or infirmity.[13]

Wellbeing in school environments is often approached as remedial – something that will stem or address problems – when it could be approached as enabling young people to achieve their potential, promoting resilience, creativity and independence. Health and wellbeing is not just about safeguarding, daylight, acoustics and ventilation, it's also about capability, which includes having choice and agency. In the post-COVID-19 world, physical environments for learning will need to be comprehensible, manageable and meaningful. A brief for a school, thinking only about wellbeing and capability, might be very different. We have seen during the recent lockdown period that schools are not just places to fill young people with knowledge. What if school design briefs were created around delight, happiness, values, community relationships and social experiences?

These points were explored in a June 2020 report by Scott Brownrigg entitled *What If Schools Were Designed for Wellbeing?*, following an online round-table discussion organised in collaboration with educationalists the-learning-crowd. Panellists including a head teacher, local authority client, and the Department for Education head of design, discussed how school design can support the health

13 'World Health Organization (WHO) Definition of Health', https://www.publichealth.com.ng/world-health-organizationwho-definition-of-health/.

Figure 6.1 A Brief for Wellbeing, by Scott Brownrigg and the-learning-crowd.

Figure 6.2 Hilltop School, Hyderabad, by DesignAware, completed in 2019, where generous space standards and a site-specific response have facilitated community engagement and social distancing.

and wellbeing of pupils and teachers in the post-COVID-19 world. The resulting report identified three key drivers for wellbeing in school environments:

- outside space
- community connection
- inclusive design.[14]

Education designers need to build a case around the increased use of and connection to landscape and consideration of the microclimate around schools. Not least because, as well as wellbeing, it offers vital sustainability benefits in terms of biodiversity, reducing heat gain, reducing solar gain, and other positive benefits. Sustainability must include inclusivity so schools can meet as many needs as possible, without adaptation, and reduce support needs. If buildings are going to endure and last for 100 years, they have to be adaptable without the need for significant capital investment.

DesignAware, an emerging practice based in Hyderabad, were approached four years ago by an educational trust running a charity school in a makeshift hall. They already had plans designed by an engineer and asked the practice to complete the design and make it ready for construction. On visiting the site, they discovered that it was part of a cliff. The plans they already had were designed for flat terrain. DesignAware were asked to redesign from scratch, and offered their work pro bono.

14 'Report: What If Schools Were Designed for Wellbeing?', Scott Brownrigg website, 29 June 2020, https://www.scottbrownrigg.com/company/news/report-what-if-schools-were-designed-for-wellbeing/

The resulting building, Hilltop School (see Figure 6.2), was specifically intended to serve students residing in the heritage zone of Golconda, a primarily low-income neighbourhood, who may otherwise drop out of school early. The school provides breakfast and midday meals for the students, and sometimes also offers rations for their families, free of cost, recognising that it is not only students but their entire families that need to be helped to uplift the community.

Completed in 2019, the school has already demonstrated its resilience and adaptability. Managing costs by making use of the craggy terrain and a simple flexible palette of materials, it has already acquired more local meaning and relevance. The school has now become a community centre during weekends and vacations, and serves as an awareness centre and makeshift clinic for the community. In the post-COVID-19 world, where raising awareness and educating families about best health and safety practices will be vital, this place serves that purpose. The school does not require redesign for social distancing as the spaces were designed in close collaboration with the teachers, students and community for the possibility of future growth, and the common spaces, as well as classrooms, are 20% larger than standard requirements.[15]

Where additional internal area is not achievable, covered outside space can extend classrooms and provide year-round use of the external

15 Takbir Fatima interview for the Virtual Design Festival 2020, https://www.dezeen.com/2020/07/08/takbir-fatima-screentime-vdf/.

V
4

environment, thereby ultimately offering more learning opportunities. This was the approach taken in the Inside-Outside School (see Figure 6.3), a 2015 collaboration between Haverstock and Cottrell & Vermeulen Architecture responding to tighter government capital budgets and the focus on modern methods of construction (MMC). Designed for primary or social, emotional and mental health (SEMH) schools, it reflected their long-held view that direct access to the outside from all classrooms is highly desirable. An extensive canopy oversails insulated timber teaching cabins, creating a flexible environment for learning outside the classroom protected from the elements. This inside/outside space has a unique character with planting and a range of different smaller intervention spaces to suit different learners' needs – pods, yurts, shelters. A tempered space that can be used throughout the year.

The idea was explored with a local authority but ultimately unbuilt due to procurement changes. The designers recently revisited the principles as a potential response to COVID-19 and other environmental challenges that require a new approach to school buildings.[16] To ensure social distancing and manage the risk of infection, gatherings of pupils in corridors and entrance lobbies will need to be avoided and group sizes in classrooms will need to be limited. Communal gathering spaces will need to be rethought. The proposal supports this by giving all classrooms direct access to the outside, making it possible to arrive at school without moving through corridors. Generous circulation spaces make it possible to keep a social distance and reduce crowding. What is a playground solution for rainy days can also double up as open-air classroom teaching to help maintain social distancing and provides a higher-performing naturally ventilated solution.

While the proposal for the Inside-Outside School conveniently addresses some challenges of post-COVID-19 reopening, ultimately the solution seeks to create a healthier school where children and young people embrace the outside and undertake equitable amounts of learning inside and out. There is a strong relationship between deprivation and the prevalence of obesity in the UK,[17] and this approach to the design of a school celebrates active learning, creating more kinaesthetic learners.

This approach also supports inclusion. Knowing that they can easily access the outside assists some children and young people with SEMH difficulties to regulate their emotions – giving them choices that make them more comfortable and ultimately more resilient learners. External learning offers greater scope for the curriculum by facilitating activities that need larger spaces and cannot often be undertaken in the confines of a classroom. For some children and young people this access to broader skills is vital for them attaining cultural capital.

16 'The Outdoor School' webinar, led by Claire Barton of Haverstock and Richard Cottrell of Cottrell & Vermeulen Architecture, Festival of Learning Spaces, July 2020, https://www.festivaloflearningspaces.com/seminar/outdoor-learning/.

17 A. Briggs, 'The Economic, Environmental And Social Factors That Shape Our Health Are The Key To Tackling Obesity', *The Telegraph*, 29 July 2020, https://www.telegraph.co.uk/global-health/science-and-disease/economic-environmental-social-factors-shape-health-key-tackling/.

Figure 6.3 Visualisation of the Inside-Outside School, designed in 2015 by Haverstock and Cottrell & Vermeulen Architecture – designed around covered outside space to enable outdoor learning and unrestricted circulation all year round.

This prefabricated solution reflects an industry- and sector-wide move away from traditional construction. The change has a number of drivers including a reduction in embodied carbon and energy consumption. The London Energy Transformation Initiative (LETI) – a network of over 1,000 built environment professionals made up of architects, engineers, clients and many others – are working together on a path to a zero-carbon future. Their *Climate Emergency Design Guide* sets out the approach, targets and benchmarks for each sector, including schools. By 2030, 100% of all new buildings will need to operate at net zero, which means that by 2025 100% of all building must be designed to net zero.[18] A Passivhaus approach will be needed to meet many of the standards.

18 London Energy Transformation Initiative, *Climate Emergency Design Guide*, January 2020, https://www.leti.london/cedg.

Figure 6.4 Harris Academy Sutton, Surrey, by Architype, completed in 2019 – the largest low-energy Passivhaus school in the UK.

The UK's first Passivhaus secondary school, and the largest Passivhaus school in the UK, is Harris Academy Sutton (see Figure 6.4) in Surrey, designed by Architype.[19] Stepping from four to two storeys at the boundary between the Royal Marsden Hospital Campus and neighbouring houses, it will ultimately accommodate 1,275 pupils and 100 staff. Sensors monitoring air quality tell teachers when to open or close windows, busting the myth that Passivhaus standards require a fully sealed environment. Although the capital cost has been higher, the architects predict that the energy costs in use will be 80–90% less than those of a comparative standard school.

19 L. Mark, 'Massivhaus: Harris Academy Sutton by Architype', *Architects' Journal*, 22 November 2019, https://www.architectsjournal.co.uk/buildings/massivhaus-harris-academy-sutton-by-architype.

Scott Brownrigg are testing this prediction on two almost identical nursery schools being delivered for West Lothian Council: St Mary's Bathgate following the practice's well-established flexible fabric-first Optimum School principles,[20] and Blackridge Early Learning & Childcare Centre (see Figure 6.5) following Passivhaus principles. The project includes a long-term commitment from all parties to work with learners, staff and operators to optimise operation on both sites. An academic research partnership with Napier University will capture data from construction verification testing and ongoing performance monitoring, providing a true performance comparison for the operation measured against the as-designed theoretical performance model.

Like many other post-industrial regions, West Lothian is a diverse and complex mix of challenging social, cultural and regeneration influences. This project has the next generation at its heart and from inception the council were determined that these early-years centres would be located to influence two communities which draw upon a wide demographic in their catchment. The long-term influence of these young learners from these diverse communities is regarded as being integral to the net-zero-carbon strategy for the region. The council's Early Years team wanted not only to create space which would support learning, but also centres which would inform, adapt and influence young minds, parents, staff and operational teams to become net-zero achievers.

20 'Optimum Schools', Scott Brownrigg website, 1 February 2016, https://www.scottbrownrigg.com/company/news/optimum-schools/.

This brief required the architects not only to rethink how space is distributed within the built enclosure – to provide larger, grouped and more flexible spaces – but also to reimagine how the Scottish Government space metric could be applied to deliver more meaningful learning space and sensory environments around the centre. Internal and external environments are melded into a seamless space to create educational equity between inside and outside.

From a learning perspective, the easy leap into the external environment directly supports safer, happier and healthier learning. From a social equality perspective, the spatial design actively encourages the safe and controlled integration of parents and carers – a vital component in supporting young developing learners, enabling them to become positive influencers and effective contributors for many years to come.

Worldwide, students themselves have also now taken an interest in the potential for school design to address global challenges. The United Nations Sustainable Development Goals are the focus of the graduate programmes at the Royal Danish Academy of Fine Arts, Schools of Architecture, Design and Conservation (KADK). 'Circular economy' principles and 'Design for Disassembly' inspired Maja Olsson to propose an easily adaptable cross-laminated timber school for students with impaired hearing (see Figure 6.6).[21]

21 *Dezeen* staff, 'Ten Projects from KADK Graduates Offer "Solutions to the Major Challenges of Our Time"', 9 July 2020, Virtual Design Festival website, https://www.dezeen.com/2020/07/09/kadk-royal-danish-academy-fine-arts-vdf-school-show/.

Figure 6.5 Blackridge Early Learning & Childcare Centre, designed by Scott Brownrigg to Passivhaus standards to be monitored as part of a long-term research project with West Lothian Council and Napier University, begun in 2020.

Young people are well aware of the climate emergency and ecological crisis. They have been leaving school to protest about it. School environments provide an opportunity to help young people understand their place in the world and the impact of their behaviour and the built environment on the planet. The Brighton Waste House, completed in 2014 as Europe's first permanent building made of approximately 90% waste materials, and creating 25% more energy than it consumes, was commissioned by the University of Brighton from architect Duncan Baker-Brown to demonstrate that a real construction project was an excellent pedagogic tool for students. During the 12-month construction process more than 750 pupils from local primary and secondary schools visited and learned about the circular economy from the site and even contributed waste that they had collected.[22] School buildings can and should be a learning tool. What lesson should they be teaching?

22 D. Baker-Brown, *The Re-Use Atlas: A Designer's Guide Towards a Circular Economy*, London: RIBA Publishing, 2017.

Figure 6.6 Timber Architecture & Circular Design – a proposal for a school for students with impaired hearing based on the 'Design for Disassembly' principle, by Maja Olsson, MA Architecture, Royal Danish Academy of Fine Arts, 2020.

Expanding School Space

UNICEF points out that, over and above basic access to early-years, primary and secondary education, the provision of 'positive, welcoming and safe learning spaces' is crucial to overcome cultural and emotional barriers to participation in education, including fear of institutions, shame regarding economic status, a sense of alienation, and lack of confidence, and to developing a range of capabilities through education.[23] Research carried out during the UK lockdown by Holly Passmore, graduate psychologist, provided evidence that the pandemic has created some new psychological barriers. Learners are feeling both excited and scared about returning to the school environment. Arrival and transition, a sense of security and empowerment, and opportunities to retreat or withdraw were all identified as key to successfully overcoming these fears. Holly challenged a group of architects in Scotland to respond to her research and provide design ideas to 'turn fear into curiosity' – to give children a sense of confidence and empowerment for a positive experience of their return to school.

Amongst the responses catalogued in Holly's resulting publication *Inclusive Learning Environments Post-Covid*, Holmes Miller Architects proposed extended covered arrival space, as part of a 'creative, inclusive, and immersive learning landscape' (see Figure 6.7).[24]

23 H. Taylor and S. Wright, *Urban Schools: Designing for High Density*, London: RIBA Publishing, 2020, p 15.

24 H. Passmore, *Inclusive Learning Environments Post-Covid*, August 2020, p 16, www.linkedin.com/in/hollypassmore/.

Figure 6.7 Arrival Space, Immersive Early Years Design (2020) – a building model for a pre-school curriculum by Holmes Miller.

Figure 6.8 HELO (Happy Education and Learning Outside, 2020) by ERZ Studio – a structure to support outdoor learning made from recycled materials.

As well as providing a managed transition space for children returning to school, this also provides a practical waiting area for parents, enabling comfortable physical distancing.

ERZ Studio recognised the need to support additional outdoor learning. Their proposed HELO (Happy Education and Learning Outside) lightweight modular learning pods (see Figure 6.8) are constructed from recycled materials and include hand sanitising stations and composting toilets to support hygiene requirements and enable outdoor learning to be extended for longer periods. Child-scale, fully accessible, sensory, tactile and biophilic, HELO offers benefits both in terms of wellbeing and adventure.

Inspired by seeing makeshift tents being used by some nurseries in Denmark, Curl la Tourelle Head Architecture (CLTH) visualised and published a concept for 'tent classrooms' to provide additional socially distanced capacity and access to fresh

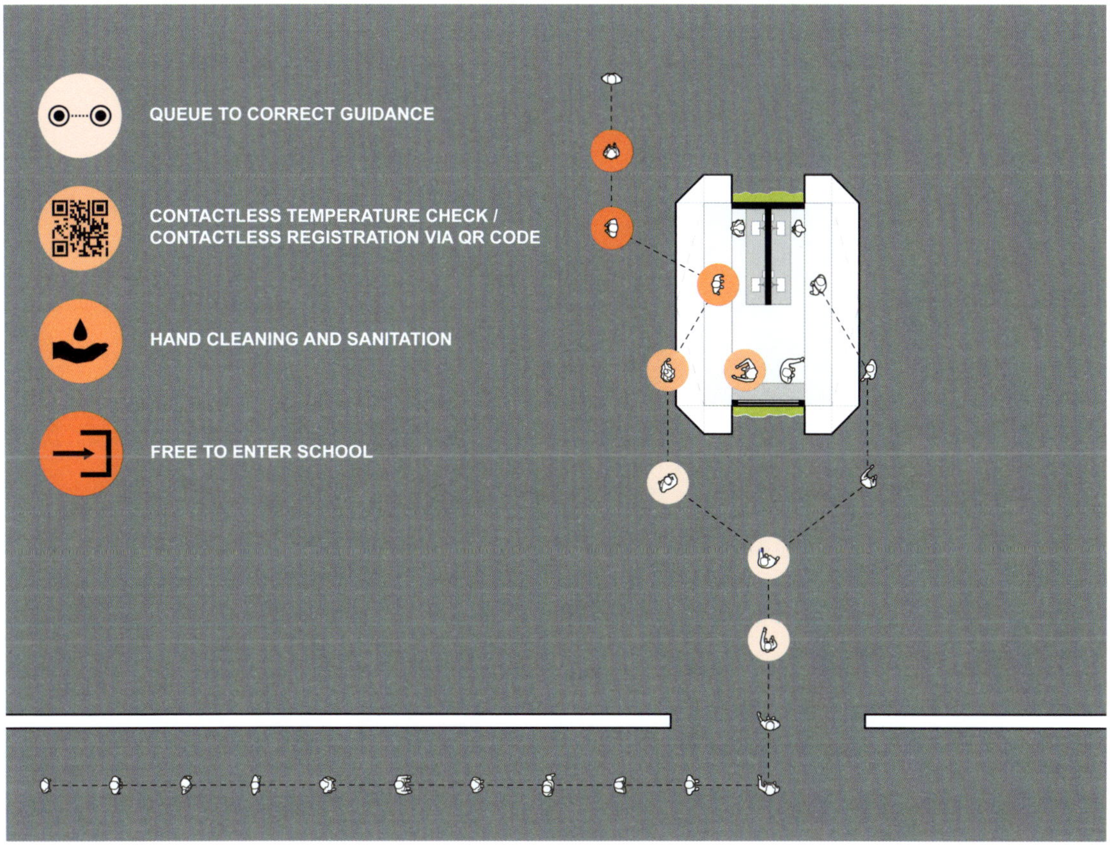

Figure 6.9 MOSSI (Mobile Outdoor School Support Initiative) Pod (2020) by Scott Brownrigg – example use as a welcome area.

air (see Figure 6.10 overleaf). Where schools lacked playing fields, they could be sited in local outdoor spaces and configured for a range of uses including handwashing stations. CLTH speculate that these outdoor schooling spaces, necessitated by coronavirus social distancing, could lead to an evolution of the concept of outdoor learning and a wider rethink of school design, particularly in the UK.[25]

Scott Brownrigg have combined a proposal for additional space for schools and a way to break down the nervousness that some children or parents might feel about returning to school with a longer-term opportunity for outreach and local connection. The MOSSI (Mobile Outdoor School Support Initiative) Pod (see Figure 6.9) is conceived as a sustainable modular timber structure on wheels, designed to be affordable, easily relocatable, reusable as a reception and welcome space, hygiene station, outdoor group teaching space, playground cinema or mobile exhibition space for the school fete, and repurposable – temporarily or permanently – as a high-street pop-up shop. The latter usage could particularly encourage local businesses to

25 N. Hitti, "Education Spaces Will Never Be The Same Again" Says Roar Report', *Dezeen*, 17 June 2020, https://www.dezeen.com/2020/06/17/education-design-post-coronavirus-roar-studio-report/.

Priority over oncoming vehicles

Figure 6.10 Pop-Up Schools (2020): reclaiming the street, by Curl la Tourelle Head Architecture.

engage with the school through sponsorship of a pod in return for use of it during school breaks. The tactile timber structure could accommodate green walls or roof, solar panels, could provide Wi-Fi and simple outdoor services to support outdoor learning, and would be designed to be towed by a domestic vehicle to minimise operational challenges for the school.

Dubai-based design studio Roar gathered a group of 10 professionals including designers, teachers, a doctor, a psychologist and academic researchers to produce a white paper entitled *7 Perspectives: How COVID-19 will Transform the Design of Education Spaces*.[26] While extending the capacity of school buildings was highlighted, the report also outlined design ideas for modifying existing spaces including using movable furniture, movable space dividers and folding walls to repurpose spaces underused during the school day such as dining halls. In addition, the specification of fittings and finishes can mitigate hygiene concerns – anti-microbial materials, touchless taps and automatic-opening or fixed-open doors. Engaging graphics on the floor and walls, rather than institutional warning signs, are a more integrated way to message changed rules.

While the contributors noted that some of the curriculum had been delivered very successfully online, students and teachers were missing specialist equipped physical teaching spaces such as science labs, sports facilities and arts rehearsal or performance spaces. They also highlighted concerns about equity. While 'hybrid learning' or 'blended learning' – a mix of digital, physical, remote and face-to-face learning – might relieve the pressure on existing school space and be adopted easily by some schools, it is reliant on students having access to digital devices, internet connectivity and a space to focus quietly at home. School may be the only place students can find that space to learn. ADP Architecture's report *The Future of Learning Spaces* highlighted similar concerns.[27]

As this research identified, providing space to manage the ongoing health risk and psychological impact of the pandemic is necessary for students, staff and families. Designers and teachers believe that schools and colleges could benefit from a changed environment – particularly needing co-working spaces, including quiet pods for studying, one-on-one meeting spaces and small breakout areas. Counselling rooms, 'defensible' spaces for vulnerable individuals, and sanctuaries and retreat spaces of all kinds and for all ages will contribute to helping school communities settle back into learning. If conversations between educational psychologists and architects, triggered by the pandemic, continue, all schools will benefit.

26 Roar, *7 Perspectives: How COVID-19 will Transform the Design of Education Spaces*, June 2020, https://designbyroar.com/roardesign/wp-content/uploads/2020/06/White-Paper-on-Education-Design-1.pdf.

27 ADP Architecture, *The Future of Learning Spaces*, May 2020, https://www.adp-architecture.com/insight-the-future-of-learning-spaces/.

Blurring the Edges of School

During the Second World War, Ernő Goldfinger presented his vision of the reconstruction of a post-war Britain in a series of exhibitions mounted for the Army Bureau of Current Affairs (ABCA). In the 1943 ABCA exhibition entitled 'Health', Goldfinger proposed a blueprint for improved housing, sanitation, working conditions, schools and diet. The RIBA Photography collection includes the images he intended for use on an exhibition display board. Images of families, schools and children are integral to this vision.

Confirming this vision 50 years later, in 1996 the second United Nations Conference on Human Settlements (Habitat II) passed a resolution to make cities liveable places for all. The conference declared that the wellbeing of children is the ultimate indicator of a healthy habitat, a democratic society and good governance. The provision of education opportunities at the heart of cities is key to children's wellbeing. Alongside policies and plans to manage urban growth and ensure access to infrastructure and services, architectural design can play an important role in addressing barriers to participation in education.

Along with the quality of the built environment, space standards matter to human health. A recent World Vision report on COVID-19 highlighted the risks to children in urban contexts.[28] Overcrowded, inadequate housing and lack of public open space, as well as public toilets, is an issue that has been particularly highlighted during lockdown. Neighbourhood deprivation affects individual health outcomes.[29] Children in polluted cities are more likely to suffer from obesity.[30] Poor health outcomes and exclusion cost the economy money, as well as wasting human potential.

Schools add value to city environments. This value is not just social. Since 2015, the Economist Intelligence Unit's 'global livability ranking'[31] has assigned a score for over 30 qualitative and quantitative factors for cities worldwide across five broad categories of stability, healthcare, culture and environment, infrastructure and education. The addition of a good school has been shown to increase prices for homes in the catchment area.[32] Schools can become the focal point for a new development, creating a centre that may not otherwise naturally arise, around which the community can be created. The importance and value of schools as a community resource and civic space has grown in the context of the loss of a number of community facilities in the UK – libraries, Sure Start centres, even local shops – over recent years.

28 World Vision International, *COVID-19 Aftershocks: A Perfect Storm*, May 2020, https://www.wvi.org/publications/report/coronavirus-health-crisis/covid-19-aftershocks-perfect-storm.

29 H. Fisher and A. Reuben, 'Your Childhood Neighbourhood Can Influence How Your Genes Work – New Study', *The Conversation*, 26 June 2020, https://theconversation.com/your-childhood-neighbourhood-can-influence-how-your-genes-work-new-study-141543.

30 S. Weedy, 'Children In Polluted Cities "More Likely To Suffer From Obesity"', Child in the City website, 25 June 2020, https://www.childinthecity.org/2020/06/25/children-in-polluted-cities-more-likely-to-suffer-from-obesity/.

31 https://www.eiu.com/topic/liveability.

32 'Best Schools Add £18,600 To Average House Price', BBC News website, 20 March 2017, https://www.bbc.co.uk/news/uk-england-39327149.

School playgrounds also add value to neighbourhoods. One in eight British households has no garden and the percentage of homes without a garden is higher among ethnic minorities.[33] Green space, particularly, adds value for everyone and, unsurprisingly, estate agents anticipate that access to outside space will be high on the agenda for urban residential purchases post-COVID-19.[34] Good-quality landscape design and trees have demonstrable asset value.[35]

The *Making London Child-Friendly* report published in March 2020,[36] just as London went into lockdown, emphasised the importance of the physical, as well as social, urban infrastructure for health and safety. The United Nations Convention on the Rights of the Child recognises the right to play and participate in cultural life. Safe outdoor environments that facilitate independent mobility are key. If we want to prevent a resurgence of the dominance of cars, as children return to school, we need to make our streets great places to walk and cycle for children and adults alike. Design can improve 'liveability' for children and their families in urban environments.[37] Well-designed spaces for children, and therefore for families, are assets at the heart of liveable, healthy cities.

Students of architecture have been particularly drawn to ideas about integrating schooling across the city environment, testing and visualising the idea of the 'dispersed school' identified in the 2020 book *Urban Schools: Designing for High Density*.[38]

University of Oregon students explored sustainable design at the urban scale, proposing in one project – the Albina Community Centre by Odessa Cleavenger – to combine child development and environmental education at the centre of the 'historically underserved neighbourhood on Portland's East Waterfront' to provide a range of learning and collaboration opportunities.[39] National University of Singapore graduate Tan Xin Yuan considered the influence of housing as a typology on building individual identity and values beyond the traditional pedagogy of what a school can teach.[40]

33 Office for National Statistics, 'One In Eight British Households Has No Garden', 14 May 2020, https://www.ons.gov.uk/economy/environmentalaccounts/articles/oneineightbritishhouseholdshasnogarden/2020-05-14.

34 J. Armstrong-Fox, 'How Will The Housing Market Change Post Covid-19? Seven Predictions From Property Lawyers Collyer Bristow', Inside Conveyancing website, undated, https://insideconveyancing.co.uk/news/how-will-the-housing-market-change-post-covid-19-seven-predictions-from-property-lawyers-collyer-bristow/.

35 Christopher Neilan, *CAVAT (Capital Asset Value for Amenity Trees) – Full Method: Users' Guide*, The London Tree Officers Association, January 2017, https://www.ltoa.org.uk/documents-1/capital-asset-value-for-amenity-trees-cavat.

36 Mayor of London *et al.*, *Making London Child-Friendly: Designing Places and Streets for Young People*, London: Greater London Authority, March 2020, https://www.london.gov.uk/sites/default/files/ggbd_making_london_child-friendly.pdf.

37 'Showcasing Global Examples of Child-Friendly Urban Design', Child in the City website, 1 May 2020, https://www.childinthecity.org/2020/05/01/showcasing-global-examples-of-child-friendly-urban-design/.

38 Taylor and Wright, *Urban Schools*.

39 *Dezeen* staff, 'University of Oregon Students Spotlight Five Sustainable Urban Design Proposals', Virtual Design Festival website, 9 July 2020, https://www.dezeen.com/2020/07/09/university-of-oregon-vdf-school-shows/.

40 *Dezeen* staff, 'Architecture Graduates from National University of Singapore Future-Proof Their City', Virtual Design Festival website, 7 July 2020, https://www.dezeen.com/2020/07/07/national-university-singapore-architecture-vdf-school-shows/.

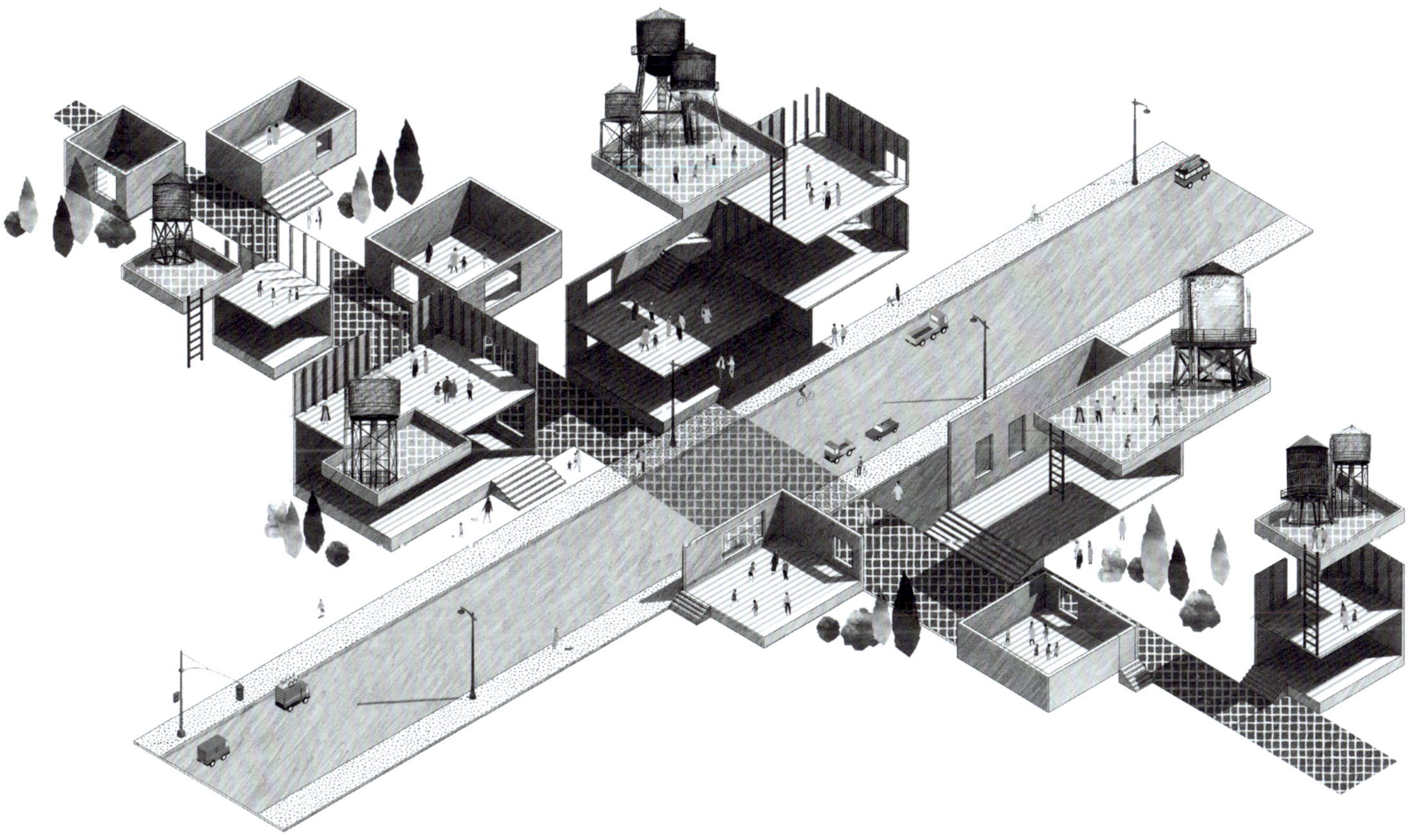

At Cambridge University, Charlie Edmond's 'Void Pedagogy' imagined a decentralised and regenerative school in Tokyo that brings established rural project-based learning approaches into void spaces – a 'children's village' in the city.[41] Julia Cabanas sought to address segregation and disconnection in New York schools, and challenge the strict zoning system, by distributing learning over several urban blocks, tying community, cultural and education venues together, and transforming school into a shared neighbourhood space – 'Harlem as School' (see Figure 6.11).[42]

Given that much of our behaviour is dictated – or at least influenced – by our environments, new building technologies, building typologies and community engagement projects can inform the necessary adjustments we need to make to meet these aspirations and to accommodate the 'blended learning' approach we are expecting will continue.

Figure 6.11 Harlem as School (2020) by Julia Cabanas, University of Cambridge – illustrating how a dispersed school model can help create neighbourhood spaces for urban integration and connection.

41 'Year 5: Charlie Edmonds – Void Pedagogy, Tokyo, Japan', University of Cambridge Architecture Society website, 2020, https://cambridgearcsoc.com/Charlie-Edmonds.

42 'Year 5: Julia Cabanas – Harlem as School, New York, USA', University of Cambridge Architecture Society website, 2020, https://cambridgearcsoc.com/Julia-Cabanas.

Next Steps

To future-proof schools for a world where we live with COVID-19, or another pandemic, and climate change, these ideas illustrate how existing and proposed educational facilities must be designed differently to meet the needs of children and society by:

- supporting a balance of physical and digital learning
- optimising access to outside and the quality of the outdoor learning environment
- promoting hygiene, welfare, safety, health and wellbeing
- meeting wider local needs – welcoming community integration and inclusive access
- addressing climate change – zero carbon, flexible, adaptable and resilient
- offering an environment designed to be a tool and resource for learning in itself.

While we've all been working and learning at home, many of us have developed a greater appreciation for the architecture, built and natural environments in our neighbourhood. As we emerge from lockdown we need to remember to hold on to this experience and jealously guard the things we've missed the most. Seeing schools, playgrounds, libraries and cultural and entertainment places closed has been heartbreaking for children as much as adults. And while many parents and educationalists have embraced the opportunity for a different kind of education away from exams and timetables, others have feared for vulnerable children and the loss of educational progress as well as impact on mental and physical health. Pupils, parents and teachers alike have missed being part of the community of school. Schools offer far more than mono-functional institutions. They should be woven into the social and material fabric of communities to meet all their needs.

> 'We now have an opportunity to retool and re-energize schools and schooling so that it looks very different than the place we all learned in.'
>
> ···➔ PRAKASH NAIR, SCHOOL ARCHITECT[43]

43 https://prakashnair.com/.

CHAPTER 7

UNIVERSITIES AND COLLEGES

IAN TAYLOR

IAN TAYLOR

Ian has extensive university project experience in the UK, and internationally with the University of Washington in Seattle and the Princess Sumaya University for Technology in Jordan. He leads Research and Innovation at Feilden Clegg Bradley Studios (FCBStudios), is a member of the Higher Education Design Quality Forum research group, and is Visiting Professor at University College London's Institute for Environmental Design and Engineering.

Introduction

Post-pandemic design needs buildings that are welcoming, economic, functional, adaptable and safe.

It is the architect who should be the most empathetic designer of the construction professionals. The architect should have the skills to judge how people will react to space, how dimensions influence movement, how distance and acoustics impact on speech legibility.

It is the architect who should lead the briefing process, listen, and help the client prioritise their requirements. It is the architect who should spend the time to understand how well or not the existing buildings in a college or university estate are performing and so inform the design of the next projects.

The pandemic has forced us all to have renewed concern for people's health, happiness and activities when inside a building or outside in a space. Architects should lever this concern to join up the design and construction process – by involving academics and students as well as facilities and maintenance staff in early-stage briefing, and by encouraging innovation in building services and structural design, and building construction, to deliver end products that are well commissioned and perform as intended. We need to get the simple things right: built quality, air, light and landscape.

The pandemic forces everyone in higher education to reassess the value and purpose of proximal interaction with others. Students and researchers, alongside their supervisors and lecturers, need to develop new ways to interact. Administrators and the social wellbeing and health and estates teams are all forced to re-evaluate what is most critical for the success of their university and college.

It is the outcomes of the activities that the physical and built environment facilitate which are at stake. The serendipitous encounters which lead to new thinking and social relationships are now at risk of becoming physically outlawed.

Which pre-existing interactions are compromised when healthcare distancing and controls are superimposed on the estate? The possibilities for online communications have become more important parts of all our lives. Their uptake for use in learning environments has now been given a

Figure 7.1 Brunel University by Richard Sheppard, Robson & Partners, completed in 1966. The intensity of discussion and chance meetings outside lecture theatres and in social spaces remain important aspects of student life. Since the 1970s the diversity of the student body has widened, and the importance of these break or social areas been recognised, but such interaction is now challenged by the pandemic.

new impetus after years of mixed scepticism and enthusiasm. Tertiary education courses already operate in a digital dimension, but the digital and physical structure and associated networks are likely to have developed independently and may not yet be fully complementary. The enforced mass testing exercise over the 2019–2021 academic years will demonstrate areas of relative success and failure. By 2025 one of the key developments will be a maturing of a new structure where the virtual and physical are integrated, and potentially interchangeable, creating more flexible and robust systems that will be better able to respond to future pandemics and disrupters.

Alongside the health pandemic, the climate emergency demands reassessment of HE/FE operations, estate management, procurement and development. These two issues are interrelated, and solutions which improve outcomes against both sets of criteria will have the most profound impact, improving both the performance and standing of those institutions that lead the way towards a healthier low-carbon future.

Future changes to the HE/FE physical environment should reflect the size and pedalogical and social character of each institution, which varies widely. In 2018–19, there were 2.38 million students studying at UK higher-education institutions.[1] These range in size between over 150,000 (at the University of London) to under 1,000 students, with the gross internal area of HE estates totalling more than

1 'Higher Education in Numbers' (2018–19), Universities UK website, https://www.universitiesuk.ac.uk/facts-and-stats/Pages/higher-education-data.aspx.

22 million sqm.[2] The further-education sector in England serves 1.4 million adults and 0.75 million 16–18-year-olds in over 8 million sqm.[3]

The numbers of students in postgraduate learning and research programmes in comparison to undergraduates varies by institution: nine UK universities are postgraduate only, eight split about 50:50; and of the 132 others, half are between 20% and 30% postgraduate. Some FE colleges specialise in adult education, others are serving only 16–18-year-olds. Some pride themselves on high hours of contact 'teaching' time, others on the strength of their research. Some campuses provide on-site housing for the majority of their students, others serve more dispersed communities with many students remaining based at their parental home. It is clear that these communities need varied solutions to many aspects of the COVID-19 pandemic.

The requirements from the physical space will undoubtedly alter but an opportunity arises for a metamorphic change that can not only offer a new approach to blended learning but also address historic ills that have exacerbated problems relating to the climate emergency, social inclusion and student wellbeing. The post-COVID-19 landscape could accelerate the delivery of the university of the 21st century: crossing the boundaries of HE and FE, engaging more fully with their local community.

2 Association of University Directors of Estates, *Executive Summary of the AUDE Higher Education Estates Management Report*, 2019, https://www.aude.ac.uk/news/publications/ems-report/.

3 Association of Colleges, *College Key Facts 2019/20*, 2019, https://www.aoc.co.uk/sites/default/files/AoC%20College%20Key%20Facts%202019-20.pdf.

What are the Particular Challenges for Tertiary Education Design?

Will the requirements of change in tertiary education after the pandemic simply mirror society or will certain features begin to dominate thinking?

The demand for tertiary education will remain as strong as ever. There could be increasing emphasis on subjects that support independent careers – demand is rising for postgraduate study and entrepreneurship support for individual business development spin-offs coming out of research in science and information technology for example, whilst FE colleges providing vocational training may be in the resurgence.

Increased awareness of the impact of the physical environment on health and climate change should drive greater focus on a range of issues in design, to the overall benefit of the process:

- more consideration of the direct impacts of space on human interaction
- more joined-up thinking on the relationships between space and teaching and learning styles
- increased focus on the importance of safe housing to create the college experience
- greater emphasis on environmental performance
- increased consideration of social good
- increased links with the local community to engender joined-up and supportive local places
- more emphasis on equality of access to the socially, or ethnically disadvantaged and elderly cohorts.

Greater consideration of these aspects in project briefs will generate better architecture through more considered discussion of the impacts of the built environment upon behaviour, learning outcomes, resource use and operational performance.

The sector should be wary of technological solutions which are based on reduced interaction between people, limitations on the use of spaces, and surveillance. People learn from people. The strength of a college's reputation is built not only upon the quality of its teaching staff, research and facilities but also the ease of access to these assets. Students also recognise these benefits, and are now becoming more demanding for contact time in order for their fees to be justified.

The physical restrictions that the pandemic has forced upon us are challenging the tertiary education sector in subtly different yet significantly more expansive ways in comparison with schools. Firstly, school education is available to every child as a right – with only a minority purchasing, or choosing, an alternative route. Whilst the introduction of league tables and parental choice do mean that options are available, the standard curriculum and exam frameworks mean that variations in teaching styles and facilities lead to a relatively limited range of variations between school estates, often defined by class size and the quality of facilities. Secondly, within tertiary education the range of environments, specialisms and facilities is much greater than in schools – being generated by the more diverse learning pathways on offer which have been developed for different subjects. The extent of one-to-one teaching, equipment use and interaction with others varies. Thirdly, many tertiary education providers also offer residential and whole-community facilities, leading to providers having to consider the issues raised within all the sectors covered in this book, with the challenges posed by the pandemic having impacts on each part of their estates: residential, workplace, heathcare, hospitality, retail, civic/cultural and masterplanning and placemaking.

The breadth of impact is wide. Alongside local authorities there are no other institutions in the UK that manage such diverse property portfolios, including self-guided and taught learning environments, specialist research facilities, workplaces, social, sport and catering facilities, and housing.

The immediate challenge for the sector since early 2020 has been the continuation of the delivery of teaching and research. For teaching this has meant a full immersion into the world of online tools, enormously accelerating a shift that has been ongoing over the last decade. For the 2020–21 academic year this is being consolidated to such an extent that many new methods are likely to become permanent features of university teaching in the future. The use of large lecture theatres will be assessed below. Flipped teaching which utilises both online material and group working sessions will increasingly become the norm. Access to all spaces, but perhaps especially laboratories and workshops, may be extended over longer hours to allow for lower densities of occupation whilst still providing access to all students.

The courses which could be hardest hit in the short term may be those which feature group working and physical collaboration and those activities that demand close human contact: medicine, physiotherapy, drama, theatre, music, beauty, team sports, and group workshop and laboratory collaboration. Teaching and learning will carry on though, and new processes and interactions will start to develop to substitute for those activities deemed too unsafe.

By 2025 the introduction of a vaccine will have hopefully removed the need for physical distancing, but the risk of a future pandemic with a new strain requiring a different vaccine will remain, leaving the emergency distancing issue as a risk that building design will have to consider from now on. There are news sets of criteria now – for building users, owners and operators. All are currently concerned that buildings should encourage healthy practices relating to distancing and engagement with others, and physical features such as ventilation and cleanliness should be of a standard that is not putting them at risk. In the medium term this could start to generate new criteria for building refurbishment and new-build projects, but ones which should basically return to time-proven principles of good design for people.

There are a number of general design features which will become more desirable over the next few years; and as many university estates are microcosms of society, featuring all the building typologies considered in this book, observations in the other sections of this book will no doubt generally apply here too. Within the context of tertiary education there are four overarching themes worthy of comment before addressing particular impacts on areas of the estate.

Fresh air and daylight

Building users and clients will have an increased awareness of visibly more natural systems – developing preferences for opening windows over mechanical ventilation, and access to fresh air, daylight and nature over deep-plan, sealed and artificially sustained interior environments. Mechanical ventilation can and will provide more reliable fresh air, but it is not visible. Opening a window is a specific and definite action by the occupants, which can give a significant boost to their confidence.

Adaptability

The adaptability of space will become paramount again. The pandemic has given us all a lesson in change management – how well we have been able to incorporate change and adapt both our behaviours and estates gives us insights into how we might need to prepare for the possibility of even more disruptive events through different pandemics and climate-change impacts in the future. So flexibility will start to become a design driver again: the investment in renovation works or new buildings designed to be specifically bespoke to only one function and layout may become less desirable.

Low-carbon, loose-fit

'Long-life, loose-fit' will be changed to 'low-carbon, loose-fit': the awareness of building component life and the enormous impact of the embodied carbon of construction materials and components and of the construction and maintenance process will need increasing scrutiny as we decide how to invest our limited carbon budget to provide the lowest risk but greatest benefit. The reuse of components at the end of their useful life in their first building configuration could start to enable shorter lifespans for interior fit-outs to be viable without large embodied carbon impacts. The provision of spaces that can be subdivided or adapted over time with moveable furniture to give flexibility of space planning could quickly adapt to both new learning styles or physical distancing pandemic restrictions. At the other end of the scale, the investment into quality materials that will enable very long building life could justify some increased initial carbon investment in construction materials, as long as this is also backed up by carbon-neutral or regenerative operation to compensate for the initial high hit. It must now be remembered that an immediate requirement of the climate emergency is to reduce carbon impacts now – and not to use excessive carbon resources now for relatively low carbon savings annually thereafter.

External spaces

Students are becoming increasingly aware of the climate impacts of our material environment,[4] and whilst the carbon and environmental impacts of building construction are now becoming an important issue to them, the quality of the external campus space in which they sit is of equal concern. Welcoming and safe external spaces on campus will become increasingly important as social and working environments (despite the British weather!).

4 Student climate survey carried out by YouthSight for the Higher Education Design Quality Forum (HEDQF), May 2020, results summary to be published by HEDQF: https://www.hedqf.org/research/.

Figure 7.2 Sainsbury Laboratory, Cambridge, by Stanton Williams, completed in 2010. A design that celebrates the visibility of human endeavour: encouraging contact without compromising circulation, clearly showing who is in the building and how much space there is to occupy safely.

Challenges for the Use of Space

Lecture theatres and seminar spaces

Much lecture-style teaching is being transferred to online modes, potentially becoming a fixture for the future rather than a short-term bandage. In higher and further education there will be a shift away from the use of large lecture theatres for general content delivery in timetabled teaching. The shift towards flipped learning and increasing use of online platforms, supplemented by individual and small group tutorials and discussions, will help even out circulation flows inside teaching and learning buildings, avoiding large gatherings and crossovers associated with the lecture room timetabling. Whilst such moments had offered some potential for socialising and meeting, these changeover periods were not ever that conducive to lingering and exchange. However, the pre-meet before lectures was always a good point for students to talk about coursework or general social anecdotes, and it is these informal occasions and incidental meetings that we are all missing.

Income from conferencing use of lecture halls and seminar facilities over holiday breaks in the academic year, alongside the letting of student accommodation and use of catering facilities, had become a useful income stream which the pandemic has now put at risk. The future viability of this dual use will be under increased scrutiny in the future.

Large lecture theatres could still be desired for special star lectures and offer group working environments with enhanced technology and ventilation, allowing students to operate in small isolated groups, like that designed in FCBStudios' Myhal Centre, University of Toronto, completed in 2018 (see Figure 7.4). Flexible seating arrangements allow different configurations (loose fit). The

Figure 7.3 The Richmond Building, University of Bristol, remodelled by FCBStudios (completed 2016). Founded on the tenets of efficiency, sustainability and identity, which were all lacking in the existing building, the renovation has created more accessible and inclusive spaces, encouraging the use of the stair and new open spaces created around it. The four phases of renovation of the 1960s student union has dramatically improved its energy performance from an EPC rating of 'E' (111) to 'B' (42).

Figure 7.4 The Auditorium at the Myhal Centre for Engineering Innovation and Entrepreneurship (MCEIE), University of Toronto, Canada, by FCBStudios and Montgomery Sisam, completed in 2018. The 500-seat interactive auditorium has been designed to facilitate audience engagement by allowing students to engage in a dialogue with the professor and with one another.

space is designed with collaboration in mind, with cameras and screens to share activities across it and connect to those who can't attend. It will be interesting to see if these spaces offer more flexibility over the next academic year than more traditional layouts.

Large flexible floors which offer many potential learning environment styles through temporary partitions or moveable furniture can offer adaptability for changing pedagogy (or pandemic). The use of wall-mounted screens in learning zones where digitally enabled learning shown to individual student devices is broadcast to be visible to others passing the space can give a flavour of activities being pursued. There is a desire for learning to be more visible, for connections across the academic body to be encouraged, and working with physical space and digital technology together will start to lead to new space typologies. The webcasting of lectures, seminars and tutorials will allow those shielding or those only able to attend remotely to join in, improving inclusivity.

Tutorial rooms

Whatever the physical distancing rules enforced, most colleges will have a range of small rooms or open-plan areas to enable small group teaching and project workspace. In open-plan areas the acoustics will influence the ability of adjacent groups to work independently. In good weather some activities may be able to transfer to external and semi-external settings (see 'External space' section below).

Specialist teaching settings

- Laboratories: science, medicine,
- Workshops: engineering, computing, law
- Studios: art, dance, theatre, music, sport, beauty

Unless users can be kept in differentiated team groups where distancing is relaxed, these facilities will throw up difficult timetabling, density and cleaning challenges, potentially requiring the relocation of equipment to optimise use. Courses which feature high levels of interpersonal skills will require new combinations of design and management solutions to help enable interactions to continue.

Learning support and social spaces

- Libraries
- Social learning spaces
- Student centres
- Food and drink

These places are important parts of college life – and for many the main communal features. It will be especially important to introduce natural and passive constraints to circulation and access in these spaces, so that the imposition of future lockdown might be possible with minimal impact on the character of the environment. The introduction of timetabled booking of facilities, rooms and study seats in these shared facilities could help avoid abortive circulation in search of places to sit or meet.

Food and drink spaces will be subject to similar rules to public facilities, and so any temporary regimes regarding health and safety will be better

Figure 7.5 Exeter Library, Exeter, New Hampshire, by Louis Khan, completed in 1972. The ingredients of healthy library design – individual workspaces next to opening windows with views to landscape and clear circulation routes.

understood by the users. The location of these facilities adjacent to external usable areas will allow future flexibility if internal constraints are reintroduced in the future.

Connecting spaces and cores

A reliance on the use of lifts for vertical transportation will be replaced by acceptance of the use of staircases, especially if these also offer the views, daylight and ventilation that will become so desired. Checking that staircase and circulation layouts could offer one-way circulation if ever required, while maintaining fire safety, may become standard best practice. The temporary retrofit of existing buildings has demonstrated the advantages of wide corridors and stairs, as well as the provision of multiple stairways to enable one-way up/down circulation to be introduced to reduce contact points. Open-plan extensions to circulation used for informal meeting can easily become passing places in a more distanced world.

Clarity of circulation principles will be needed to ensure pinch points and queuing areas are available adjacent to spaces with potentially restricted access such as kitchenettes and toilets, and the design of toilets themselves will need greater consideration of circulation and handwashing facilities than before. Administering distancing criteria is easier in single-cubicle layouts containing both WC and hand basin, than the use of shared wash-hand basins.

Figure 7.6 University of Sussex by Sir Basil Spence, completed in 1967. Colonnaded circulation routes allow students to relate to the landscape as they travel around the campus. Speaking to the BBC's *Town and Around* programme in 1963, Spence said: 'I feel that one of the most important things is that a university should give the student a feeling of confidence.'[5]

It is easy to consider how many people can safely sit in a room to suit specific distancing requirements, but anticipating the interactions between groups of people waiting to enter or exit a large room is more challenging. IT service providers are offering enhancements to CCTV systems to help administer access and density enforcement by number-counting and facial-recognition technologies, but such measures will not be able to prevent bunching or induce social distancing at those control points themselves. The onus should be on the students rather than the university to ensure compliance with distancing.

Meanwhile there will be more technological solutions introduced such as contactless access and automatically opening doors, allowing circulation without any human or physical contact. Even if appropriate, such features should not be introduced if these remove all personal human and safe tactile welcomes to a building, which most students and academics enjoy as friendly thresholds in their community.

A diverse range of circulation routes will encourage opportunities for collaboration and interaction, but in times of pandemic they also increase the risk of infection. An unintended consequence of very rigid circulation routes which prohibit wandering and alternative routes to the same destinations, is that serendipitous connections and meetings could be discouraged. Mapping people movement at early design stages will allow such issues to be discussed with the client and users.

External space

Students like to socialise, relax and study in outdoor spaces. This is neutral territory, which if attractive, protected from adverse weather and surrounded by greenery, provides a valuable resource. The good design of landscape around

5 'Sir Basil Spence: University of Sussex', National Records of Scotland website, undated, https://webarchive.nrscotland.gov.uk/20170903013043/http://www.basilspence.org.uk/learning/buildings/sussex-university.

and near to buildings provides healthy settings for the student and academic community. Learning by sitting in a group under a tree is an ancient and emblematic image of education: coming together in a symbolic place of shelter to share knowledge.

In the post-pandemic world such spaces will provide release in comparison to the more constrained interiors. Out-of-town campus universities often offer attractive grounds which have become intrinsic features of the character of the institution. Urban settings are often more challenging both in their public/private separations and the impact of higher density on the opportunities for the integration of external space. Some have traditionally physically set themselves apart from their town (as the quads and courts of Oxford and Cambridge colleges) but there is an increasing desire from urban universities and colleges to make their education more visible and welcoming, and for them to create a public realm which helps define their space and extent and offer safer, better and accessible environments, with facilities and quality landscaping as part of the cityscape.

Universities can develop under-used public realm to provide accommodation, circulation, social and waiting spaces. Outdoor spaces could be managed to support varying needs or temporary facilities. Enhanced control of spaces could allow more permeable façades and multiple entry points to surrounding buildings. These spaces offer opportunities to adopt 'temporary urbanism' installations that allow greater flexibility in finding a 'new normal' or new campus models.

The dense city university projects by Grafton Architects in Lima, Milan, Kingston (see Figure 7.7) and the LSE now on site offer exemplary precedents for the incorporation of external circulation spaces to be colonised by university members – mixtures of public and semi-private realm that connect with the urban context. Alongside the social and placemaking benefits of this approach, there can also be cost benefits: to incorporate areas of unheated and protected external space as circulation and meeting places can offer more space at lower cost than if these were all internal, though to make these robust and attractive requires ring-fenced budgets for external spaces and landscaping.

Developing the engagement and vitality of campuses by encouraging students to spend longer on campus has been critical in improving student experience and inclusion, especially with students from outside the UK. This has resulted in reduced drop-out rates, improved grades and an increase in further-education career paths (such as PhDs).

The spaces between

In temperate climates there is more significant use of external spaces for learning, and less differentiation between inside and outside. In our own more northern climate in the UK similar relatively benign conditions can be created for large periods of the year in covered but unheated spaces either adjacent to, or surrounded by, interior space. With some shelter from wind and rain, and enabling low sunshine to penetrate, external spaces like old walled gardens can provide comfortable microclimates. Even with added roofs, the fact that such spaces can be created

Cafe

at lower cost per unit area than fully heated and controlled internal space could encourage greater demand for such spaces on campus in the future. In times when universities have been seeking to encourage students to stay on campus for longer periods of the day ('sticky campus'), the provision of large flexible naturally ventilated spaces, covered courtyards or galleria-type volumes could offer good socially distanced environments in times of pandemic risk and a whole range of more intense uses at other times. More frequent use of such intermediate spaces over longer periods of the year could encourage more flexible approaches to clothing – perhaps coming to campus with a raincoat and winter jumpers, and continuing to wear these in social and learning settings, could also start to reduce heating requirements and so reduce carbon impacts in operation of the estate.

There is the opportunity to consider external or tempered circulation zones, which can assist in reduction of infection, and with reduced heating and building costs can be an environmentally friendly and cheaper option for the provision of more area.

Administration

- Academic and staff services
- Estate and procurement services

As with other office work in all other sectors, the pandemic has demonstrated the robustness of remote working, with some benefits arising from the time generated through gained commuting time, alongside the challenges to collaborative work and the lack of face-to-face meetings.

It may be that there will be elements of university and college administration that can continue with some remote working, but student-facing support, wellbeing and academic services will still want to deliver personal engagement.

It is interesting to postulate whether administrative space requirements may fall in the future, giving potential for the expansion of teaching and learning facilities. Space requirements for administration and some subject areas may be able to reduce significantly – lowering overheads and easing neglected investment over the years. These buildings can then be redesigned/repurposed to meet post-COVID-19 requirements.

The arguments that have been held over individual academic offices in the last few years will be given a new twist by the pandemic. New models of academic office use may emerge, engaging with remote working and encouraging cross-collaboration whilst reducing space requirements on campus. Conversely some academics may wish to return to single academic offices which offer opportunities for controlled engagement with small numbers for tutorials.

Residences

Student housing offered by Universities is generally individual rooms in shared flats of between four and 12 students, often with shared toilets, bathrooms, kitchen and living spaces. Infection control is very challenging, and especially difficult in units without en-suite facilities. There are challenges relating to the creation of a balance between cross-fertilisation

Figure 7.7 Town House, Kingston University, London, by Grafton Architects, completed in 2020. External terraces and circulation routes up and around the building create usable spaces, add character and make the interior more efficient.

of ideas between students from different subjects, and cross-contamination of COVID-19. Until vaccinations are available, institutions are likely to follow different solutions to the concept of community 'bubbles' in accommodation which they manage – with some potentially grouping by subject so distancing in classes can then be reduced, while others are specifically wanting to keep accommodation mixed between subjects studied to retain cross-fertilisation between students when this is considered important to the character of their college. In settings where students will be coming from home environments and privately rented shared accommodation alongside college accommodation, limitations to group sizes will have little impact. Common-sense precautions within accommodation, as elsewhere in college facilities, alongside good management of anyone in contact with people contracting the virus is probably the sensible way forward.

Challenges in Context

Community engagement

By 2025, FE colleges and universities serving their local communities may be thriving, as both the climate emergency preferences around travel and pandemic travel restrictions may still be encouraging more local decisions for education and lifestyle. Universities will have established more certainty over numbers of foreign students attending, following the 15 years before the pandemic when the numbers of international students from China have tripled whilst all others have remained relatively stable.

In mid-2020 it was predicted that the cash lost to universities as a result of the pandemic could be up to 20%, leading some – including a number of Russell Group universities – to be in severe financial difficulty.

Student numbers are now very important to the local economy of many university towns. The Sheffield Central parliamentary constituency has the largest number of students in the UK at around 60,000; Bath's two universities host 21,000 students, one-quarter of the city's population; whilst 9,000 students in Aberdeen make up one-third of the population. The relationships between towns and colleges will become stronger over the coming years, as their interdependences become more clearly articulated and their mutual support increases. Designers should develop strong communication tools to help enable institutions to engage meaningfully with local communities and politicians, and continue early planning authority discussions so initiatives are seen in the full context of local development.

Mobility

The location of residences and academic and social facilities will influence the significance of mobility solutions at each college. There will be increasing demand for zero-carbon, safe and healthy transport solutions with increased cycle facilities, pedestrian routes and electric charging points. The immediate health priority will start to influence decisions taken by prospective students relating to the location of the college chosen and its distance from housing. FE colleges, which already tend to have students pursuing courses who live nearer than at a university, could stand to benefit from this concern, while the proximity of student residences to a campus will become a more significant factor in student choice when moving further afield.

The increasing availability of lower-carbon-impact personal transport options will counteract this trend, but there will be challenges to restrict or provide new parking facilities as the ability to travel by electric cars, scooters and bikes increases. The increased interest in vehicle-sharing clubs to those concerned to consume less in order to reduce their personal carbon impacts will be set back by concerns over transmission of the virus.

Equality, health and wellbeing

Greater equality of access for all, including the elderly and less privileged members of society will be reflected in more considered project briefing, in order to establish accessible environments which do not discriminate. Access to IT equipment at home is known to be a significant barrier. Those living in homes with limited IT access will struggle to get to university in the first place due to lack of distance-learning possibilities.

Linked to the community engagement agenda and health and wellbeing, colleges and universities will be at the forefront in developing new models for consultation and occupancy evaluation to ensure their estates are fully supporting their educational access agendas. The social inclusion agenda must prioritise space and facilities for students requiring access to computers and desks, who may not have these at home. Grants to support homeworking should be considered, and mental health issues closely supported to reduce impacts from isolation and stress, which were already a significant issue on campuses.

Contact with nature / opportunity to embrace biophilic design

The increasing interest in health and the benefits of landscape and biodiversity as a result of the pandemic will translate into greater consideration of, and funding allocation for, landscape. In settings where there may be funding for renovation and adaptation of existing buildings, the main visible investment made could become the public realm and landscape around them.

Carbon

Architects are well placed to lead estates teams towards the portfolio of measures that will have maximum benefit quickly.

Because air-quality health fears will increase the demand for improved ventilation, many spaces could increase the use of mechanical ventilation, leading to a rise in energy use, whilst other areas become more passively controlled, and naturally ventilated and lit. Internal target temperatures in winter might need to be pushed lower, but better clothing, and access to views and landscape, compensate. Design for well-ventilated open-plan teaching delivery using digitally enabled models could become the norm, and exceptional pandemic events will be dealt with using better-planned contingency measures.

The carbon issue, on the other hand, is more fundamental and known. The climate emergency demands very prompt action and

Figure 7.8 Verandah Walk at James Cook University, Townsville, Queensland, Australia, by Wilson Architects, completed in 2017. This scheme joins existing buildings across the campus, creating a curved walkway with a cantilevered roof directing attention to the landscape and the library. Four pavilions extend out from the path and operate as connected outdoor learning spaces. Nearby fountains create a cooling effect and atmospheric background noise.

change. Standards and expectations need to be challenged to deliver lower operational carbon performance, and architects must develop the knowledge of embodied carbon in order to be able to advise colleges of the best routes to lowering their impacts over the next decade and support them in ambitions towards carbon neutrality as soon after 2030 as possible.

New Design Values in Tertiary Education

The new client values – economy, adaptability, carbon neutrality, health, equality, wellbeing and biophilic/regenerative design – will start to become the key drivers for innovation in the HE and FE sector. The Extinction Rebellion school generation will start to choose their places of study and living based on more sophisticated expectations for their environment, whilst the thought-leading academic institutions will want to demonstrate their commitment to tackling the climate emergency. Architects, engineers and contractors will be expected to rise to this challenge, and will need to have the skills and tools to effectively provide solutions to the problems set out.

Architects must acknowledge the problems faced by the sector and recognise both the short-term priorities and longer-term goals of their sector clients. One of the greatest challenges is planning for change.

In April 2020 the worst-case financial impact scenarios for UK universities envisaged a 75% drop in foreign students and a 20% drop in UK students.[6] By mid-August universities and colleges were facing potential growth in UK student numbers as a result of the exam results fiasco. It is absolutely clear that the adaptability of the estate is paramount. The potential continuing risks from the pandemic need to be addressed to offer safe, healthy environments for study and research in the offer to encourage movement and adventurousness of students and academics to pursue their interests.

If architects can rise to the occasion and engage with HE and FE clients to help establish economic and healthy occupation of their estates, and support them in practical ways to maximise the benefits of their existing buildings and external spaces, they can start to engage again in how best these estates should most naturally develop over time. In the light of the climate emergency there must now be a presumption in building retention and renovation before demolition and replacement, unless carbon accounting studies and functional inadequacy demonstrate otherwise.

With intelligent briefing that sees the opportunities in prioritising healthy adaptable spaces and maximising the use of existing assets, good design can be levered to address the symbiotic requirements of our health and that of the planet. The universities and colleges should take the lead and demonstrate what is possible – for it will be good for their own survival as well as the communities they serve.

6 P. Dolton, 'The COVID-19 Pandemic Is Causing a Crisis in the UK Universities', *Vox*, 31 May 2020, https://voxeu.org/article/covid-19-pandemic-causing-crisis-uk-universities.

CHAPTER 8

INFRASTRUCTURE AND PLACEMAKING

SARAH FEATHERSTONE

SARAH FEATHERSTONE

Sarah is an architect and director of Featherstone Young, and a member of VeloCity, an all-female, multidisciplinary team, presenting a strategic vision that looks at how we can grow villages differently, by disincentivising car use and making radical change to planning policies. The team also includes: strategist Kay Hughes of Khaa; architect Petra Marko of Marko&Placemakers; architect Annalie Riches of Mikhail Riches; planner Jennifer Ross of Tibbalds Planning and Urban Design; and engineer Judith Sykes of Expedition Engineering.

Introduction: Gentle Radicalism – New Approaches to Growth in the Countryside

Increasingly the housing crisis in the UK is placing huge pressure to build in the countryside but with solutions that only concentrate on urban centres and new developments along roads. We see many smaller village settlements struggling to survive with the loss of community facilities, an increasingly ageing population, a lack of housing diversity and a 'NIMBYism' approach to any new development. Growth in villages has been constrained and little thinking has been given to how we support and reinvigorate them. As land is running out around towns, we need to radically change planning policies and behavioural patterns to bring about bold and progressive strategies that plan for the future of the countryside and create sustainable places supported by new movement infrastructure.

The ideas VeloCity, an all-women team of industry experts, has been developing over the past few years look at one way to tackle some of these issues and our focus has been to work with existing villages. They are rural settlements that already have a strong sense of place and by linking them as clusters through a fine-grain network of cycling and walking routes, they can collectively grow and support the community facilities they have lost and be less reliant on the car.

The VeloCity proposition sits within a wider context of initiatives both historical and current, located in the UK and internationally, that put into practice what good growth can look like and the social, environmental and economic benefits it embraces. Several of these are referred to in this chapter which, by collectively bringing together different initiatives, puts across a strong case for new approaches to deliver innovative and sustainable movement and placemaking in the countryside.

Now more than ever there is an appetite for change. Whilst the COVID-19 pandemic has brought great tragedy and highlighted huge social inequalities, arguably the climate emergency has a far more devastating long-term impact. More positively, the pandemic has given us the opportunity to see that the kind of radical change we need to save the planet is feasible. Less aviation, less car use, less commuting, less pollution, more working from home, more sustainable transport, more localism, more responsible agriculture, are all beneficial to our environment. It has also shown that significant behavioural and societal change can happen – and happen quickly.

It has demonstrated there is an appetite for change, but to bring this forward we need time to slow down and evolve a long-term strategy to rethink how we can do things differently. Within our industry there is a sense of caution to the government's recent post-COVID-19 strategies: Project Speed and Build Build Build. To put in place greener, slower travel and more sustainable building models people will also need to think more collectively. Naomi Klein captured this when she spoke about the importance of slowing down and the 'empathy' and 'softness' the pandemic has elicited in people.[1]

With transport infrastructure traditionally leading on many new developments, there is often little joined-up thinking with placemaking and how they can collectively form cohesive communities. This chapter makes a deliberate shift from urban-centric strategies to ones that tackle issues in the countryside – particularly rural settlements which for many are dispersed, disconnected and isolated and where people's daily journeys are wholly car-dependent. In the words of Sadie Morgan of the National Infrastructure Commission:

> As a country, we are moving into a decade where many big infrastructure and housing projects are being delivered. It will be design that defines the legacy they leave behind. We must make sure that our housing and infrastructure adds to the life of our cities and countryside, that it is fit for purpose, designed for the needs of all, is not wasteful of the world's resources and most importantly stands the test of time.
>
> VeloCity focuses on the very real issues facing our rural communities. It develops a vision of sustainable growth that is sympathetic to its environment, innovative and forward thinking. It shows the importance of connecting joined up strategic thinking with the people and places on the ground. I very much hope that this vision is the beginning of a cultural change; an acceptance of the need to deliver for the future generations in a way that respects our past.[2]

1 Naomi Klein interview with Katharine Viner, *The Guardian*, 13 July 2020, https://www.theguardian.com/books/2020/jul/13/naomi-klein-we-must-not-return-to-the-pre-covid-status-quo-only-worse.

2 Foreword to the VeloCity Manifesto: *Growing Villages Differently*, 2020, pp 6–7, https://velocity651476576.files.wordpress.com/2020/05/velocity_manifesto_may2020.pdf.

Figure 8.1 VeloCity: growing villages differently.

Emerging opportunities in a post-COVID-19 world

So where do we go from here?

It is now quite clear that we all need to think and live differently and embrace more radical thinking in order to achieve the paradigm shifts necessary to sustain the environment. If there is anything positive coming from this virus, it is the opportunity to see that this kind of radical change is possible and is already starting to be played out. This chapter introduces a number of emerging opportunities which align with the five principles set out in the VeloCity manifesto:

- **Opportunity over decline** – providing new places to live and work
- **People over cars** – creating more sustainable movement networks
- **Compact not sprawl** – keeping the special character of our countryside
- **Resilient not fragile** – promoting sustainable environments, health and wellbeing
- **Connected not isolated** – linking communities with shared resources to benefit all.

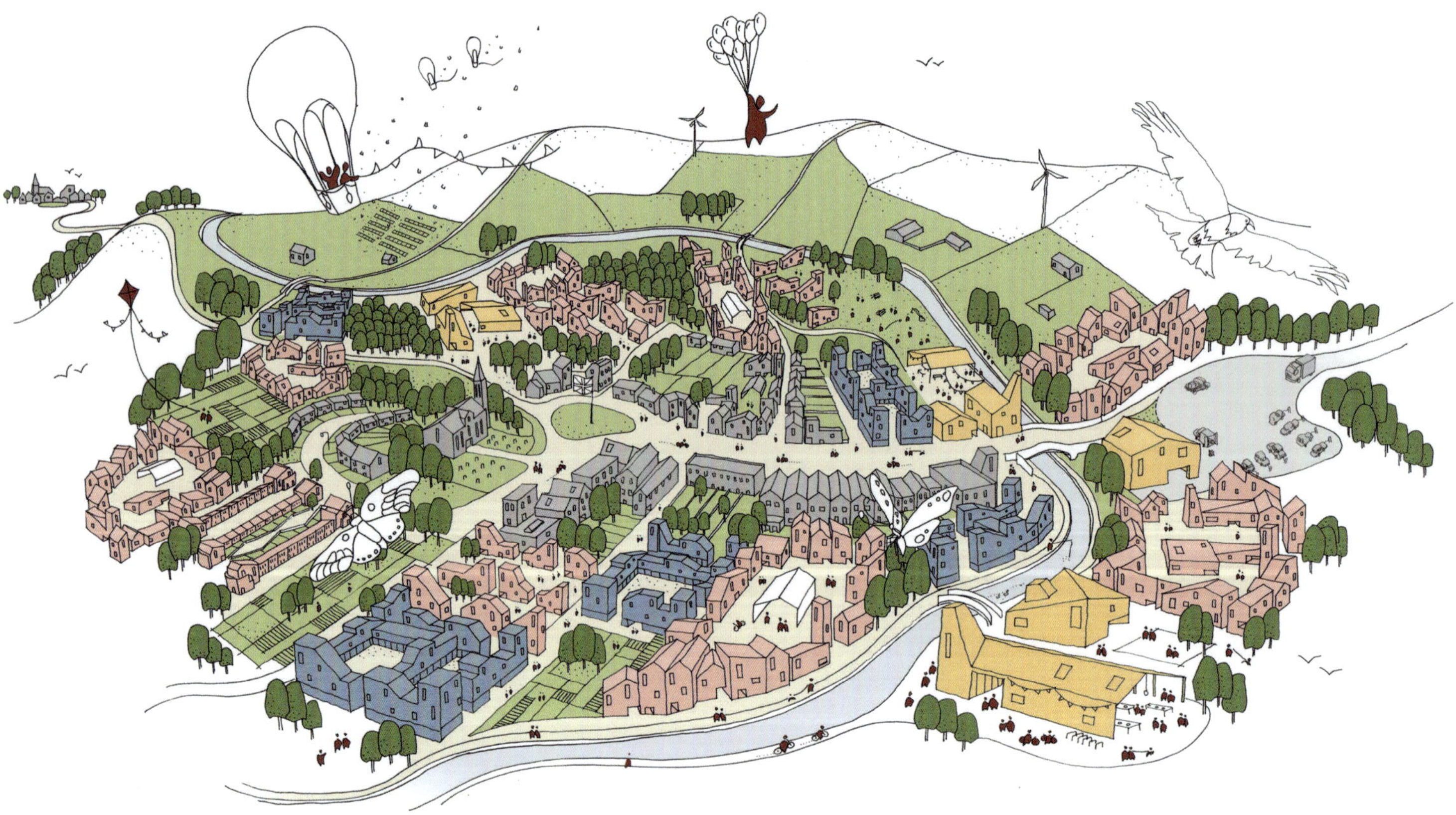

Figure 8.2 VeloCity: reimagined village.

Opportunity over Decline – Providing New Places to Live and Work

Why the countryside?

There are hundreds and thousands of villages proliferating in our countryside that have a strong sense of place, yet we see village life dying. Often some of the most desirable and protected places in the UK, villages are also at the same time seeing significant poverty, lack of jobs, ageing populations and housing stock, lack of investment, lack of accessibility, lack of housing diversity and a NIMBYism approach to any new development. Yet the village and village life has much to offer people in terms of community, access to the countryside and quality of life, and this is where we should focus our attention – reinvigorating villages so they can thrive again and become more sustainable places.

With the countryside making up 85% of the UK land area but only 18% of the population living there, the pressure to build new homes in rural areas is increasing, but with solutions that largely concentrate on urban centres and new developments along roads. Growth within smaller settlements is constrained and little thinking has been given to how we support and reinvigorate them.

A 2008 study by *The Observer* and the Commission for Rural Communities identified scores of small communities in decline and in so doing confirmed that, 'Across the country: 95 per cent of village halls are struggling to stay open, 27 village pubs are closing a week, 800 village shops are shutting each year, 400 garages and filling stations are closing each year, 100+ churches of all denominations are closing each year, 7 rural schools are shutting annually, 90 cottage hospitals are under threat.'[3]

The opportunity to advance a more place-based strategy for development in the countryside is already in the making.

There are over 10,000 villages in England, set only 2–3 miles apart, and they offer an opportunity to advance a strategy which can alleviate housing pressure on the towns and turn villages into well-connected places for 21st-century living.

In simple terms it is about integrating with what is already there and tapping into the sense of place.

The VeloCity concept grows existing villages as a cluster, with new homes built to a higher density within each village so as to reach an optimum size that supports and brings back the local shop, pubs and schools they have lost. It is also a strategy that puts a stop to the current development we see happening in villages: small-scale, low-density sprawl that follows roads out of villages, forming hard edges with the existing community and surrounding countryside. These forms of development mimic approaches to town and suburban housing developments which are seemingly at odds with the character of a village and with time see villages conjoining and losing their individual identity.

3 A. Hill, 'How Our Villages Are Fighting to Stay Alive', *The Observer*, 14 September 2008, https://www.theguardian.com/uk/2008/sep/14/ruralaffairs.britishidentity.

The potential to unlock land for more new housing within villages offers a more sustainable alternative which keeps villages distinct and walkable and protects the surrounding countryside; but in order to implement this, planning and transport policies must be turned on their head. We need to demonstrate that what are currently seen as unsuitable locations can actually accommodate future growth. This is not only a matter of lifting policies protecting heritage and environmental locations; it is also about reviewing policies on site allocation. Here we have a chicken-and-egg scenario: potential sites for new housing in rural areas is based on a village having good existing services and transport links, which means many smaller villages are deemed unsuitable for new housing and consequently remain unsustainable.

Who owns the land poses further challenges to any large-scale legislative changes needed to develop rural areas differently. Guy Shrubsole in his 2019 book *Who Owns England?* states that 50% of England is currently owned by less than 1% of the population and that this is largely made up of wealthy landowners, 'the aristocracy and landed gentry'.[4] Today how this land is managed has a huge impact on the affordability of housing, the way we grow our food and how much space we set aside for nature.

Historically the countryside has been a backdrop to conflict and political uprisings – feudalism, class divide, land rights, economic depression and two world wars – which have seen philanthropists, industrialists, idealists, radicals and revolutionaries all experiment with better ways of rural living, with utopian visions ranging from new model villages to farm colonies to current-day garden villages. These models demonstrate that at specific moments in time, visionary thinking can bring about radical changes in the countryside. Post COVID-19 is one of those moments and an opportunity to rethink the way we manage and distribute land to tackle our housing crisis and protect the earth's resources. Building new towns and villages in the open countryside can't be the only way, and releasing land within existing settlements at land values that can sustain truly affordable homes, work and community facilities has got to be the way forward.

During the pandemic we have seen calls to the government from the likes of CPRE, the countryside charity and Shelter to put in place mechanisms that reduce high land values and provide more affordable housing, and these calls reflect the urgency of where and what kind of new housing should be built. The national audit conducted by University College London for CPRE and published in January 2020 found that most new housing is so poorly designed it should not have been built and that design outcomes scored progressively worse as projects moved away from urban cores, reduced in density and were built on greenfield as opposed to brownfield sites.[5] It follows that such unsuitable sites located away

4 R. Evans, 'Half Of England Is Owned By Less Than 1% Of The Population', *The Guardian*, 17 April 2019, https://www.theguardian.com/money/2019/apr/17/who-owns-england-thousand-secret-landowners-author.

5 Place Alliance, *A Housing Design Audit for England*, January 2020, https://www.cpre.org.uk/resources/housing-design-audit-2020/.

from community facilities also lead to more car-reliant transportation, which in the case of people living in affordable housing is likely to be a luxury they can't afford. This is echoed by the BBC report on Transport for New Homes that found young couples are 'trapped in car dependency'.[6]

So if we can build more compact, light-footed homes within villages, not outside, we not only have an opportunity to create healthier and more socially cohesive villages but also to retain their quintessentially picturesque qualities. The *Living with Beauty* report by the Building Better, Building Beautiful Commission (BBBBC), launched in February 2020, refers to higher densities as 'gentle density', which in this case aims to respect and build on the traditional village character, and place emphasis on movement by people rather than the car.[7]

Gentle densification in the countryside can also protect undeveloped open land between villages and allow it to be sensitively used as a shared resource for community-run food production, amenity space, local energy generation and enhanced ecology.

Shifting minds

For many, the British village still evokes a romanticism which has endured to the present day with popular representations such as BBC Radio 4's *The Archers* and the CPRE's 'best kept village' competitions. However, such examples of popular culture also acknowledge the pressing issues facing our villages and people's growing concerns of how to tackle them. BBC1's *Countryfile* regularly gives exposure to the social, employment, mental and physical isolation facing rural communities, and *The Archers* has seen the villagers fighting to save their local shop and farmers. Employment trends before the virus already saw a move towards flexible working with 14% of the UK workforce comprising homeworkers, increasing to 22% in rural areas.[8] This is now accelerating and will almost certainly help invigorate villages, creating a need for new places to live, work and share resources.

To turn minds and gain support of local communities the potential benefits must be communicated well, and people must feel they have a proper stake in future development of their places. The Localism Act of 2011 goes some way to giving people a greater say on local decisions and where housing should be built in their communities. Work undertaken by Hana Loftus of Public Practice, recounted in her paper *Growing Villages*, explores the frustrations and rewards localism offers to village communities in the South Cambridgeshire district.[9] Interestingly she has found that people are not against development in their villages per se and that many people recognise villages need more

6 R. Harrabin, 'Young Couples "Trapped in Car Dependency"', BBC News website, 24 October 2018, https://www.bbc.com/news/science-environment-45956792.

7 Building Better, Building Beautiful Commission, *Living With Beauty: Promoting Health, Well-being and Sustainable Growth*, January 2020, https://assets.publishing.service.gov.uk/government/uploads/system/uploads/attachment_data/file/861832/Living_with_beauty_BBBBC_report.pdf.

8 UK Government, 'Home Working', May 2019, https://assets.publishing.service.gov.uk/government/uploads/system/uploads/attachment_data/file/805021/Home_Working_Final_May_2019.pdf.

9 H. Loftus, *Growing Villages: How Should Village Growth Be Shaped in Rural Areas?*, London: Public Practice, May 2019, https://www.publicpractice.org.uk/resources/growing-villages.

housing to renew and sustain village life. From this research it seems what is important to them is a more collaborative process and its aesthetic quality.

This is perhaps what was missed in the BBC2 programme *The New Builds Are Coming*, where the planner and developer are pitted against the local community with their plans to build 500 new homes on the edge of their Oxfordshire village.[10] Here, what was on offer by the developer was suburban-style housing bolted on to one side of the village with no regard to integration with the existing community. What was missing was any dialogue or appreciation that there could be alternative and better ways of doing this.

Landed estates can lead the way

Who owns the land plays a significant role in how the countryside evolves and as already mentioned, a large proportion of the UK is owned by big landed estates whose actions over hundreds of years have shaped the landscape and lives of people living there. Whilst some owners have failed to protect the environment and the interests of the wider community, others have looked to do things differently. The rewilding scheme at the Knepp Estate in Sussex, and the 2,000-acre organic farm at Sheepdrove on the Kindersley Estate in Berkshire, are good examples of this.

Blenheim Estate in West Oxfordshire is another (see Figure 8.3). The VeloCity team were fortunate to be introduced to representatives from the Estate, who own 12,0000 acres of land comprising a stately home, parkland, a working farm and much land within and around several villages on its fringes. As a large landed estate, a holder of local property and a large employer they are deeply rooted to the area and recognise their responsibility to those who live and work in and around Blenheim today but also to those who will follow in future generations. VeloCity's vision chimed with their rethinking and ambition to create better-connected communities, and more responsible housing that disincentivises car use, has a low carbon footprint and values the land's natural capital.

A number of the villages around the Blenheim Estate are poorly connected and suffer from various intractable issues already discussed in this section – an ageing population, high house prices, a lack of and declining levels of services, high levels of congestion and a lack of accessibility to alternative, more sustainable modes of transport.

Based on this context VeloCity developed a strategy with Blenheim that takes a more joined-up look at the estate and the surrounding villages (see Figure 8.4). Having walked and cycled the estate and consulted with key stakeholders, we were able to explore in detail all aspects of village life. This built up an initial picture of the various barriers and opportunities facing the area, culminating in a sketchbook of ideas and strategies that present a roadmap to build out over a 20-year plan.

10 *The New Builds Are Coming*, directed by Richard Macer, two episodes, first broadcast on BBC2, 31 January and 7 February 2018.

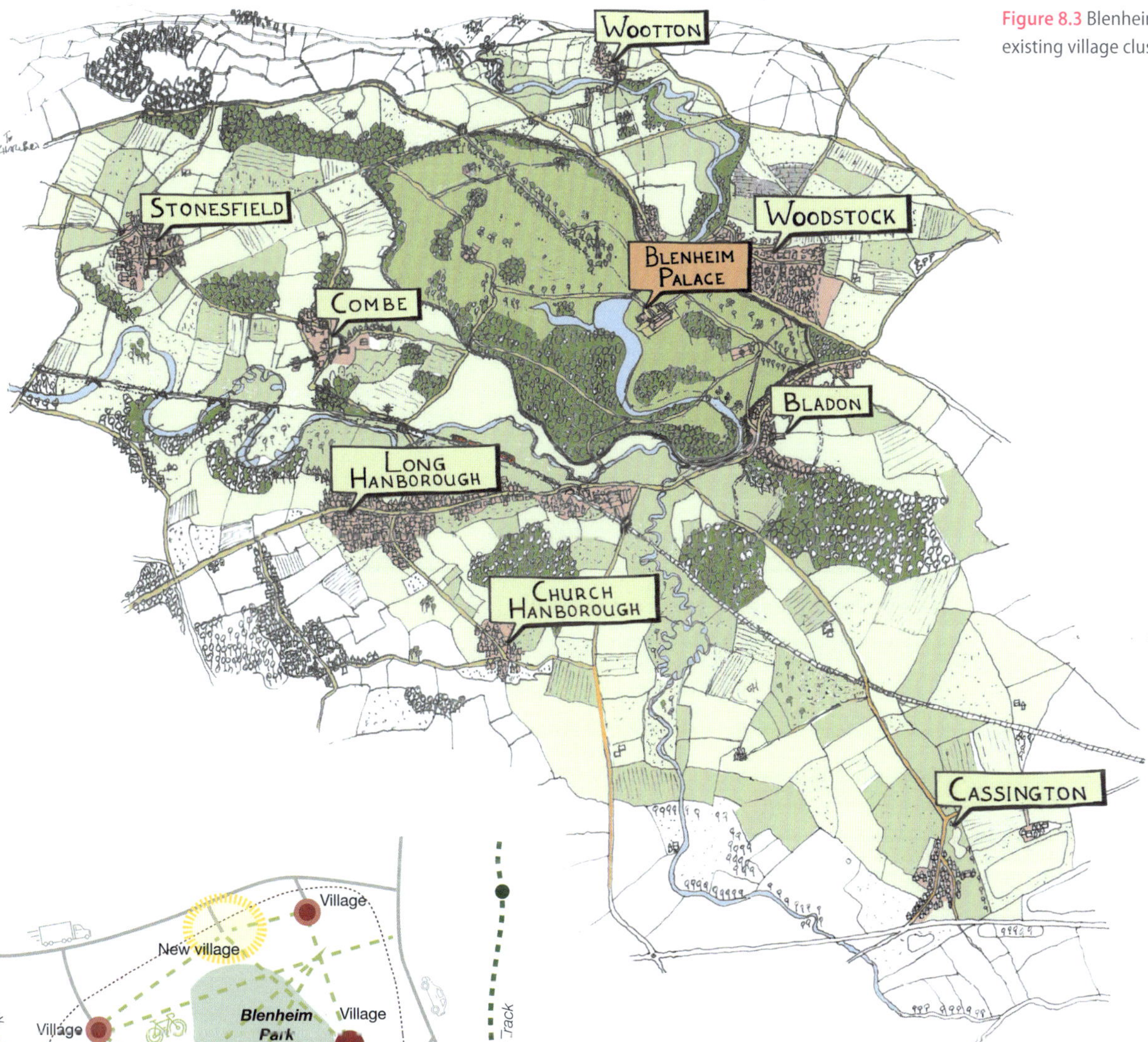

Figure 8.3 Blenheim existing village cluster.

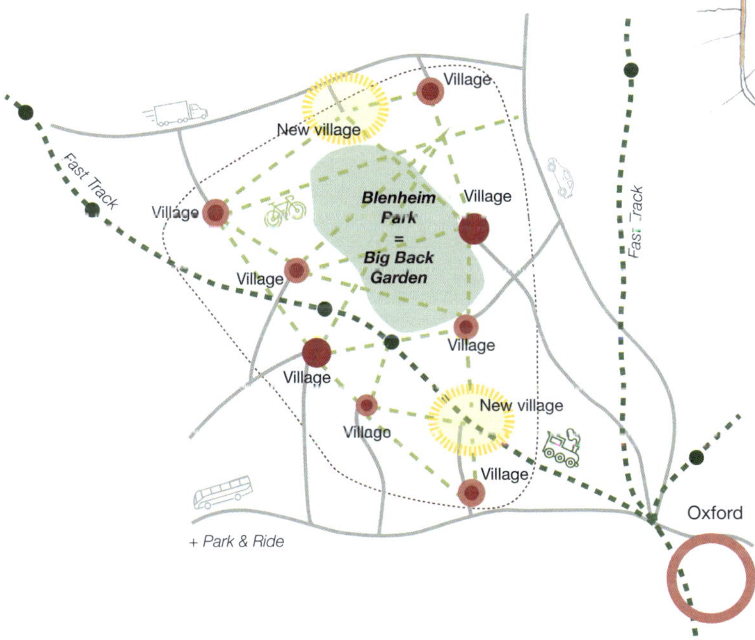

Figure 8.4 Diagram showing VeloCity's vision for the Blenheim village cluster.

The strategy enables the Estate and villages to work and operate together to deliver a thriving cluster of all eight villages with realistic alternatives to movement by car. Short-term initiatives see bridleways across the estate trialled as new cycle routes, providing more direct connection between villages so that local journeys to school, work, shops and train station are made quicker and safer. These can then develop into an integrated network of cycle and walking routes combined with transport sharing options and local delivery initiatives using electric vehicles that will reduce movements in HGV traffic, promote new community work hubs, deliver alternative approaches to planning, provide new affordable housing that sits within villages and bring forward new approaches to farming practice, food production and land management.

The delivery of this all-encompassing future growth strategy will be led by Blenheim Estates as landowner, developer and long-term steward of the land, putting them in a position to lead the way and have wider influence on other landed estates. However, delivery will depend on partnering with not only a multiplicity of local stakeholders and communities living and working in the area, but also the public sector which can help fund more sustainable farming practices and environmental measures as well as invest in alternative transport modes and facilitate the reversal of high land values and planning policies which currently place huge constraints on growth in the countryside.

People over Cars – Creating more Sustainable Movement Networks

One of the greatest challenges facing both countryside and urban areas is climate change, and our ever-increasing reliance on car travel is a big contributor.

Vehicles contribute to 80% of air pollution breaches and 34% of greenhouse gas emissions.[11] In their *National Infrastructure Assessment*, the National Infrastructure Commission is urging the government to speed up its preparations for electric and autonomous vehicles.[12]

The COVID-19 lockdown has seen a significant decrease in car use and air travel. People are walking and cycling more as part of their daily routine, providing huge physical and mental health benefits. Less air and car travel improves air quality: Stanford University has calculated that the reduction in air pollution in China caused by the current economic disruption has saved approximately 20 times more lives there than have been lost due to the infection.[13] That's an incredible statistic and will see many more people wanting to move from cities to the countryside for better air quality. Furthermore, Cycling UK has found that if

11 M. Taylor and S. Laville, 'Revealed: Thousands of Children at London Schools Breathe Toxic Air', *The Guardian*, 24 February 2017, https://www.theguardian.com/uk-news/2017/feb/24/revealed-thousands-of-children-toxic-air-london-nitrogen-dioxide.

12 National Infrastructure Commission, *National Infrastructure Assessment*, 10 July 2018, https://nic.org.uk/studies-reports/national-infrastructure-assessment/.

13 I. Kottasová, 'China's Coronavirus Lockdown Curbs Deadly Pollution, Likely Saving the Lives of Tens of Thousands, Says Researcher', CNN Health website, 17 March 2020, https://www.cnn.com/2020/03/17/health/china-air-pollution-coronavirus-deaths-intl/index.html.

cycling increased to 25% of annual journeys by 2050, it could yield a cumulative annual benefit of £42 billion.[14]

Well before the COVID-19 pandemic there was ample evidence that more cycling and walking benefits our health and improves social ties and the local economy. Research by the European Cyclists' Federation (ECF) found that already at current levels in Europe 'cycling produces global benefits of 150 billion euros per year', in contrast to the negative impact of motorised road transport estimated at €800 billion per year in a recent study by European Commission.[15]

Furthermore Sustrans, the ECF and the Union Cycliste Internationale (UCI) have done a lot of work around the benefits of pursuing a cycle/pedestrian-led strategy which makes compelling reading.[16]

Summarised below are some of the key highlights found in a number of reports:

- The US study *A Global High Shift Cycling Scenario* shows that cycling can have a substantial positive impact on the world's future, saving nearly $6 trillion globally over the next 15 years and dramatically improving quality of life. Benefits also include a reduction in urban transport CO_2 emissions by about 7% compared to business as usual, rising to more than 10% reduction by 2050.[17]
- The results of a survey by the British Chambers of Commerce put the annual cost of congestion at £17,350 per business, or over £23 billion for British businesses as a whole.[18]
- The NHS recommends 150 minutes of moderate physical activity per week. This works out as 30 minutes per weekday: for example, cycling about 7 miles or walking 1.6 miles.[19] Research by Sustrans in their 2013 report *Increasing Business through Sustainable Travel* suggests that workers using the cycle network, compared to the average worker, take approximately half the number of days off, resulting in a £13.7 billion annual boost to the British economy.
- Work also undertaken by Sustrans confirms that smaller-scale projects and investment in sustainable transport create more jobs per pound invested than road construction and thus present very good value for money.[20]
- In terms of jobs, there is a lot of evidence to show that continued reduction of car use through improving sustainable transport infrastructure provides more jobs than it destroys.[21]

14 British Cycling, 'It's Time to Choose Cycling', 16 May 2020, https://www.britishcycling.org.uk/campaigning/article/20200516-campaigning-news-14-million-ready-to--ChooseCycling-in-biggest-transport-revolution-for-a-generation-0.

15 European Cyclists' Federation, *The Benefits of Cycling: Unlocking Their Potential for Europe*, December 2018, https://ecf.com/sites/ecf.com/files/TheBenefitsOfCycling2018.pdf.

16 European Cyclists' Federation, *The Benefits of Cycling*.

17 Institute for Transportation & Development Policy and the University of California, Davis, *A Global High Shift Cycling Scenario*, 12 November 2015, https://www.itdp.org/2015/11/12/a-global-high-shift-cycling-scenario/

18 British Chambers of Commerce, *The Congestion Question: A Business Transport Survey*, 2008.

19 'Exercise', NHS website, https://www.nhs.uk/live-well/exercise/.

20 Sustrans, *Active Travel and Economic Performance: A 'What Works' Review of Evidence from Cycling and Walking Schemes*, 2017, https://www.sustrans.org.uk/media/4472/4472.pdf.

21 Sustrans, *Active Travel and Economic Performance*.

To reinvigorate villages one of the key issues we need to tackle is recalibrating the movement network and making people in the countryside less reliant on cars. For commuters, folding bikes and electric scooters make multimodal travel easy and convenient. Options for the school run include the bike bus and bikes with facilities to carry children, and a good option for last-mile journeys is the use of electric buggies and electric vehicles which can also serve for local waste collection and deliveries.

We are behind the curve

Many cities and governments elsewhere in the world are making ambitious plans to transform the way people move and connect with each other. Paris's '15-minute city' is a concept proposed by scientist Carlos Moreno, inspired by the work of activist and urban theorist Jane Jacobs, and has been recently implemented in the French capital by its female mayor Anne Hidalgo. It advocates self-supporting neighbourhoods created by people walking and cycling no more than 15 minutes to get to school or work, and addresses issues of climate change, car pollution and quality of life. Other cities have followed, with Milan being one of the first in Europe to introduce a forward-thinking scheme in response to the COVID-19 crisis, reallocating street space from cars to cycling and walking. Milan is a small, dense city, 15km from end to end, with only 1.4 million inhabitants, 55% of whom use public transport to get to work and with an average commute of less than 4km,[22] making a switch from cars to active modes of travel potentially possible for many residents.

What we found out elsewhere

With research funds secured from RIBA and the William Sutton Prize from the Clarion Housing Group, VeloCity has been able to make study trips to a number of places where cycling and walking predominate. One trip was to Copenhagen where we met with Gehl Architects' Andreas Røhl and Lærke Jul Gagner. Their practice's pioneering approach to pedestrianising spaces and moving cycling and walking to the top of the movement chain stems from Jan Gehl's focus on human interactions – an early influence in his architecture career from his psychologist wife Ingrid Mundt.

Andreas, who was formerly director of the bicycle programme at the City of Copenhagen, outlined some of the incentives that could help recalibrate the movement chain, including reduced tax if you cycle, good integration with public transport, making cars less attractive by locating parking further out, safety (especially for women and children), consistency of rules and a range of associated services. Cycling needs to work not only for the sports fanatics and early adopters, but also for people of all ages and capabilities. 'Happiness', both said, was important, and not surprisingly Denmark consistently ranks at the top of the world's happiness index.

22 L. Laker, 'Milan Announces Ambitious Scheme to Reduce Car Use After Lockdown', *The Guardian*, 21 April 2020, https://www.theguardian.com/world/2020/apr/21/milan-seeks-to-prevent-post-crisis-return-of-traffic-pollution.

Figure 8.5 The VeloCity team exploring the Byhusene car-free housing project in Copenhagen, by Vandkunsten Architects, completed in 2016.

Drawing back to how we could reinvigorate villages through a slower-speed infrastructure, we discussed what is unique about the English countryside – what elements make people perceive it as charming and picturesque. Alongside the church, cottages and farm buildings, the pub was seen by our hosts as one of the most defining features. A place of refuge, an extended living room where the community meets, a shared platform.

We went on to visit the classic 'Potato Rows' – terraced houses built in the 1870s by the first workers' housing association to provide healthy and cheap homes following the cholera epidemic. Recently the residents' association won a battle to stop them being flattened for a motorway, and today the streets between the Potato Rows are shared-surface 'home zones'. Whilst not entirely car-free, they do prioritise pedestrians and cyclists and allow life to unfold beyond the houses' front porches.

The 'potato row' model has been an inspiration for several new housing schemes in Copenhagen, including the Byhusene project – 110 houses by Vandkunsten Architects in the new Islands Brygge neighbourhood, completed in 2016 (see Figure 8.5). Here the houses are more compact and rather than have large private gardens and front-of-house car parking, space is given up for shared streets, free from cars entirely, and a shared 'commons' – a green space in the immediate vicinity which supports this communal living model. We experienced the success of the shared streets first hand, observing numerous toddler ride-ons scattered around freely. One porch had an integrated blackboard forming a little outdoor classroom. There were no fences around front gardens and the transition from public to semi-private space was achieved through subtle changes of surface from paving to gravel, lawn and planting. For us, whilst in an urban context, Byhusene is an inspirational car-free neighbourhood that makes cycling and walking the easy choice and offers the opportunity for social networks to grow and evolve.

As a result of the COVID-19 pandemic, the UK government has made some significant changes to encourage more cycling and walking. During lockdown they introduced a £250 million emergency travel fund to encourage people to adopt a more active travel plan – walking and cycling – if they can't work from home. This has brought forward positive measures for pedestrians and cyclists, with pop-up bike lanes, wider pavements and safer junctions. In July a further investment was made with the government kick-starting a £2 billion cycling and walking initiative, Gear Change, that sets out a comprehensive, long-term vision to increase active travel.

With more people cycling and spending time outside, there has been greater support for all sorts of small-scale enterprises including the resurgence of bike co-ops and repair shops helped by the government's release of £50 bike-repair vouchers. Just being outside enjoying the fresher air has allowed us to imagine how much better life would be without the car. 'Let's turn car parks into nature parks. Car parks into bike hire docking stations. Car parks into community farms and allotments. Car parks into mini-forests, to let cities breathe' read a mid-2020 tweet from environmentalist Guy Shrubsole in response to a survey commissioned by the Ministry of Housing, Communities and Local Government that indicates there are a staggering 50,000 acres of car parks in England which have the potential to be used for housing and, who knows, maybe other uses too.

Embedding the benefits of walking and cycling into how we go about our daily lives has got to be a good thing, and with the impact of COVID-19 bringing more initiatives forward, it would be good to see these being directed not just to cities but also to the countryside.

Compact not Sprawl – Keeping the Special Character of our Countryside

In the UK we identified and visited a number of rural or semi-rural places where housing was either more compact and/or included car-free initiatives and approaches that involved communities in the decision-making.

The remote, picturesque village of Dent in the Yorkshire Dales was a particular stand-out (see Figure 8.6). Set high up in a valley, it has narrow cobbled streets with small terraced workers' cottages, many of which are listed, and provide for a predominantly farming community but with a growing seasonal tourist economy. It has its own train station (highest mainline station in England) on the Settle–Carlisle line, located further up the valley 7km away at Cowgill, and unbeknown to us was visited by Ian Nairn in the 1970s as part of his BBC series *Across Britain*. In his programme he applauds the same qualities that we witnessed when there – a very dense compact village with a strong village community, and cars parked outside the village. Apparently the villagers themselves were so keen to keep the village

Figure 8.6 Dent, a picturesque village in the Yorkshire Dales.

WELCOME TO MARMALADE
NO THROUGH
ROAD

Figure 8.7 Marmalade Lane, Cambridge: a car-free street.

car-free that they built a Grasscrete® field for car parking on the edge of the village that blends with the surrounding landscape – now that's community spirit for you! What is also interesting about Dent is that its built density is very high yet people consider it to be a most charming and picturesque place, which attracts many visitors during the tourist seasons.

We went on to include a number of other visits – notably to Marmalade Lane on the edge of Cambridge (by Mole Architects, completed in 2018; see Figure 8.7), which had similar shared streets and common spaces to those found at Byhusene, and to Poundbury in Dorset (by Léon Krier, built from 1983 onwards) with its large green open spaces deliberately located on the edges in order to make its centre more compact and walkable.

In the words of the BBBBC, 'a beautiful place is a place in which people wish to walk, rather than a place that the car helps them to avoid',[23] and it seems clear from this research that cycling and walking as the mainstream form of movement can shape the way places are planned and the way people communicate and relate to one another. Their report goes on to make recommendations to the government as to what makes a good 'place', and one of these is the need for more skilled teams and innovators within local authorities to help put design and placemaking at the heart of the process and bring communities together to combat NIMBYism.

Now more than ever we need to be light-footed and agile when creating new homes. Fears that high-density living has helped spread the virus can't be a reason to avoid densification – far bigger threats such as population growth have contributed to this pandemic. Low-density sprawl is particularly prevalent in rural areas, and if we are to keep villages as distinct places and respond to environmental pressures, we need to stop this kind of growth and give land back to the open countryside, making it accessible to all.

Shrubsole's wishlist of what we could do if more land was freed up included allotments. During COVID-19 many more people have signed up for these and, according to recent data from the Association of Public Sector Excellence, the average waiting time has hugely increased, with up to 18-month waiting lists for over 400 people in some areas.[24] This fuels the mounting calls for the release of more land for public use. With the government, the Ministry of Defence, the Church of England and others all owning vast swathes of land, more could be done to open up the countryside.

23 Building Better, Building Beautiful Commission, *Living With Beauty: Promoting Health, Well-being and Sustainable Growth*, January 2020, p 11, https://assets.publishing.service.gov.uk/government/uploads/system/uploads/attachment_data/file/861832/Living_with_beauty_BBBBC_report.pdf

24 R. Smithers, 'Interest in Allotments Soars in England During Coronavirus Pandemic', *The Guardian*, 10 August 2020, https://www.theguardian.com/lifeandstyle/2020/aug/10/interest-in-allotments-soars-in-england-during-coronavirus-pandemic.

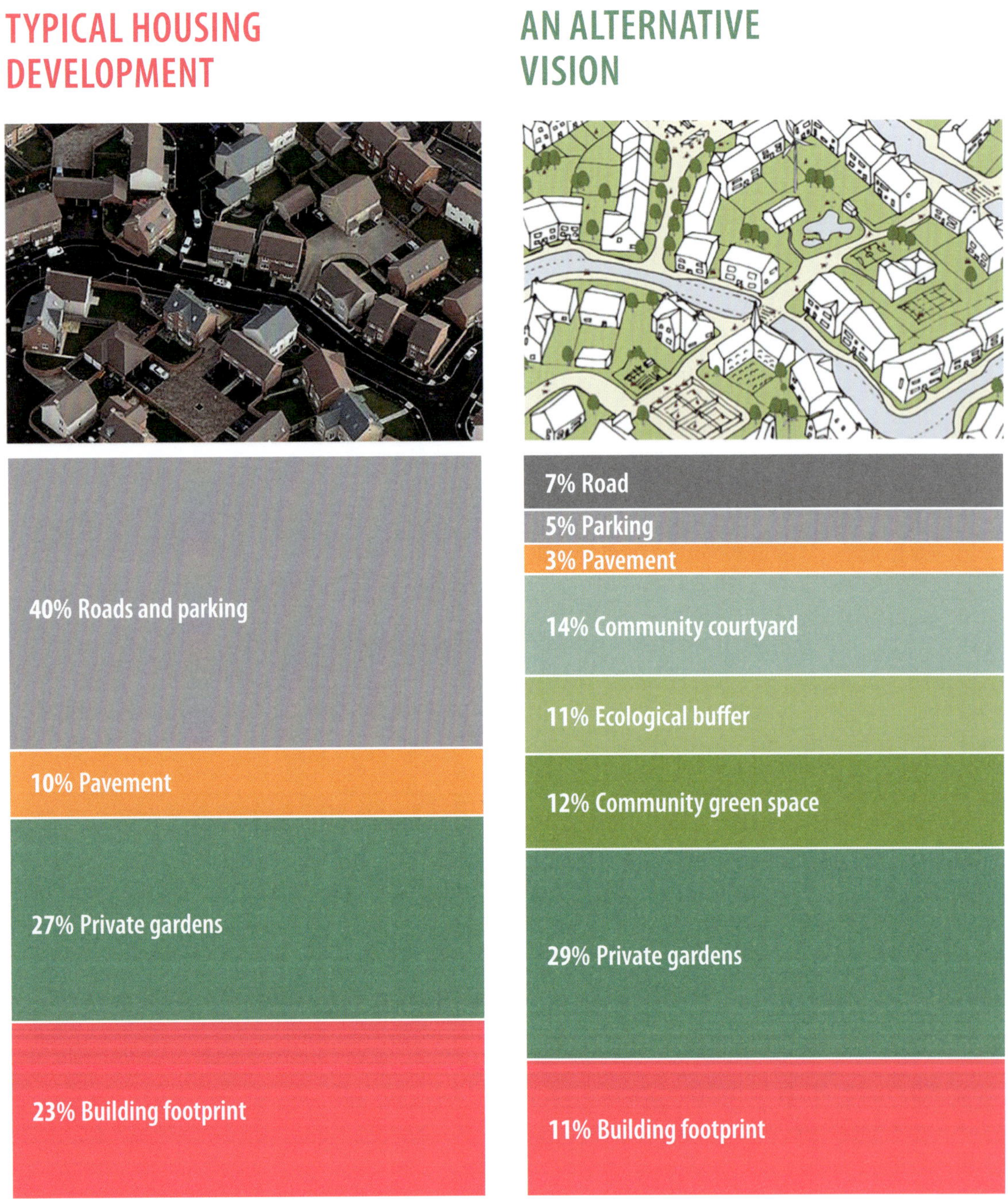

Figure 8.8 A landscape-led alternative to typical housing developments, with more space for people and the environment.

More space, less car

In a typical housebuilder's development the proportion of space given to open green spaces and community facilities is frighteningly low. With more attention to the spaces in between and priority of people over cars, it is possible to posit an alternative landscape-led approach which gives less primacy to the car and creates a more light-footed, compact development with meaningful green space for people and the planet.

If we place this in the context of the countryside, the case is even stronger. A village brings different characteristics to those of a town – compactness, walkability and immediate access to surrounding countryside. Low-density suburban models boosted by the car boom of the 1960s and 1970s are no longer appropriate and are eating up too much land and destroying our natural environment. Village greens have been eroded to provide car parking, pavements have been given over to wider roads, and new homes require bigger footprints to accommodate garage and front drive. Pollution and safety are an increasing concern as villages are used as shortcuts to avoid the congested main roads. Many residents have had enough and see strategies that reduce car use as an increasingly attractive option. VeloCity's strategy to reinstate the historic bridleways and footpaths as new cycling and walking networks offers safe and healthy travel options which not only ease the pressure on existing overstretched infrastructure, but are also cheap to put in place and reduce upfront costs compared to any greenfield development.

The thinking recognises that existing villages can better support the services they need collectively rather than on their own, and in doing so are able to retain their own distinct and individual characters. A village cluster can be one of five or six forming larger 'town clusters' all within a 7-mile cycling distance of a train station (see Figure 8.9). With time the clusters will become virtually car-free as public transport and cycling and walking become the main forms of movement, with vehicular movement kept to the edges. These village clusters share similar principles to those of the Garden Village movement, the difference being that one is concentrated around a single new village whilst the other is made up of a series of dispersed villages, which we refer to as Villages in a Garden.

This strategy has wider application across the UK countryside, and a countywide proposal has been submitted to local authorities in Oxfordshire who have invited people to submit ideas for the Oxfordshire Plan 2050 as they look for opportunities to do things differently and create a more sustainable future across the county. With their support it will enable Blenheim to lead the way as a pilot scheme and deliver on their pledge to secure a viable long-term future for the estate and villages.

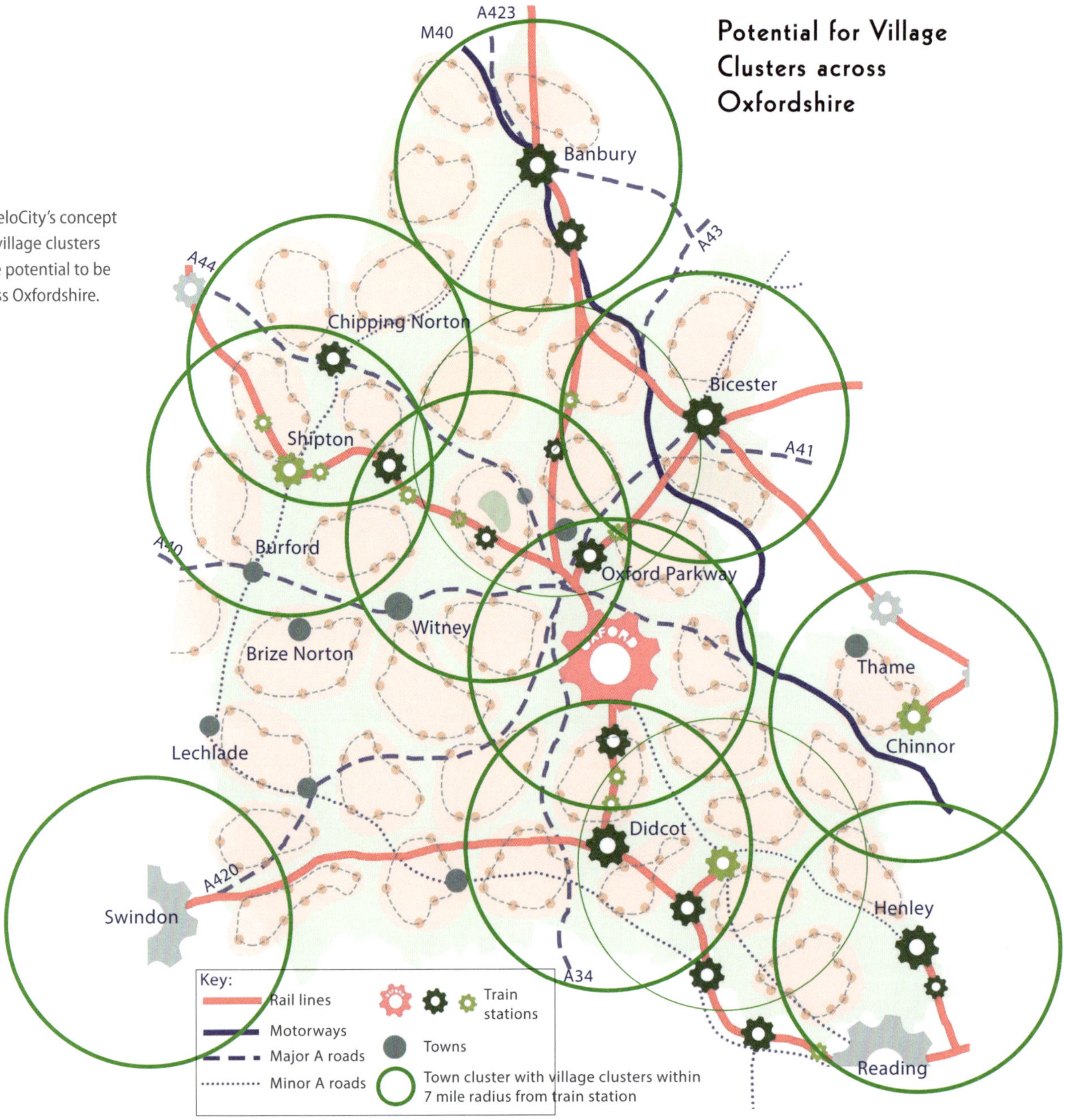

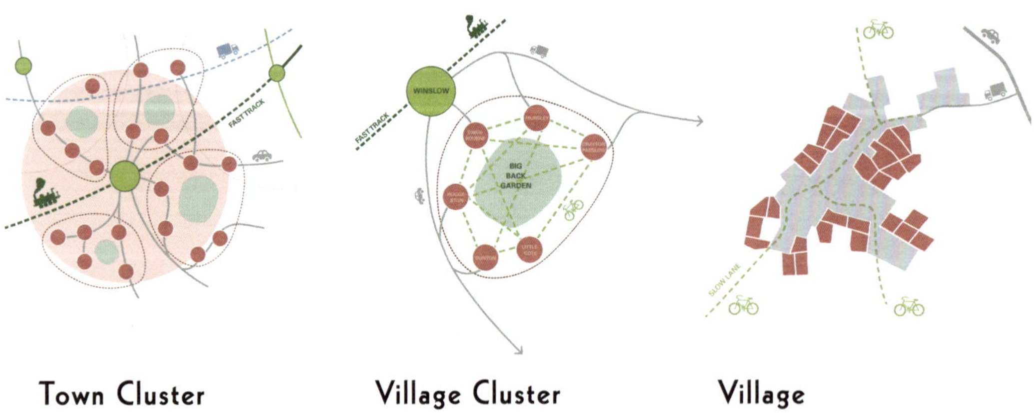

Figure 8.9 VeloCity's concept of scaleable village clusters that have the potential to be applied across Oxfordshire.

Resilient not Fragile – Promoting Sustainable Environments, Health and Wellbeing

> We are the first generation to know we are destroying the planet and the last one that can do anything about it.
>
> ---→ TANYA STEELE, CHIEF EXECUTIVE OF THE WORLD WILDLIFE FUND[25]

It doesn't take a crystal ball to see that over-reliance on the car is not a siloed issue and the type of environment we build – from housing through to public spaces and infrastructure – will also have a big impact on climate change and determine everything from air quality to mental health and productivity. Whilst the COVID-19 pandemic has brought great tragedy and highlighted huge social inequalities, arguably the climate emergency has a far more devastating long-term impact with the potential to wipe out the whole of humankind and many other species.

We are living beyond the earth's carrying capacity, with devastating loss of precious habitats and climate-change impacts. In the UK alone, 58% of all species have declined dramatically in the last 70 years and we have lost 97% of our wildflower meadows as a result of urbanisation and more intensive agricultural practices.[26] We also see the social consequences of economic growth through concentration of wealth in cities, growing inequality, social exclusion and the breakdown of social networks.

There are significant associated health impacts, with the estimated cost of heat-related mortality at £150 million by 2050.[27] In the UK, nearly one in three children leave primary school overweight,[28] and for the first time since the Second World War, growth in life expectancy has stalled.[29] And of course, mental health issues are on the increase. Food is purchased shrink-wrapped with no thought as to the impact on soils and ecosystems in the hinterland.

Extinction Rebellion, Greta Thunberg, David Attenborough, Friends of the Earth and many more public figures and organisations are all calling for a radical shift in behaviour over climate change. As a result of the overwhelming evidence

25 E. Nicholson, 'Humans Have Caused Wild Animal Populations To Drop By 60% Since 1970 According To WWF's Living Planet Report 2018', BBC Wildlife website, 31 October 2018, https://www.discoverwildlife.com/news/wwf-living-planet-report-2018-60-per-cent/?fbclid=IwAR3mBvbn5g9JOYHyD8zj7YacYmBnO5i0Iv-b-7La0Lr5I4N-1bxa8CN0ht4.

26 State of Nature Partnership, *State of Nature 2019*, 2019, https://www.wildlifetrusts.org/sites/default/files/2019-10/State-of-Nature-2019-UK full report.pdf.

27 K. Brown, 'The Hidden Problem of Overheating', Committee on Climate Change website, 8 August 2017, https://www.theccc.org.uk/2017/08/08/hidden-problem-overheating/.

28 A. Packham, 'One In Three Children Leave Primary School Overweight, Creating "Norm for XL Uniform"', *Huffington Post*, 1 September 2016, https://www.huffingtonpost.co.uk/entry/children-overweight-obese-finish-primary-school_uk_57c7e06ae4b01e359229bc76.

29 M. Bulman, 'Life Expectancy In UK Stalls For First Time On Record, Government Statistics Reveal', *The Independent*, 25 September 2018, https://www.independent.co.uk/news/uk/home-news/life-expectancy-uk-latest-ons-government-healthcare-age-elderly-health-a8553701.html.

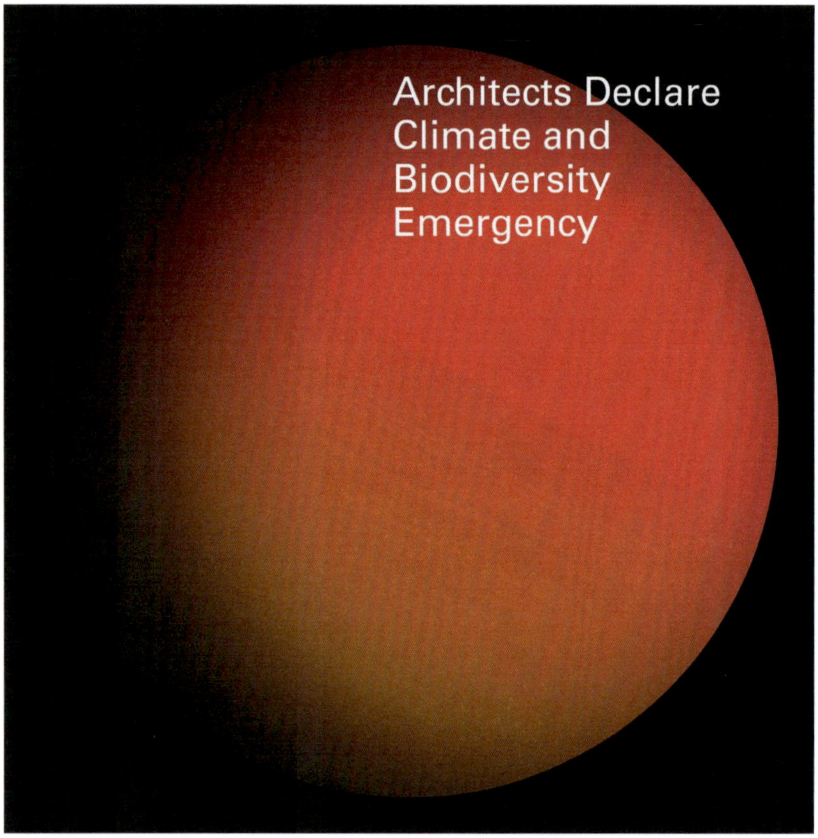

Figure 8.10 Calls for a radical shift in behaviour over climate change.

of the impacts of climate emergency on the health and wellbeing of people and our planet, the UK government has pledged to meet a net zero-carbon emissions target by 2050. Over 70% of local authorities have declared a climate emergency, with many seeking to achieve this target by 2030.[30] Professional bodies representing architects, engineers and landscape designers have also declared it, with hundreds of practices signing up to the pledge to take action.

The world population continues to rise, and in the UK alone it is projected to reach 72.4 million in mid-2043, increasing by 10.3% from 2018 with the proportion aged 85 or over predicted to almost double.[31]

Post COVID-19 we need to create a more balanced ecosystem that doesn't prioritise economics and GDP over social and environmental value. We need a much fairer distribution where resilience will become key over efficiency. This could be the end of growth as we know it – the Scottish government and Glasgow are deleting 'growth' and replacing it with 'thrive', Oslo Architecture Triennale's 2019 theme was 'Degrowth' and Amsterdam has introduced doughnut economics as its post-COVID-19 plan.

And COVID-19 has shown us that now more than ever we are in a place to make this change. We have seen it, we have dramatically changed our lives. And we have seen that if our governments are so minded, they too can change and have already demonstrated they can find millions to invest in this change.

Change to how we travel, change to farming practices, change to work habits, change to the way we support our families and community, change to our health and housing provision, change to the way we protect our environment and how collectively we can bring forth these changes.

30 'List of Councils Who Have Declared a Climate Emergency', Climate Emergency website, 6 October 2020, https://www.climateemergency.uk/blog/list-of-councils/.

31 Office for National Statistics, 'National Population Projections: 2018-Based', 21 October 2019, https://www.ons.gov.uk/releases/nationalpopulationprojections2018based.

But meaningful change requires time to pause and rethink. The government's post-COVID-19 strategies Project Speed and Build Build Build feel too quick and will just give momentum to do things the way they have always been done – that is, remaining wholly dependent on the big housebuilders who as we know are notoriously resistant to change. Furthermore, relaxation of planning policy will only weaken our protection laws, particularly in relation to our environment and climate change, and we will likely end up seeing more carbon-generating projects and many on new roads. The problem here isn't the planning system, it's a lack of funding it, a lack of the ambition that can encourage good people to be proactive and creative.

So we need to slow down, make time to evolve a long-term strategy and ask what kind of delivery and planning mechanisms can enable change, and what kind of housing we want to build for future generations. Naomi Klein captured this in a recent interview, saying, 'when you slow down, you can feel things … From its very beginning, the virus has forced us to think about interdependencies and relationships.'[32]

32 Naomi Klein interview with Katharine Viner, *The Guardian*, 13 July 2020, https://www.theguardian.com/books/2020/jul/13/naomi-klein-we-must-not-return-to-the-pre-covid-status-quo-only-worse

Connected not Isolated – Linking Communities with Shared Resources to Benefit All

Collective action and a sharing economy

This softness and shift to greater interdependencies chimes with VeloCity's call for a more 'gentle radicalism'. And maybe gentle radicalism alludes to what women can contribute to the shaping of the spaces and places we live in. As we struggle to readdress the gender imbalance in many walks of life, not least in our transport and construction industries, we see men still leading on key decision-making. Even the land on which places are created is predominantly owned by men thanks to the feudal system of male primogeniture whereby women are excluded from inheriting land and titles from their fathers.

It is interesting that some of the cities we cited as being ahead of the curve are ones where women have instigated or designed them. Paris's '15-minute city' for one, and Barcelona another, also leading the way with a female mayor and a collective feminist agenda that are making major transformations to the city. And so too in the countryside. Aspects of the VeloCity proposition bring forward qualities which arguably can be attributed to women being involved and acting collectively. The following suggests a few aspects that women have approached differently:

- **working with what is there** – not wiping the slate clean and building new places from scratch, more typical of an alpha-male approach

- **our movement patterns** – statistics show that men's and women's daily journeys are different; more women travel on foot and use public systems than men. If we can encourage more people to go about their daily life within a much smaller area and combine a number of tasks in one journey, this will not only be better for the environment but also offer greater opportunity for informal social interactions which currently the car denies
- **shared spaces** – the public spaces we use are often quite segregated and research has found that women feel more comfortable in spaces that are less prescriptive and more adaptable. VeloCity's Big Back Garden – a collective space that a cluster of villages encircle and which people crisscross when travelling between villages – is one such space that has the flexibility to offer a range of community activities: leisure, food production, tree-planting and much, much more.

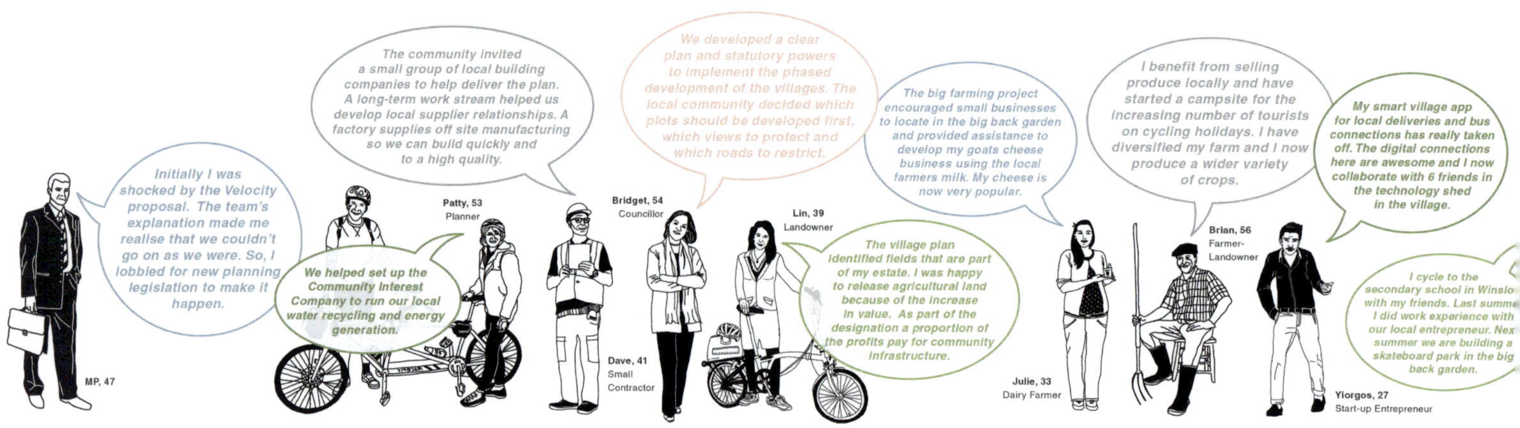

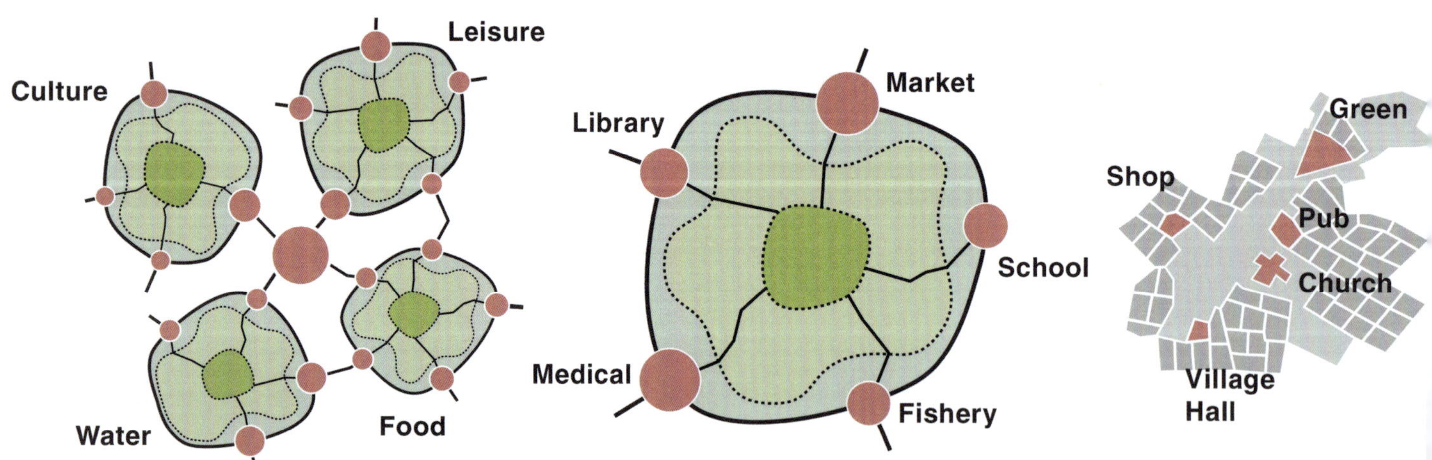

Figure 8.11 Collective action and a sharing economy.

Whilst it is hard to say definitively that these approaches are unique to women, they nonetheless have a tenacity and foresight that is shifting the dial and thinking about how we might adapt and grow our cities and villages differently to meet the social and environmental challenges of the future. Christele Harrouk wrote a piece in *ArchDaily* entitled 'What Can Cities Imagined by Women Look Like?' where she quoted, 'Cities are supposed to be built for all of us, but they aren't built by all of us.'[33] So if we can make changes whereby more women and a more diverse representation of people work in our industry, then maybe we can reverse this situation and collectively bridge the gender gap.

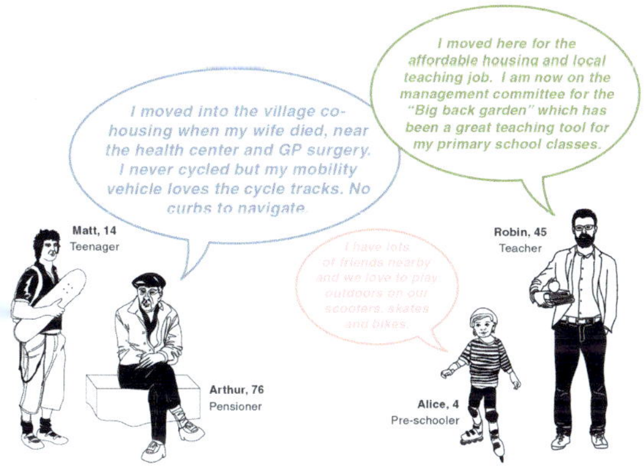

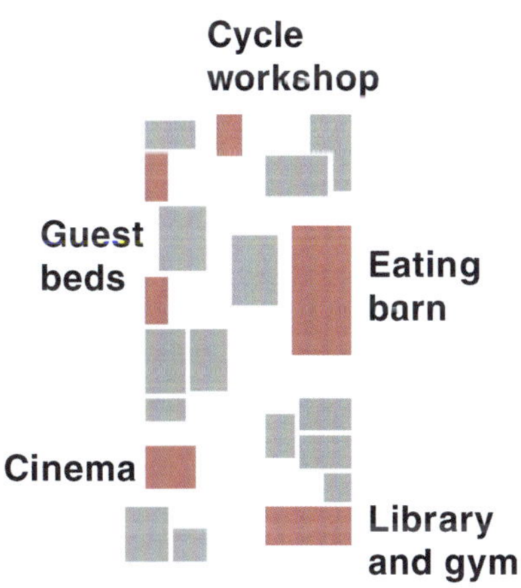

A collective, sharing culture runs across all scales of the VeloCity proposal – from the way in which regional village clusters offer different specialisms, through to the shared resources each village can offer, through to the shared dining space you might find in a new housing scheme. On the big scale it is about understanding the social and economic issues affecting community life – the critical mass needed to support everyday services and the application of collective, sharing principles that abolish the 'NIMBY' mentality. At the small scale it is an opportunity for communities to take control and reclaim village life (see Figure 8.11).

33 C. Harrouk, 'What Can Cities Imagined by Women Look Like?', *Archdaily*, 25 December 2019, https://www.archdaily.com/927948/how-can-cities-imagined-by-women-look-like-the-case-of-barcelona.

Emerging Opportunities in a Post-COVID World

> It has been the collective action embodied in public services provided by the state that is seeing us through the [COVID-19] crisis ... We will only be able to deliver and secure our future to guard against future crises if we ensure our new society is founded on a participative democracy blossoming within our communities but also within the economy and at work.
>
> ···→ JOHN MCDONNELL, SHADOW CHANCELLOR OF THE EXCHEQUER, APRIL 2020[34]

Instead of stagnated and outdated attitudes to rural development, the pandemic shows radical change is both possible and desirable. Making changes to planning and transport structures, creating better-quality housing and taking advantage of modern technological advancements will all allow us to shift negative perceptions of development in rural areas. The opportunities offered by localism – driven by less commuting, less car use and more sustainable local transport – show how rural areas can drive innovation and be a true place for gentle radicalism.

34 J. McDonnell, 'Out of the Coronavirus Crisis, a New Kind of Britain Must Be Born', *The Guardian*, 3 April 2020, https://www.theguardian.com/commentisfree/2020/apr/03/coronavirus-crisis-new-society.

Figure 8.12 VeloCity's future village cluster.

ACKNOWLEDGEMENTS

CHAPTER 1 – Nicola Gillen

As with all things, this piece of writing has very much been a team effort. In addition to the generous contribution of time and ideas from my co-authors, I gratefully acknowledge Bryan Berthold's, Despina Katsikakis's, Tomas Polster's, Andrew Phipps's, Hiral Patel's and Argent's contributions in preparing this chapter.

CHAPTER 2 – Pippa Nissen

We would like to thank Caroline Collett, Elin Simonsson and Amelia Bloore for all their help with this chapter.

CHAPTER 3 – Julia Park

These things are invariably a team effort. As well as the contributors named within the chapter, I'd like to thank my colleagues Rachel Serfling, Olivia Smith and Matthew Goulcher at Levitt Bernstein, Claire Bennie of Municipal and everyone else who offered advice or allowed us to draw on their work.

CHAPTER 4 – Adam Scott

There is no way in a month of Sundays that everything we've covered in this chapter is down to me. On the contrary, I am the lucky beneficiary of the know-how of a whole host of extremely wise owls, some of whom we have met, most of whom we have not. Whether developer, architect, entrepreneur, designer, writer, asset manager or consultant, I am extremely grateful to each and every one of them. They are: Andy Pratt, Ashley Munday, Carrie Ho, Charlotte Boyens, Claire Barrett, Dave Waddell, David Morris, David Tickle, Ed Humbert, James Scroggs, Josh Artus, Juliet Kinsman, Fiona Scott, Friedrich Ludewig, Guy Hollaway, Lloyd Lee, Mark Bourgeois, Matthew Shang, Natalie Louey, Nigel Costain, Paul Semple, Rachel Calton, Rory Martin, Roger Madelin, Ross Bailey and Sachiko Osawa. It goes without saying that any errors are mine and mine alone.

CHAPTER 5 – Sumita Singha

I am grateful to the following people (in no particular order): Aiko Nakada, architect, for her assistance in translation and for writing a section; Koichi Suzuki (Director, International Projects, K.ITO Architects & Engineers); SS Tokyo (photographer); Michael Woodford (Director, White Arkitekter); Timothy Soar (photographer); Kengo Kuma & Associates; Daichi Ano (photographer); Ashley Wu (CPG Corporation); and Ruairi Reeves (Director, Medical Architecture). Also, grateful thanks to my colleagues in the NHS for the many soundbites and pieces of information that helped in the writing.

CHAPTER 6 – Helen Taylor

This chapter has been made possible by the commitment, passion and vision of architects and their collaborators working to make great school environments. I must particularly thank and acknowledge my colleagues at Scott Brownrigg, Sharon Wright of the-learning-crowd, Bruce Glockling, Crawford Wright, Hilary Macaulay, Takbir Fatima, Claire Barton, Brian Vermeulen, Richard Cottrell, Catherine Harrington, Helen Murray, Holly Passmore, Mark Ellson, Felicity Steers, Wayne Head, Simon Bumstead, Claire Mantle, Laurika Olayvar, and everyone involved in LETI – the London Energy Transformation Initiative, all of whose excellent work is integral to this chapter. I must also thank the practices and students of architecture who generously shared their exciting design ideas and who gave me more images and projects than I was able to include. I promise to find a way to acknowledge their work elsewhere. And of course – any mistakes are all mine.

CHAPTER 7 – Ian Taylor

My thanks to FCBStudios' Jo White and Dr Joe Jack Williams for their contributions to the chapter, and Caroline Ellerby, Fliss Childs and Jenny Stephens for photograph support.

CHAPTER 8 – Sarah Featherstone

We thank our critical friends: Joanna Averley (Chief Planner, Ministry of Housing, Communities & Local Government); Harriet Bourne (Director, BBUK (Landscape)); Mel Dodd (Associate Dean, Central Saint Martins (academic)); Richard Lavington (Director, Maccreanor Lavington Architects (architect)); Hilary Satchwell (Director, Tibbalds Planning and Urban Design (urban designer/architect)); Mike Wells (Director, Biodiversity by Design (ecologist)); Jane Wernick CBE (Consultant, engineersHRW (engineer)); and David Lawrence (CAG Consult (economist)). In addition, many thanks to: Sadie Morgan OBE; Tom Holbrook (5th Studio); Alicia Picaro; Simon Conibear (Duchy of Cornwall); Hana Loftus (HAT Projects); Claire Curtice; Meredith Bowles (Mole Architects); Blenheim Estates; and Clarion Housing Group.

INDEX

IMAGE CREDITS

Introduction

pp 0–1 photo David Barbour; p 3 photo Philip Vile; p 5 photo Paul Raftery, pp 6–7 Foster + Partners

Chapter 1

pp 10, 11, 13, 16–17 Cushman & Wakefield; pp 14, 37–9 Argent / John Sturrock; p 20 Our World in Data; p 21 Source: IEA (2020), https://www.iea.org/commentaries/working-from-home-can-save-energy-and-reduce-emissions-but-how-much. All rights reserved; pp 34–5 The Collective; p 40 Argent Related Cityscape

Chapter 2

p 42 © seanpines.co.uk; pp 43, 46, 51, 60, 64–5 photos Gareth Gardner; pp 45, 50 Nissen Richards Studio; p 47 photo Robin Maggs; p 49 photos Nigel Luckhurst © Britten Pears Arts; p 54 photo Jim Stephenson; pp 56(t), 59 photos Dan Dunkley; p 56(b) photo Will Holt; p 58 photo David Christian; p 66 RIBA Collections; p 68 photo Sushma Jansari; p 71 Courtesy of the Natural History Museum, London

Chapter 3

p 74(t) Emily Gray Photography; pp 74(b), 81 Pollard Thomas Edwards; pp 75, 82, 90, 92, 99 photos Tim Crocker; p 77 photo Rob Rhodes; p 80 Proctor & Matthews Architects; p 85 photo Fanny Blanc; pp 89, 93, 97 Levitt Bernstein; p 95 LETI

Chapter 4

p 104 photo Alex Maclean; p 105 photo by Bossi. Creative Commons Attribution-ShareAlike 2.0 Generic licence (CC BY-SA 2.0): https://creativecommons.org/licenses/by-sa/2.0/; p 107 jax10289 / iStock; p 112 Frasers Property; p 114 photo Jack Thurston; pp 116–17 Place Intelligence; p 120 Appear Here; pp 122–3 photo Lauren Commens; p 124 Yoo Capital; p 125 Bikini Berlin; p 126 photo Nicole England; p 127 Hammerson plc; p 128 Cedric Price fonds, Canadian Centre for Architecture; pp 129,131 Charlotte Boyens at FreeState; p 134 Argent / John Sturrock

Chapter 5

pp 136–40, 139–40, 146, 149–53, 162 photos Sumita Singha; p 141 SS Co., Ltd. Kenichi Ohno; p 145 Joe Low / RIBA Collections; p 155 Kengo Kuma Associates; pp 156–7 CPG Consultants Pte Ltd; p 158 Medical Architecture, photo Tim Crocker

Chapter 6

pp 164, 167, 174, 179 Scott Brownrigg; p 169 Ujjwal Sannala / Akhila Rao; p 171 Haverstock; p 172 Jack Hobhouse/ Architype; p 175 Maja Olsson; pp 176–7 Holmes Miller; p 178 erz Ltd, August 2020; pp 180–1 Curl la Tourelle Head, Image by Darc Studio 2020; p 185 Julia Cabanas 2020

Chapter 7

p 188 FCBStudios; pp 189, 198 Architectural Press Archive / RIBA Collections; pp 193–4 photos Hufton+Crow; p 195 photo Industryous Photography; p 197 photo Xavier de Jauréguiberry; p 200 photo Denis Gilbert; pp 204–5 photo Andrew Rankin

Chapter 8

p 208 photos Agnese Sanvito; pp 210–28, 232–35 Velocity; p 230 Architects Declare